TARGET FUNDING

TARGET
FUNDING

A Proven System to Get the
MONEY & RESOURCES
You Need to Start or Grow
Your Business

KEDMA OUGH, MBA

New York   Chicago   San Francisco   Athens   London
Madrid   Mexico City   Milan   New Delhi
Singapore   Sydney   Toronto

1 2 3 4 5 6 7 8 9   BNG   24 23 22 21 20 19

ISBN   978-1-260-13236-6
MHID   1-260-13236-6

e-ISBN   978-1-260-13237-3
e-MHID   1-260-13237-4

The views and opinions expressed in this publication are those of the author and do not necessarily reflect the views or opinions of Federated Investors, Inc., or its affiliates.

McGraw-Hill Education books are available at special quantity discounts to use as premiums and sales promotions or for use in corporate training programs. To contact a representative, please visit the Contact Us pages at www.mhprofessional.com.

To Farmingdale State College,

for believing a young girl could impact the world

if given the opportunity to do so

CONTENTS

PART FOUR
Funding for Inventions and Innovation

PART FIVE
Funding for Startups and Small Businesses

PART SIX
Funding for the Unbankable

PART SEVEN
Ready, Set, Fund!

FOREWORD

I wish I had this book when I started my first business.

I have long admired Kedma Ough, and this great book, *Target Funding*, only underscores what I already knew: Kedma is a committed, super-smart, talented, skilled, ardent advocate for entrepreneurs.

She is not the Wonder Woman of Small Business for no reason!

An entrepreneur herself, Kedma is clearly passionate about helping small businesses succeed. Whether it is her work with Small Business Development Centers (SBDCs), or speaking at industry events, or her work with inventors, or now, here, with this excellent resource, Kedma's mission is to help small businesses succeed.

Lucky you.

As mentioned, this book would have been so helpful when I started my entrepreneurial journey. Back in the day, I was an unhappy lawyer in a big firm with big dreams of small business. That is, I longed to leave the "comfort" of the firm and start my own law practice. The issue, as it is for so many aspiring entrepreneurs, was money. Where would I find it? How would I find it? What were my options?

In the end, I cobbled together a smorgasbord of funding—a little savings, a loan from a friend, an advance on an inheritance, and some credit card advances. It worked, but it was far from ideal.

Instead, had I had *Target Funding* available to me, I would have learned about a universe of options that I had no idea were available:

- Funding options specifically for veterans, people with disabilities, women, or other diversity groups
- Community Development Financial Institutions (CDFIs), which offer microloans and often other types of business loans
- Targeted sources of debt funding and equity funding
- Grants and government contracts

It's here. It's all here.

The good news for you is that not only do you in fact have this book available to you, you have Kedma Ough as your guide. That means that one of the country's leading small business advocates (indeed, she is a past winner of the Small Business Administration (SBA) Small Business Champion of the Year Award) will explain, in plain English, what your options are and which might make the most sense for you.

So, if you are looking to start and fund a business, you have most certainly come to the right place.

As I said, lucky you!

Steve Strauss
USA TODAY Small Business columnist
Author, *The Small Business Bible*

PREFACE

Sometimes when people walk into my office and see the beautiful space of a well-established company headed by a confident entrepreneur, they think, *Wow. She's lucky to have had all this good fortune.* They often presume I come from privilege or that success came easily for me.

Nothing could be further from the truth. My childhood was difficult, to put it mildly. As a child, I was often sad and anxious. When I was old enough to realize my situation, I felt vulnerable and trapped. Books provided a means of escape, and I dreamed of going to college, hoping that a degree would be my ticket to a better future. At age 14, I also got my first glimpse of entrepreneurship when I spent a year living in Ireland with my grandmother, who was a fourth-generation entrepreneur. She was such a savvy woman, and I fell in love with the idea of being a businesswoman, too.

After graduating high school, I went to a community college, and that is when my life really changed—but not in the way I'd hoped. I was living with a volatile person, and I was in really bad shape emotionally and psychologically. One night during an evening class I was taking, I got a 911 page from my therapist. I hurried to a pay phone to call her, and she told me that the violent person I was living with had contacted her. "You need to leave the college now!" she said urgently. "He's on his way there, and he said if he finds you he is going to kill you!"

I ran to the parking lot, but I was in such a panic that I couldn't remember where I'd parked. As I frantically looked for my car, I saw the person's car driving slowly back and forth near the entrance to the lot. My legs felt like quicksand, and I was screaming but no sound was coming out. My only thought was, *Run, Kedma, run!* Just then I spotted my car and ran toward it, ducking down and dashing between vehicles. Staying crouched down, I opened my car door just enough to grab my books, the only thing I cared about, and ran back to the pay phone. I called a friend, who came and picked me up on the other side of campus, out of sight of the parking lot. Meanwhile, the perpetrator continued to drive back and forth, searching for me.

It was unsafe to go back to my place of residence. In fact, the person posed such a threat to me that I literally went into hiding. I had no money, no job, no car, and I was homeless. I stayed with a friend at first, and a group of friends banded together to find me my first home and purchase items for me to live there. It was an illegal basement apartment in a squalid house in what was essentially a ghetto. But that cockroach-infested hovel was my safe haven for five years. In addition, my friends helped me find my first full-time, minimum-wage job as a bill collector. In my interview, I communicated that I was in hiding, and if they hired me I needed to have my information held with the strictest of confidence.

The problem was that I couldn't afford my education. One of my professors, who was among the few people who knew about my situation, encouraged me to petition the college for a hardship scholarship. So I wrote a letter to the college's finance committee explaining the painful circumstances I was facing, and I was called in for an interview. After answering a few questions, I pled my case, stating that I'd lost everything—my home, my family, my car, my identity—and the only thing I had left to live for was the opportunity for an education. Afterward, I was directed to wait in the secretary's office while the committee deliberated on my case. As I waited nervously, I asked the secretary for a pen and a sheet of paper. I wrote a letter to God, having little faith that my request would be heard since God had never showed up to help me before. In the letter I promised that if the scholarship committee would give me a scholarship, I would use my education and abilities to help other people in need for the rest of my life.

About two hours later, I was summoned back to the conference room. One of the committee members walked over to me and said, "Kedma, please stand up." My knees shook as I rose from the chair. The woman took my hand and shook it, saying, "Thank you for the woman you are. You're getting a full scholarship to this college."

Because that small group of people believed in me when they had no reason to, I set out on the path that led to where I am today. And I made good on the promise I'd made in that letter. But it didn't happen quickly or easily.

It took five years to get my bachelor's degree, the last three at a local university, on a full scholarship from the hospital where I worked as a bill collector. The whole time, I continued to work full-time and to live in the basement apartment. My goal was to become a business coach, because I realized there were two ways to positively affect someone's life: in the home or in business. Being a business consultant rather than a family counselor, I could not only help people in their personal lives, I could also help give them the financial means to move their lives forward.

After graduating from college, I moved across the country to Arizona, where I'd never even visited, didn't know a soul, and had no job. I thought, *Oh, big me. I have a degree. Of course someone will hire me*! It didn't take long for me to realize that an undergrad degree in business did not guarantee the position I'd trained for and the paycheck I'd hoped for. I started out working as a temp and then was hired as a customer service rep at a call center.

A few months later, the call center closed that entire operation, and I was part of a massive layoff. Suddenly, I was jobless at a time when the job market was abysmal. The regional reemployment center offered two programs: assistance finding another job or a small business training program to help prepare me to start my own business. I decided to give entrepreneurship a try.

I came up with a great idea that combined the cozy comfort of a bed-and-breakfast with a luxury spa experience and spent three months researching the market and developing a business plan. At that point, my business counselor at the reemployment center, Sandra Hoy Johnson, told me, "Okay, you're ready! It's time to move forward."

I made an appointment with a loan officer at the branch where I'd done my personal banking for several years. I handed him my shiny new business plan and told him I wanted a loan for my unique B&B offering full spa services.

"How much are you looking for?" *$300,000.*

"Is this for a startup?" *Yes.*

"Have you ever owned or operated a bed-and-breakfast or health spa?" *No, but I frequent them and have researched them extensively.*

"Do you have any collateral?" *Well, I have a beat-up old car, worth a few thousand.*

"Do you own a home?" *No, I rent an apartment.*

"Do you have any money to put down?" *No.*

"Do you have family or friends who can lend or invest in the business?" *No.*

"Who is your current employer?" *I've been unemployed for a few months, since my last employer closed its offices.*

At that point, the loan officer looked me straight in the eyes and said, "We can't help you. You need to go get a job."

That pissed me off, and when I'm pissed off, I make things happen. So I took my business plan, which he hadn't even looked at, and walked out, even more determined to find a way to launch my business.

By the time I got back to my apartment, I'd lost some of that steam. I knew I had a great business idea, but the only funding option I thought might be available to me had just turned me down flat. Then I had an aha moment: Why did I need to own the B&B? I didn't. I could provide spa services to an existing B&B. Within six months, I opened my business, and I didn't need any startup capital. My team of practitioners—from massage to acupuncture, pedicures, facials, aromatherapy, mud baths, you name it—got a percentage of the customer fees, the B&B owner got a percentage, and I got a percentage. That business model was different from the one I'd worked months to create, but it worked. So many people bury their ideas in the Cemetery of Dreams because they aren't willing to negotiate their dream. They'd rather kill the dream than start small and move forward from there.

My business was a hit and earned a nice profit. But after a while I realized the liability risk that was involved in working on people's bodies and decided I didn't want to subject myself to that kind of risk. So I closed my business and got a job as a corporate sales trainer in Colorado. Teaching 100 telemarketers a month how to engage the consumer, break through reluctance, and make the sale honed my negotiation and communication skills. It helped give me the backbone to handle the resistance, problem solving, planning, and dealmaking that being a successful business owner requires.

One day I got a call from Sandra, the director of the reemployment center in Arizona, who had become and still is my best friend. She said, "Kedma, there's a big job opportunity at the Women's Business Center here, and they're looking for someone like you—a business degree, has owned her own business, background in sales." I got the job as the Women's Business Center Director for the SBA in Tucson. Our clients were socially and economically disadvantaged women who were business owners or wanted to start a business. Finally, I was fulfilling the promise I'd made when I wrote that letter asking for divine intervention so I could get my education. For the first time I felt like I was doing what I was meant to do. *This is why I'm here; this is why I exist.*

During that time, I fulfilled another life goal. I completed a master's in business administration through Troy State University's weekend program at the Davis-Monthan Air Force Base in Tucson.

But soon after getting my dream job at the Women's Business Center, I experienced a major blow, and it was a double whammy. I left my troubled marriage, and it impacted my financial situation. When we divorced, I was left with our communal debt, which was significant, and I was advised to file for bankruptcy. In one fell swoop I lost my husband and my good credit. As I walked out of bankruptcy court, I felt humiliated and defeated. It was one of the lowest points in my life.

Two weeks later, I got a Capital One credit card in the mail. The interest rate was really high and the credit limit was only $200, but it gave me such a boost that it might as well have been $200,000. I jumped up and down in my apartment screaming "Capital One, you believe in me!" Then, I had an aha moment: What if I could find a way to help other people like me—with no or insufficient collateral and no credit or bad credit, or even a bankruptcy—obtain funding. That became my mission, and over the next 15 years, I was obsessed with uncovering funding sources and other resources for good people whose circumstances inhibited their ability to secure traditional financing.

To that end, I continued working as a business counselor at the Women's Business Center in Tucson. Soon I began to work with minorities and people with disabilities in addition to women. I also served on the finance committee for the state vocational rehabilitation program and taught entrepreneurship and business leadership at the local university. I loved helping people help themselves by becoming successful business owners!

In 2002, I left those positions to relocate to Oregon, get married, and start a family. My first business interview in Oregon was with the

Portland Development Commission. During one of those interviews I met an amazing guy, Tyrone Henry, who said something that lit a spark in me. "Kedma, I can get you a job at PDC, but think of all the people who will never have the opportunity to work with you because you will be limited to PDC's parameters." At that moment I knew I had to start another business.

I launched my company, AVITA, in 2003, to provide business advising to people with disabilities. I rented a 150-square-foot office for $150 a month, but I wasn't sure I could afford the rent, so I shared the office with a friend. We each paid $75 for 75 square feet. I remember my landlord saying, "If you can't pay $150 a month, you may not be ready for business." He wasn't the only one who was skeptical about my venture. When I began AVITA, several colleagues were convinced that a company targeting socially and economically disadvantaged business owners would never make a profit. AVITA grew 300 percent in gross sales in the first 12 months. I hired people and moved into a 300-square-foot leased office, and then a 1,000-square-foot leased office, and in 2008, I purchased my 2,000-square-foot office. Today, I serve as the semi-absentee owner of AVITA, which focuses on assisting women, minorities, and clients with disabilities in achieving their business goals.

In 2006, I launched the Micro Inventors Program of Oregon (MIPO) to help independent inventors bring their products to market. I did that until 2014, when I became the director of the Mount Hood Community College Small Business Development Center in Gresham, Oregon. Finally, I was working at a community college, where it all began, paying it forward to other students and entrepreneurs! From 2005 to 2009, I was also the director of the Women's Business Center for the Oregon Native American Business Enterprise Network (ONABEN). Through that experience I had the opportunity to coauthor *Indianpreneurship*, an entrepreneurial curriculum designed for Native American businesses.

I have dedicated my life to removing the barriers to business success for those who are socially and economically disadvantaged. One of the biggest barriers to successful business ownership is undercapitalization. For almost 20 years, I have made it my mission to find and to open the doors to funding opportunities for those who are usually denied access to traditional funding options. I have helped more than 10,000 people understand how to fund their small business ventures so far, and through my work and this book, I will continue to help other people realize their business ownership dreams.

This is how I'm paying forward the scholarship I received so long ago. I will never forget that group of people who believed in me when I did not believe in myself. It's my bucket-list dream to one day go back to that community college as a keynote speaker and share my story with the graduating class. I am eternally grateful for the opportunity the college gave me to pursue my dream and do what I was meant to do. As a business advisor, I never judge someone by whatever circumstances they are facing. I believe that with the right opportunities, resources, and funding, anyone can lead a life filled with possibilities. And I am living proof of that.

Kedma Ough

INTRODUCTION

As a fifth-generation entrepreneur and as a business counselor to entrepreneurs and small business owners for more than 20 years, I understand the desire and often the financial need to create a business of one's own. I also know firsthand, from both my personal and my clients' experiences, that business ownership comes with both rewards and challenges.

One of the biggest and most daunting challenges faced by most entrepreneurs is finding the funds to get the resources they need to launch, build, sustain, and grow their businesses. From working extensively with entrepreneurs who happen to be women, veterans, immigrants, LGBTQ, people of color, people with disabilities, and of modest means, I also realize that funding a business can be more difficult for some than others. For some, those difficulties and inequities become insurmountable barriers that diminish or dash their entrepreneurial dreams.

Difficulties and inequities do not deter me. In fact, they motivate me to work on eliminating the problem. And when I see a barrier, I go into superhero mode to remove it. So I made it my mission to find solutions to the business funding challenges confronting so many people.

I researched. I brainstormed. I talked with bankers, investors, lean startup gurus, business development experts, industry thought leaders, successful inventors, and successful entrepreneurs. I also talked with many aspiring entrepreneurs and inventors whose ventures didn't work out. I actually learned more from listening to their stories of failure than their stories of success.

During that time of intense investigation, alternative forms of business funding began to emerge and gain traction. At the same time, conventional forms of business funding also began to change, sometimes to the detriment of and at other times to the benefit of startups and small businesses. I studied them all and continued to keep my eye on the ever-evolving world of business funding. I learned a lot from my research and from all those gurus.

But I learned the most from working with my clients to help them find the funding they needed for their ventures. They're the reason I searched high and low to unearth every funding option available to small businesses, startups, and independent inventors. They're the reason I dug deep to learn how each funding option worked, as well as its pros and cons.

What evolved from those experiences—of searching for the best funding opportunities for each individual client—was a smarter way to navigate the business-funding maze. I developed a method for zeroing in on the funding opportunities that most closely align with the needs and characteristics of a particular business, similar to target marketing, which many companies use to market to their most likely customers. Target Funding™, as I named it, enables entrepreneurs to find the funding opportunities aimed at businesses like theirs, based on specific variables—such as the location, industry, stage, and size of the business and the demographics of the entrepreneur.

Through my work as a small business counselor—via my consultancy, AVITA Business Center; the SBA Women's Business Center and Small Business Development Center; workshops, seminars, and other venues—more than 10,000 individuals have learned how to target the right funding solutions for their businesses. With this book, I am taking the next step in the journey I began many years ago in the secretary's office of the dean of Farmington College, when I made a promise to dedicate my life to helping other people break through the barriers standing in the way of the life they have envisioned for themselves.

Now, to be clear, this book is *not* about wringing all of your business funding out of your personal finances—saving every extra dollar, giving up vacations, cutting up your credit cards, working two or three jobs, skimping on the essentials and comforts of life. Frankly, I am tired of the self-help business funding books that state the obvious: that you're going to have to put your own money into your business. And then rehash the same old threadbare options for bootstrapping a business and the same old conventional business financing options—bank loans and investors. Of course, as a business founder and owner, you're going to use some of your personal resources for your business—but not *all* of your assets, and never so much that it jeopardizes your financial well-being. Of course, you're going to launch and run your business as economically as possible—but not if it means going so lean that it undermines your business. Of course, you're going to seek bank loans and investors, if you qualify. The reality is, most people don't have the personal resources to fund a business, nor do most people qualify for conventional business financing during the start-up phase of their ventures. That's why I went in search of a better way to fund a business. That's why I wrote *Target Funding*.

The book you are holding in your hands provides core information about the myriad funding options available to startups, small businesses, and independent inventors along with a road map for finding the funding opportunities that best align with your business. This book also includes real-life business funding success stories as well as examples of actual funding sources for each funding option presented. (Just keep in mind that lenders, grantors, investors, and other funding sources change their offerings from time to time, and companies, organizations, and programs sometimes change hands or close their doors.)

May this book guide you, inspire you, and enable you to get the funds you need to launch and grow your business. I hope the knowledge you receive from this book also enables and inspires you to pay it forward to another entrepreneur searching for a way to make their business dream come true.

PART ONE

The New American Dream

A Business of One's Own

The Opportunity

Innovation, Entrepreneurship, Small Business Ownership

Mom, apple pie, and baseball may be quintessentially American. But nothing is more integral to American culture than innovation, entrepreneurship, and small business. People grow up in and emigrate to the United States believing that here, in the land of opportunity, anyone with a good idea and a lot of gumption can turn that idea into a successful business. We not only believe it, we witness it over and over again: "everyday" Americans who create a new product or service, or put a new spin on an existing product or service, or build a new business from the ground up, or breathe new life into an existing business—and prosper from their ingenuity and efforts. We are inspired by these enterprising innovators in our midst. And most of us aspire to the all-American dream of being our own boss.

Economic individualism—a fancy term for achieving financial independence as an inventor, entrepreneur, or business owner—is deeply rooted in US history. America was founded and settled by innovators and capitalists who set down roots and set up shop, literally and figuratively, across this vast land. Many of the world's greatest scientific discoveries, technological inventions, and societal advancements have come from American inventors and entrepreneurs. The nation's citizens have continually founded and built private enterprises in every industry sector—agriculture, transportation, manufacturing, education, healthcare, financial services, entertainment, communication, information, and more. Some grow into midsize companies and others into large corporations or global conglomerates, but the majority remain small businesses.

In fact, small businesses comprise 99.9 percent of all US businesses, employ almost 48 percent of all US employees, and produce more than 50 percent of nonfarm private gross domestic product (GDP). As a champion of small business, I wholeheartedly agree with the following statement from a report by the management consulting firm McKinsey & Company:

> No hero stands taller in the nation's political and business psyche than the small-business owner. With good reason. Small businesses, defined as companies with fewer than 500 employees, account for almost two-thirds of all net new job creation. They also contribute disproportionately to innovation, generating 13 times as many patents, per employee, as large companies do.[1]

THE AMERICAN ENTREPRENEURSHIP REVOLUTION

Despite the steadfast economic heroism of Main Street businesses, many people buy into the myth that corporate America is the primary generator of jobs and innovations in the United States. This misconception stems, in part, from the economic dominance of large corporations during the late nineteenth century and twentieth century, which gave rise to the popular notion that "what's good for big business is good for America." Corporate employment—which came to include a decent wage, a 40-hour work week, paid vacation time, worker's compensation insurance, health insurance, and often a pension—became the preferred path to job security. Entrepreneurship became an occupation of the elite, and innovation became the domain of government institutions and large corporations. Although small business remained vitally important to the US economy, it took a back seat to corporate America, and smaller enterprises often struggled to stay afloat or to grow.

Then, the 1980s ushered in a new age of American entrepreneurship, sparked and propelled by mass corporate layoffs and job-threatening mergers as well as by new societal mores, educational opportunities, scientific discoveries, technologies, and sources of capital. Between 1980 and

2004, according to a Baylor University study, more than 5 million jobs were lost at Fortune 500 companies while 34 million new jobs were created at small businesses. The number of US small businesses also doubled, increasing from 14.7 million in 1977 to 29.6 million in 2007.

Computer and telecommunication technologies combined with a changing business environment spurred a boom in home-based businesses, from 6 million in 1984 to 15 million by 2014. Today, more than half of all US small businesses are home-based, and more than two-thirds of American entrepreneurs start their businesses at home. Launching from home is a great way to minimize overhead costs, leaving more startup capital for building the business. In some cases, a home-based business can also enable you to spend more time with your family and pursue other interests.

Enactment of new franchising laws in 1979, which reduced the risk and expense of owning a franchise, also enabled more people to become business owners. Today, more than 750,000 franchisees, up from 356,000 in 1980, offer a variety of products and services through 2,500 franchise companies spanning 80 industries. What's more, the demographic of franchise ownership has also been shifting, with an increasing number of women, minorities, baby boomers, millennials, and veterans becoming franchisees.

The entrepreneurship and small business ownership revolution that emerged in the 1980s has continued to grow and gain strength. Today, 60 out of 1,000 American adults are small business owners, and every month more than 500,000 US adults found or cofound a business.[2] According to the US Small Business Administration (SBA), more than half of Americans either own or work for private companies with fewer than 500 employees, and those small businesses create two out of every three new jobs in the United States each year. An upsurge in Internet enterprises has also contributed to the accelerated growth of entrepreneurship, with 3 in 10 US jobs now held by self-employed entrepreneurs and their employees.[3] Small business played a significant role in the country's recovery from the Great Recession, too, creating 60 percent of new jobs between 2009 and 2013.

Since then, the rate of business startups has slowly but steadily increased, reaching prerecession levels by 2017. Another positive development is that startup growth has occurred not only in large urban metropolitan areas but also in midsize metropolitan areas.[4] Revenues, profits, and diversity ownership are also on the rise for both new and existing small businesses.[5]

Numerous surveys have consistently shown that more than half (53 percent) of actively working Americans consider starting their own business, and most want to start a small business. One in four corporate executives want to launch their own companies, and 66 percent of millennials, who comprise almost half of the workplace, want to start a business.

> Entrepreneurship has emerged over the last two
> decades as arguably the most potent economic
> force the world has ever experienced.
>
> —Donald F. Kuratko, Executive Director, Johnson Center for
> Entrepreneurship and Innovation, Indiana University at Bloomington

INNOVATION DRIVES ENTREPRENEURSHIP

Many years ago, a large financial institution hired me as a consultant for a substantial amount of money. I found myself in an environment in which I was a rather isolated cog in a big wheel. We workers, regardless of how high up the totem pole, pretty much stayed in our own little boxes, and had little interaction with one another. Everyone just rolled along, following concisely established processes. There was no room for innovation. The unspoken but very clear modus operandi was, here's what we want; here's how you're going to do it; and here's where you're going to stay— right there in that confining little box.

One day about a year into the position, I called my mother from work. About three minutes into the conversation, I said, "Mom, I'm having a really hard time here. It's so structured. There is no open thinking, no open dialogue. Everybody just does their prescribed jobs like robots. I feel like I'm not using my talents or creativity. I can't take it. It's killing me."

She said, "Honey, it's only eight-fifteen in the morning."

My mom's one-sentence reality check was my aha moment. If I was feeling that miserable 15 minutes into my workday, then no amount of money was worth signing away my soul. So I resigned and went back to the idea of building my own business.

Feeling stifled in your job can kill your entrepreneurial spirit, or it can incite you to put your talents and creativity to work on your own venture. The burning desire to innovate—to translate an invention or idea into a product or service that solves a problem, fills a need, or enhances lives—is the catalyst to entrepreneurship for many people.

The technology or concept that kindles your innovation may or may not be your own, and often is not. New scientific discoveries, new technologies, and new business models provide opportunities to apply those developments in innovative ways, giving birth to new products and services upon which new businesses are built. For example, think of the variety of mobile devices, accessories, and apps that have been derived from the original concept of cellular phones. Now think of all the businesses, of varying sizes and stripes, that have been launched to bring those innovations to market.

Of course, the itch to innovate is not the only reason people become entrepreneurs. As the saying goes, necessity is the mother of invention—or reinvention, in many cases. Unemployment, insufficient income, and job instability can also be mighty motivators to create your own economic opportunity by way of business ownership or self-employment. Launching a business may also provide the opportunity to prosper from doing something meaningful or enjoyable to you. Social entrepreneurship is one of the fastest growing paths to business ownership in the United States today.

People build and buy businesses for a variety of reasons—to have more flexibility, more responsibility, more creativity, or more control in their work. To create jobs for other people or a legacy to pass on to their heirs. To maximize their potential or to make more money. Or to pursue a passion. I have met thousands of aspiring entrepreneurs who dream of creating a business that aligns with their passion—and thousands more who have succeeded in doing just that.

Regardless of your motivation for starting or expanding a business, the impetus that turns intention into reality is innovation—the translation of an idea or invention into a unique product or service that customers are willing to pay for. Ultimately, that's what entrepreneurship is all about, and it's what puts the American dream of business ownership within reach of anyone with the desire and gumption to grab that opportunity and run with it.

> The secret sauce that's driven the American economy and the American success story is entrepreneurship.

—Steve Case, Chairman and CEO, Revolution; Founder and
Partner, Revolution Growth; Chairman, Case Foundation;
Cofounder and former CEO and Chairman, AOL

STARTUPS AND SMALL BUSINESSES: AMERICA'S DREAM MAKERS

More than a half million new businesses are launched every year in the United States. During the first two years of operation, these startups generate the majority of the nation's net new jobs. Most of these fledgeling enterprises will remain small to midsize companies. A study by McKinsey & Company found that, although all industries have high-growth firms, in no sector do high-growth companies account for even 5 percent of the total number of firms in any industry. Not all businesses are scalable, and not every entrepreneur aspires to create the next Microsoft, Nike, or Starbucks. Many prefer to start and stay small. But small doesn't mean stagnant. In fact, about 60 percent of small business owners plan to expand their businesses over the next one to five years.[6]

The nation's small businesses make up 99.9 percent of all US employer firms and employ five times more people than do large corporations. Year after year, the SBA Small Business Profile reports that the largest share of small business employment is with firms having fewer than 100 employees and the greatest net job gains are with firms employing fewer than 20 employees. Small business accounts for half of the US gross national product (GDP), to the tune of more than $6 trillion (2017). Creating new small businesses and energizing existing small businesses could create more than 20 million new jobs by 2025.

The gig economy also contributes to the nation's economy. Today, one in eight Americans—over 15 million people, almost 11 percent of the workforce—are currently self-employed in either an incorporated or unincorporated business. One in four self-employed entrepreneurs have at least one paid employee, and self-employed entrepreneurs have a median of three paid employees and collectively employ 29.4 million people. For the majority, self-employment is a conscious career choice, not a hobby business or a response to unemployment. By 2020, it is estimated that more than 20 percent of adult US workers, some 30 million people, will be self-employed in their own businesses.

Now, some people hold that "true" entrepreneurship means building a high-growth company that employs thousands of people and generates hundreds of millions of dollars. I say, if you create a profitable small business that provides employment for a few hundred or a handful of people, or for you and you alone, then you are a successful entrepreneur who is contributing to the economy.

At the end of the day, Americans continue to launch new companies at an astounding rate, and America's small business sector remains the country's economic backbone. Most entrepreneurs and small business owners are exactly where they want to be, and their businesses are doing just fine. In a recent survey of small business owners from a broad spectrum of industries nationwide, almost 70 percent reported that their businesses were profitable. As important, 75 percent rated their happiness level as a business owner at 8 or above on a scale of 1 to 10.

Prosperity and personal satisfaction. Those are the rewards of economic individualism—of innovation, entrepreneurship, and business ownership. The opportunity to do well doing your own thing is still the American dream. And if you can dream it, you can achieve it. But it takes a lot of hard work, a bit of luck, and access to funding and other resources.

The Challenge

It's All About the Cash

America's entrepreneurs, inventors, and small business owners solve problems, improve our quality of life, create jobs, and drive economic growth. So, when the United States drops from the world's top ranks in entrepreneurship and innovation, there is reason for concern. But not for panic. With more than 50 percent of employed adults itching to start a business, 60 percent of small business owners intending to grow their enterprises, more than 500,000 small businesses launched, and more than 40,000 patents filed by independent inventors each year, there is no shortage of opportunity for innovation, entrepreneurship, and small business ownership in the United States. Plenty of motivated, talented, hardworking people have ideas for innovations and enterprises. But it takes more than vision, determination, talent, and hard work to transform a good idea into a profitable enterprise. It also takes capital.

Of course, lack of capital is not the only or always the primary reason startups, small businesses, and inventions bite the dust. But it is often a contributing factor in the more than 60 percent of startups that fall before they fly, the 50 percent of small businesses that never reach the 10-year mark, and the 70 percent of inventions and 40 percent of patented inventions that never make it to market.

The reality is, accessing the capital you need to launch a business, or to expand or stabilize a small business, or to bring a new product or technology to market is often a challenge. It is all the more difficult when you don't know how to play the funding game.

THE FUNDING GAME

Throughout the many years I've been coaching entrepreneurs on how to find the funds they need for their ventures, I've often thought of how similar business funding is to playing chess. In chess, you have to learn the abilities and limitations of all the different chess pieces, and as you move each piece about the board, you have to strategize to stay a few steps ahead in anticipation of getting to a checkmate. In the funding game as in chess, if you don't know the capabilities of all the different players and if you don't have a strategy for maneuvering through the process, you're likely to be frustrated and, ultimately, defeated.

The first thing you need to know about the funding game is that it's not a game. It is serious business, and the stakes are high. Nobody knows better than you what you stand to gain if you come out ahead and what you stand to lose if you come up short. What you might not fully realize is that how much you stand to gain and lose directly correlates to your odds of winning, or even getting to play, the funding game. Lenders and investors can risk only so much, and they take only calculated risks in which they have a high probability of coming out on top. They expect not only to get their money back within a specified period of time but also to make a certain amount of money on that loan or investment. Even grants are contingent upon the grantor receiving something in return—such as control of how the funds are used, a say in how the company operates, or compliance with the grantor's overlying mission.

Two other things to know about the funding game are that you'll probably need to play it numerous times and you'll probably lose more times than you win. Rarely does funding come on the first try or from a single source, and rarely does a business need funding only once in its lifetime. Most people bet all their funding needs on one play—applying to one lender, one investor, or one grantor. Then, they quit the game too soon—after being rejected by that one bank, investor, or organization. I liken business funding to a pizza pie in which each slice is a funding source for a particular funding goal. To win the funding game, you need to be persistent *and* strategic. Your best shot is to identify all the funding opportunities that are a good match for your venture and then take them on, one by one, until you get the funding you need for each of your funding goals.

Another important thing to know is that you need to prepare for the game before you jump in. Most business lenders, investors, and grantors will put you through a veritable obstacle course. They'll ask for and scrutinize your business plan as well as your personal and business financial statements. They'll also assess your personal and business credit scores. They might request additional paperwork, such as bank statements, invoices, and customer orders, and will probably ask many questions about you and your venture. If you're playing the equity funding game, potential investors will also expect you to whip out a pitch deck (presentation) of your idea, product, or business model as well as your company's valuation (worth).

Here's another must-know: You must have skin in the game. That is, you'll need to put some of your own money into the business and/or put up some of your own assets as collateral. Rarely do lenders, investors and grantors provide 100 percent of funding for business expenses. And every potential funder will want to know how much you are able and willing to put in to your venture. Now, I understand that putting your own money and assets into your business can be difficult. Believe me, I have been there, at a time when coming up with even $100 for my business was a lot. But outside financing is often contingent upon the business owner covering a portion of the funding need with their own resources, and we cannot expect others to take on all the financial risk for our ventures while we invest nothing.

These basic rules of the funding game present major hurdles for most entrepreneurs, small business owners, and independent inventors. Unless they can find a way over or around them, those hurdles will eliminate some of them from the game altogether.

THE STATS AND NOTHING BUT THE STATS

To give you an idea of how the funding game is played and typically pans out for startups and small businesses, let's take a look at some telling business financing data. Since three-quarters of startup and small business funding comes from loans, credit cards, and lines of credit, we'll start there—with debt financing.

The most recent annual Small Business Credit Survey, a Federal Reserve study of 8,169 employer firms, yielded the following findings:

- 40 percent applied for credit financing (loans, lines of credit, invoice financing, etc.).

- 55 percent of business loan applicants sought $100,000 or less, and 75 percent sought $250,000 or less.

- Of the 60 percent that did *not* seek financing, 50 percent had sufficient funding, 26 percent didn't want to take on debt, and 13 percent assumed they'd be turned down.

- Of the 40 percent that *did* seek credit financing, almost half applied for bank loans—48 percent at large banks and 47 percent at small banks.

- 59 percent sought financing for expansion, 43 percent for operating expenses, and 26 percent to refinance debt.

- 70 percent of microenterprise, 54 percent of small business, and 61 percent of startup business credit applicants received less than the amount requested.

Various surveys have reported the following small business loan approval rates in recent years:

- Big banks, 23–25 percent
- Credit unions, 36–40 percent
- Small banks (the primary source of SBA loans), 46–50 percent
- Alternative lenders, 52–60 percent
- Institutional lenders (pension funds, insurance companies, etc.), 65–70 percent

Yes, you read that right. Big banks reject about 75 percent and small banks reject about 50 percent of small business loan applications. Yet, almost half (48 percent) of small business owners seek outside financing first from banks.

As for investment capital, only 1 to 3 percent of startups receive venture capital, and only 3 to 5 percent receive angel investment capital. In recent years, that has amounted to about 1,500 startups receiving venture capital and about 50,000 receiving angel capital each year. So how do the rest of the 500,000 to 600,000 small businesses that launch each year get funded?

The most recent Small Business Trends report, a survey of more than 2,600 entrepreneurs and business owners conducted by Guidant Financial and Lending Club, revealed the following:

- The most popular financing methods used by existing business owners were cash/business earnings (60 percent), friends/family (25 percent), 401(k) business financing (20 percent), lines of credit (15 percent), and unsecured loans (10 percent).

- The most popular funding methods used by new business owners were lines of credit (50 percent), SBA loans (47 percent), own cash (34 percent), 401(k) business financing (24 percent), and equipment leasing (21 percent).

- 67 percent of small business owners and 66 percent of startup founders cited lack of capital/cash flow as their top challenge.

- For new businesses, the primary barriers to obtaining funding were insufficient cash for a down payment (56 percent), lack of knowledge about financing options (41 percent), a disqualifying credit score for certain financing options (34 percent), and denied bank loans (24 percent).

Although these data vary somewhat from year to year, especially during and after an economic downturn, they accurately reflect the state of startup and small business funding in the United States over the last few decades. Fortunately, small business lending overall—from both conventional and alternative lenders—has been increasing and continues to improve as I write this book. Some progress is being made on the venture capital front, as well. Nevertheless, far too many startups and small businesses, almost 30 percent, still cannot secure outside funding. That is due, in large part, to how the funding game is being played.

WHY SO MANY STARTUPS AND SMALL BUSINESSES ARE SHUT OUT OF THE FUNDING GAME

The main reason the majority of startups and small businesses do not qualify for traditional debt and equity financing is because the risk is too high and the return on investment too low for those lenders and investors. Although most lenders and investors welcome the opportunity to finance small ventures that meet their criteria, the reality is that banks, venture capitalists, and other conventional financial institutions are risk adverse. Their priority is to mitigate their risk and make their shareholders happy. In the last 20 years, I have met very few loan officers who have ever ventured as an entrepreneur.

Lenders are bound not only by stakeholder requirements but also by government regulations to adhere to strict guidelines that dictate to whom, how much, and under what terms and conditions they can lend money. So, too, are investors required to follow stakeholder requirements and government regulations dictating in whom, how much, and under what terms and conditions they can invest capital. Some of those lending and investment criteria present insurmountable barriers to many startups and small businesses.

The Top 10 Barriers to Getting a Bank Loan

A lot of numbers go into the formula used by conventional lenders (banks, credit unions, finance companies, etc.) to determine whether to make a small business loan. The most important of those are the following.

Time in business. Two years is the minimum required by most banks. Banks rarely lend to startups with less than a year of solid revenues and without sufficient collateral. As a rule of thumb, the longer you've been in business and the stronger your financials, the more likely you are to secure a bank loan. That is because banks use historical data to predict future financial performance. If you are starting out and don't have financial statements to show sales and expenses, it is difficult to make a reliable prediction.

Loan amount. Most large banks have a minimum business loan amount of $100,000 to $200,000 and sometimes higher. Although some banks offer business loans as low as $50,000, the average small business loan in the United States is about $600,000 for large banks and $150,000 for small banks. Three-quarters of small businesses (75 percent) seek loans of less than $250,000, more than half (55 percent) seek loans of less than $100,000, more than a third (34 percent) seek loans of $25,000 to $100,000, and almost a quarter (21 percent) seek loans of $25,000.[1] Regardless of the loan amount, the bank will follow the same due diligence.

Business credit score. The FICO Small Business Scoring Service (SBSS), which is used for term loans and lines of credit up to $1 million, rates business credit on a scale of 0 to 300. The other three main business credit tracking agencies (Dun & Bradstreet, Equifax, Experian) use a scoring scale of 0 to 100. Most banks use the SBSS score because it's based on your business credit score from the other three agencies combined with your personal FICO score and your business financials. Banks want an SBSS score of 160 or higher. Since many small business owners use their own funds to launch their businesses, the SBSS score of a business that's been in operation only a few years may be low due to having little or no business debt.

Personal credit score. Your personal credit score also factors into the bank's assessment of your business's creditworthiness, on the grounds that how you've managed your personal debt is indicative of how you'll manage your business debt. Your personal credit history will also reveal any personal loans you've used to fund your business, as many startups and small businesses do, which can result in a debt load that lowers your personal credit score. Most banks want to see a personal credit score of 700 or higher. A low personal credit score can result in being denied a business loan—even when the business is financially healthy.

Down payment. Banks typically require the business owner to plunk down at least 20 to 30 percent of the financed expense. The amount of the down payment depends on the type of loan and the collateral and/or assets used to secure the loan. Coming up with a down payment is difficult for many small business owners. In fact, almost two-thirds of small business owners cite lack of cash for a down payment as their top challenge in securing funding.

Collateral. Banks almost always require valuable assets owned by the borrower to secure business loans. Should the borrower default on the loan, the bank assumes ownership of the property. Banks want collateral that can be sold for cash, such as real estate and equipment, and the cash value of those assets usually needs to be equal to or greater than the loan amount. Many fledgeling and small businesses do not own enough valuable assets to offer as collateral, and they may be unwilling or unable to use their personal assets (homes and cars) as collateral. In addition, the bank will determine the value of the collateral, and may assign a lower value on a particular asset than you would.

Debt ratio. One of the ways in which banks assess the financial stability and credit risk of a business is to measure the company's total liabilities against its total assets. For example, if your business had $60,000 in liabilities and $100,000 in assets, your debt ratio ($60,000 divided by $100,000) would be 0.6. Banks typically require a debt ratio of 0.4 or lower.

Cash flow. Banks want to see at least $1.25 in positive cash flow for every $1 of total debt payment. This provides assurance that, every month, you'll have enough money to pay the loan payment *and* all your business expenses *and* still have money left in the bank. Staying consistently, much less sufficiently, in the black is a challenge for most startups and many small businesses, even when they're profitable. The median small business has $1.03 coming in for every $1 going out, on any given day. That is not much wiggle room for unplanned expenses, delayed payments from customers, and unexpected dips in sales. Inadequate cash flow to cover operating expenses is why 45 percent of business seek financing in the first place. It's also one of the top reasons they're denied bank loans.

Revenue. Banks typically require a minimum of $100,000 to $250,000 in annual revenue, depending on the type of loan, whether and how it is secured, the profitability of the business, and other factors. Some large banks set even higher revenue thresholds, and some banks and other conventional lenders accept revenues of less than $100,000 for otherwise financially sound small businesses. Only 35 percent of small businesses generate $100,000 or more in revenue, which knocks almost two-thirds (65 percent) of small businesses out of the running for the standard bank loan.

Profitability. Banks want to know that your business is profitable enough that you'll have the liquid capital to pay back the loan. They're usually interested in both your gross profit margins (earnings less cost of goods sold) and net profit margins (earnings less all expenses) over the last few years. They might also compare your profit margins with industry averages and your direct competitors. Almost 60 percent of small businesses are profitable, 18 percent are breaking even, and 24 percent are losing money.[2] However, small business profit margins are often too narrow to meet the profitability thresholds set by most banks, and most new businesses don't break even for two or three years.

The bottom line is that small business loans tend to yield insufficient profits for big banks. Underwriting and transacting any business loan is labor-intensive. It costs about the same amount to process a $50,000 loan as it does a $1 million loan, but the bank earns considerably more profit on the $1 million loan. Consequently, many small business loan applications receive the same scrutiny as, if not more than, large business loans. In many cases, the small business owner meets with a loan officer who is not an underwriter and completes a standard loan application form, which the bank's automated credit approval system accepts or rejects the loan, without the loan officer reviewing the business plan. In other cases, based on the business owner's responses to the loan officer's questions pertaining to the five standard criteria for a bank loan (character, cash flow, condition, capital, collateral), the loan officer may suggest that the entrepreneur not submit an application because the business is not ready or eligible for a loan at that time.

That's exactly what happened the first time I applied for a business loan at a bank, one of the largest in the country. The loan officer at the branch where I'd been doing my personal banking for years didn't even bother to look at my business plan and revenue projections. He didn't even bother to run my credit score. He asked years in business (*zero*), down payment (*zero*), collateral (*zero*), and that was that. The bank's lending rules required two years in business, 20 percent down, and assets to secure the loan. And those rules could not be broken or bent for anyone.

The saying that you are more attractive to an employer if you have a job than if you're unemployed or underemployed is similar to funding. You are more attractive to a lender or investor if you have capital and assets than if you have little or no money and collateral.

The bottom line is, if your business doesn't measure up to the bank's lending criteria, you have a slim chance of getting the loan.

Why the Odds of a Getting Venture Capital Are Slim to None

One reason so few small businesses use venture capital is many founders opt out of the VC game because they're unwilling to hand over the 20 to 25 percent ownership and decision-making power that venture capitalists typically require. Others realize that venture capital is out of their reach because their businesses are and always will be too small for venture capitalists.

That still leaves tens of thousands of entrepreneurs and inventors who would gladly jump into the shark tank if given the chance. Most won't. Here's why:

Only budding upstarts need apply. Financial investors typically invest in emerging businesses with the demonstrated potential to grow rapidly and substantially in a large and diverse national or global market. Venture capitalists rarely invest in unproven business concepts and product ideas unless they are backed with a strong patent or solid research and development. Nor do venture capitalists usually invest in established small businesses that cannot be scaled to meet the VC's hefty revenue and growth requirements.

High expectations. Venture capital investing is all about the *venture*—the high-risk gamble that their investment will deliver a tenfold or higher return on investment within four to seven years. Most VCs bet on a 25 to 35 percent annual return on investment (ROI) over the lifetime of the investment, and they only bet on emerging businesses they deem capable of bringing in at least $10,000 a month in revenues and on high-revenue, high-growth established companies. Those steep return on investment and revenue requirements knock many startups and small businesses out of the running for VC capital.

Specialized investment focus. The venture capital game is dominated by technology and technology-enabled companies. In recent years, information and communications technology (ICT) companies have received the largest portion of venture capital, at more than 50 percent. The second largest portion went to lifestyle science, at more than 20 percent. Each venture capital firm focuses on one or more vertical industries—for example, the biotech and medical devices verticals of the healthcare sector. Venture capitalists focus on verticals in which they have expertise and for which there is a large and growing market. Rarely do VC firms step outside their areas of specialization, and a large percentage of small businesses simply do not fit those molds.

By invitation only. The best way, and often the only way, to get your foot in the door of a VC firm is to get a referral from a professional within their network—a financial executive, research associate, business accelerator, founder of a successful company. It is sometimes possible to make a connection with investors at industry events. Most venture capitalist firms also actively search for entrepreneurs and startups that fit their bill, in which case they initiate contact. Securing venture capital is as much about networking as it is about growth potential. Unfortunately, many founders lack those connections and are too focused on launching and building their businesses to do the networking that attracting venture capital typically requires.

Location, location, location. For several years, half of the venture capital invested and managed in the United States is in companies located in three states: California, New York, and Massachusetts. Although venture capital flows into the majority of the country's major metropolitan areas, those receiving the largest percentage of VC dollars have consistently been San Francisco Bay Area, New York City, Boston, Los Angeles, and Washington, DC. These five metro areas accounted for more than 80 percent of total venture capital investment and 85 percent of VC investment growth over the past decade (2008–2018). Other top VC concentrations are Chicago, Seattle, and San Diego. Altogether, the lion's share of venture capital has been divvied up between the same 20 or so metropolitan areas, year after year. If your business isn't located or won't be relocated in or near a VC hot spot, your odds of securing venture capital shrink accordingly.

Long, arduous process. It can take months to find and then get an audience with a venture capital firm that invests in ventures like yours. If you manage to connect with one of the firm's general partners, who then agrees to hear your elevator pitch (which you may be asked to e-mail) and likes it, you will be invited to a one-on-one meeting. If the meeting goes well, you'll be invited to give a formal presentation to the firm's partners. The game often ends there. But if you're still in the game after presenting your pitch deck, the VC firm will invite you to a few more get-acquainted meetings before determining whether they're interested in investing in your business. If they are, and if you agree to their terms, the VC firm will go through their due diligence process, which typically takes 39 to 90 days. From elevator pitch to check in hand, you're looking at six months. Add to that the months spent looking for and trying to get the attention of the right VC firm, and you've got nine months to a year into the VC game. Many startups can't afford to wait that long for an infusion of capital.

People power. Venture capitalists don't look solely at the progress and potential of an emerging business; they also look at the character and capabilities of the founding team. They want a strong, cohesive, and fully engaged management team that has a shared vision as well as the expertise, flexibility, and desire to overcome hurdles, to pivot when necessary, to go big, and to take it all the way home. They want the core team to have all the bases covered: product development, financial management, marketing, technology. Many small businesses start off with one or two founders and with insufficient capital to hire experienced managers.

Demand exceeds supply. There are 800 to 1,000 venture capital firms in the United States, and a VC firm considers 400 to 1,000 investment proposals per year. That means, on average, 900 US venture capital firms each consider 700 investment proposals a year, or 630,000 proposals. In a good year, US venture capitalists make 8,000 to 10,000 deals a year. That works out to 1.43 percent of investment proposals resulting in a VC investment.

Exit is inevitable. The ultimate goal of every angel investor and VC firm is to cash out within 7 to 10 years of initial investment, by either selling the company (M&A) or taking it public (IPO). An IPO is usually the preferred liquidity route of most investors, while an M&A is the more likely liquidity route for many startups. Most venture capitalists seek to invest in companies that stand a realistic chance of going public. For some entrepreneurs, selling a profitable growth company or taking it public after 5 to 10 years of hard work is a dream come true. For others, it's the end of their entrepreneurial dream, especially if their share of the proceeds from the liquidation of their business isn't enough to start another business. The unfortunate reality is that most startups are likely to fail before reaching either an M&A or an IPO. An analysis of 3,200 startup companies conducted by the Startup Genome Project concluded that not only will 9 out of 10 startups fail to achieve a liquidity event, they also go out of business altogether.[3]

———

The Avenue of Lost Dreams is paved with the millions of great ideas that didn't pan out because the innovators, entrepreneurs, and small business owners were unable to access the capital they needed to launch, improve, expand, or sustain their enterprises. It doesn't have to be that way. Banks and venture capital firms are valuable players in the funding game, but they aren't the only games in town, and they're not always the first or best funding option for you. You can play the funding game a different way— more creatively and strategically, targeting the funding sources that are the best match for you and your business.

The Solution

Target Funding

It may seem ironic that in the land of opportunity—where innovation and business ownership are cornerstones not only of the American dream but also of the US economy, responsible for half of all jobs and sales—the majority of startups, small businesses, and independent inventors cannot get a business loan or venture capital. When I was denied credit for my first business, I was stunned. It didn't matter that I had a bullet-proof business plan in my hand and a business degree in my back pocket. Nor did it matter that I'd had personal accounts with the bank for more than seven years. The only thing that mattered was that I didn't have the collateral, net worth, and credit score the bank required.

Fortunately, I found other ways and means to turn my idea into a successful business. Unfortunately, that is not the case for many people, whose inability to attain debt and/or equity financing often means the death of their dreams.

If you have been turned down by lenders or investors for the money you need to start, buy, improve, or grow your business, or to bring your invention to market, or to turn your passion or expertise into gainful self-employment: Don't worry about it! Other funding options are available to you right now, I guarantee it. And funding opportunities for which you do "not now" meet the criteria could be within your reach in a year or two.

Even if you do qualify for a bank loan or venture capital, I encourage you to also investigate other funding options as part of your funding strategy. In fact, I usually advise my clients to uncover and consider every dollar and every dollar's worth of resources available to them via alternative funding options—starting with those that are free. Yes, *free*! As in not having to pay it back, pay interest, or hand over a piece of your company.

Did you just experience a flutter of hope, only to have it dashed by skeptical thoughts: *If it sounds too good to be true, it probably is. If these "free" and "alternative" funding sources are legit, why haven't I heard of them before? What's the catch?* Many of my clients have asked me those same questions. And I've told them the same thing I'm about to tell you.

Those mindsets kill dreams—needlessly. Contrary to popular belief, many *proven* alternative funding options are not only attainable but also designed for ventures like yours. It's just that most people, including many business educators and counselors, don't know about these funding options. Even I didn't when I sought funding for my first business, despite having an MBA and being a fifth-generation entrepreneur.

If free money and resources are available to you to help get your business or invention off the ground or to the next level, you need to know about it! You need to know about *every* funding option, free or not, that is meant especially for entrepreneurs like you and ventures like yours. You also need a strategic plan for pinpointing and pursuing the funding opportunities that are the best for you.

I call that *target funding.* And it's easier than you might think, once you know where the funding is and have a strategy to access it.

SHOW ME THE FUNDING!

If the vast majority of early-stage entrepreneurs, small businesses, and independent inventors can't get conventional business loans or venture capital, where *do* they find the funds to start up, scale up, or shore up their businesses? According to the latest surveys of the US Small Business Association (SBA) and the National Small Business Association (NSBA), 82 to 85 percent of startup funds and 45 to 48 percent of expansion or stabilization funds come from the respective business owners and their family and friends. More than three-quarters (77 percent) of initial and early-stage funding comes from the owner's (or inventor's) personal savings, with the remainder coming primarily from personal credit cards, home equity loans, and selling personal assets.

But what about the 30 percent of small business owners who have few personal assets and a less-than-ideal credit rating? And what about those who manage to raise their own and even outside capital, but it falls short, leaving their business undercapitalized and unable to realize its potential? How do all those people fund their businesses and bring their inventions to market?

Having been in that position myself and having helped thousands of businesses in that position, I can tell you how: they find creative ways to fund their ventures. You can, too! And I'll show you how.

Regardless of whether your business is "bankable" and "investment-worthy," I encourage you to look into alternative funding options and to go after those that are right for you *before*, if not also instead of, seeking credit financing or equity financing. The more funding you get for free or at reduced cost, the less money comes out of your pocket and the better your ability to manage cash flow. The fewer equity shares of your company are held by others, the higher your percentage of your company's profits and the more control you have over your business.

I also encourage you to broaden your concept of funding to encompass more than money. Your funding strategy should include not only the money you *raise*, but also the money you *save* by getting the resources you need (materials, equipment, space, professional services) as a gift, in trade, or at a discount.

At its most basic, all business funding comes from one or more of the following:

- You, the business owner or inventor (self-funding)
- Donors (gift-based funding)
- Lenders (debt funding)
- Investors (equity funding)

What most people don't realize is this: There are multiple *funding options* within each of those four funding types, and you'll usually find multiple *funding sources* of each funding option. Sometimes the best funding opportunities for most startups, small businesses, and independent inventors are *alternative* forms of funding—all of which are actually specialized forms of self-funding, gift funding, debt funding, and equity funding.

For example, self-funding may come not only from your retirement and 401(k) funds but also (or instead) from bootstrapping, bartering, and cooperatives. Gift-based funding may come not only from family and friends but also (or instead) from matched savings grants, awards from business competitions, crowdfunding, no-cost or low-cost professional services, and grants from government agencies, business incubators and accelerators, and community organizations.

Likewise, debt-based funding may come not only by way of commercial loans from banks but also (or instead) from SBA-guaranteed loans, interest-free loans, revenue-based loans, microloans, nonprofit community lenders, online lending platforms, and "niche" lenders that focus on a specific demographic or type of business. Equity-based funding may come from crowdfunding, angel investors, and "boutique" venture capital groups that specialize in companies in a certain industry, certain location, or founded by entrepreneurs of a certain ethnicity, gender, or socioeconomic disadvantage.

You will learn about the various funding options for startups and small business as you read this book. What's more, you'll learn which ones are aimed at entrepreneurs like you and ventures like yours.

LEAN (BUT NOT MEAN) SELF-FUNDING

As attractive and as necessary as it might be to fund your business with other people's money (OPM), you will need to use some of your personal resources to fund your business or invention. But that doesn't mean you should deplete your personal assets or max out your personal credit. Unlike many business funding consultants, I do *not* advise mortgaging your home to the hilt, draining your retirement savings, tapping into your children's education funds, or selling off all your valuables. In my opinion, business ownership should be about improving your quality of life, not sacrificing it.

A self-funding strategy I do recommend is *bootstrapping*—that is, minimizing your expenses and stretching your resources. I am all for bootstrapping. In both my business and personal life, I am the queen of bootstrapping! I'm always wheeling and dealing, and I'm a shrewd negotiator. Before spending a dime, I also assess whether the expenditure is a necessity, a priority, or a luxury and then adjust my funding strategy accordingly.

That said, I won't—and strongly advise you not to—cut so many corners that it shortchanges my (or your) business, running so lean that it inhibits the value or growth of the company. Bootstrapping is about doing more with less. It is not about deferring or forgoing something that is critical to the survival and success of your business.

A few bootstrapping options to consider are:

Bartering. Entrepreneurs have been trading their wares and skills in exchange for the goods and services they need for their business for centuries. Nowadays, thanks to the Internet, you can swap goods and services with members of a local, national, or even global *trade exchange* group. These professional trade exchange networks are also known as *community exchange systems*, *local exchange and trading systems* (LETS), *mutual credit trading systems*, *time banks*, and *clearing circles*. The products or services you offer to the network may or may not be those you sell through your business. For example, a former CPA who now owns a vineyard and winery might offer bookkeeping services or cases of wine in exchange for bottle label design services or a tractor. Trading what you have for what you need is a win-win funding opportunity that eliminates the need for cash.

Buyer cooperatives. A purchasing and shared services cooperative is a nonprofit association that is formed, owned, and governed by its member businesses for the purpose of combining their purchasing power to negotiate wholesale and discounted prices for goods and services commonly used by its members. Additionally, buyer co-ops are often able to obtain a better selection and quality of products and services, better return or exchange terms, and better delivery service than a small or medium-size business could get on its own. Buyer co-ops exist for many industry sectors—from farms to restaurants, hotels, medical practices, "green" building contractors, and more. Joining a buyer cooperative can save you money and give you more bang for your buck.

> **Producer cooperatives.** Members of a producer cooperative band together
> to leverage their ability to acquire credit and to negotiate reduced prices for
> materials, supplies, equipment, and services to produce their products. Some
> producer co-ops also enable members to jointly market, sell, and distribute
> their products. Such cooperatives are typically owned by farmers, ranchers,
> fishermen, foresters, artisans, craftsmen, and small manufacturers. Joining a
> cooperative of businesses that produce products similar to yours can offer sim-
> ilar benefits to participating in a buyers' cooperative.

TARGET FUNDING MADE EASY

When I made it my mission to find money and resources for underserved
businesses, I was amazed to discover how much funding was available to a
wide range of businesses. It was as if all these funding opportunities were
being kept secret, and I'd found a treasure map marking all the funding
opportunities targeted at a certain type of business owner or business.

Most business owners are familiar with the concept of *target marketing*—in which a business identifies the key characteristics of the customers most likely to buy its products or services, and then focuses its
marketing (and often its product development) on that segment of the
market. Those characteristics are known as *variables*, and a company's
marketing strategist identifies the geographic, demographic, psycho-
graphic, and/or behavioral variables that apply to its ideal customer. For
example, although everyone buys toilet paper, customers with certain
shared variables are likely to buy plain, inexpensive toilet paper, while
those with certain other shared characteristics are likely to spend more on
toilet paper that is softer, thicker, prettier, scented, organic, recycled, or a
specific brand.

Many funding opportunities are eligible exclusively to enterprises that
fit a specific variable or set of variables. The types of variables typically
associated with business funding include:

- **Demographic.** Age, ethnicity, gender, military service, disability, sexual orientation, income level, other "diversity" variable
  (immigrant, refugee, business owner over age 50, Christian,
  Jewish, Muslim).

- **Geographic.** Country, region of country, county, state, city, neighborhood; population density (rural, suburban, urban); population size; economically distressed zone; regional industry cluster.
- **Size of business.** Microenterprise, small business, medium-sized business, annual revenues.
- **Industry sector.** Retail, financial services, technology, agriculture, healthcare, construction, creative, green, social impact, manufacturing, etc.
- **Stage of business.** Idea stage, research and development stage, startup, early-stage, growth stage, established, expansion stage, mature, etc.

Essentially, target funding involves applying the principles of target marketing to find the funding opportunities that most closely align with your variables. For example, a Native American, disabled military veteran with few personal assets who needs funding to develop a solar farm in a rural area of New Mexico might investigate potential funding opportunities for businesses having the following variables:

- Startup (small-scale)
- Small business
- Minority (specifically, Native American) business owner
- Service-disabled veteran-owned business
- Business owned by a person with a disability
- Renewable energy business (technology, sustainability)
- Rural economic development opportunity

Please note that I used the word *investigate,* which means not only to look *for* but also to look *into* something—in this case, to identify and assess all potential funding solutions for your business or invention. Although you may be tempted to then pursue every funding opportunity for which you may be eligible, that defeats the purpose of target funding. Target funding is not about casting a wide net and hauling in whatever you happen to snag; it's about cherry-picking the funding solutions that are best for you. This strategic approach to funding your business enables you to zero in on the funding opportunities that will have the most positive impact and the least negative impact on your business.

Keep in mind, too, that your funding options will change as your business grows. A funding source that might be a good fit for you now may not be in the future. Likewise, a funding opportunity that is not available or suitable now may be in the future. Target funding enables you to identify the best available solutions for your current and evolving funding needs.

Target funding begins by mapping out the potential funding options (types of funding) and funding sources (providers of a funding option) that best match your funding situation. However, before you can develop your funding map, you must first get a handle on where your business is now, what you need to do to take it to the next level, and what resources are required to get from here to there. Once you know that information, you can create your target funding map.

Creating a funding map is a three-step process that involves:

1. Identifying the expenditures and resources needed to meet your business objectives.

2. Identifying the funding opportunities for which you might be eligible, based on the funding variables applying to you and your business.

3. Prioritizing which funding solutions to target and in what sequence.

I'll walk you through that process in Chapter 20, "Creating Your Funding Map."

For now, to help you get a jump on identifying which funding solutions might be right for you, I've created the questionnaire below. Each question for which you answer *yes* indicates a variable associated with one or more potential funding opportunities presented in this book.

TARGET-FUNDING QUESTIONNAIRE

Check the YES box next to each item that applies to your business.

At what stage is your business (i.e., idea, startup, early-stage, growth stage, expansion stage)?

YES

Do you need funds for specific business advising? ❑

Do you need funds to hire an expert or mentor to advise you? ❑

Do you need funds to file a patent, trademark, or copyright? ❑

Do you need funds to build a proof-of-concept or prototype
for your product idea? ❑

Do you need funds for equipment, supplies, professional services,
or other resources to develop, launch, operate, or grow your business? ❑

Do you need funds for space in which to produce or store/distribute
your products or to operate your business? ❑

Do your specific business advising, equipment/materials,
technical assistance, and/or space needs impact the ability
to start, operate, or grow your business? ❑

Does your business qualify as a small business, per the US Small
Business Administration's current size standards? ❑

Do you have a network of individuals (family, friends, colleagues,
mentors) that support or would support your business? ❑

Are you actively involved in your local community, and does or
would your community support your business concept? ❑

Is your product or service exclusively or primarily for a certain
demographic group, such as seniors or minorities? ❑

Does your product or service provide a positive social impact,
such as helping kids with autism, reducing the number of people
facing hearing loss, or sustainably producing organic food? ❑

	YES
Does your new product or product idea have the potential to be licensed?	❏
Does your product or service appeal to the mass market (a wide range of consumers)?	❏
Can you see your products being sold via a television infomercial?	❏
Can you see your products or service being sold internationally (exported)?	❏
Can you see federal, state, and/or local government agencies purchasing your products or services?	❏
Is your product or service something that businesses, public institutions (such as hospitals and universities), and/or nonprofit organizations would consider purchasing?	❏
Can you see your products or services competing in business-plan and business-pitch competitions for awards, grants, or scholarships?	❏
Would you be able to trade your products or services for any of the funding and/or resources you need for your business or invention?	❏
Does your business provide innovative technologies or technology-enabled products or services?	❏
Is your business "creative" in nature (i.e., art gallery, photography, theater, interior design, fashion, woodworking, publishing, graphic design)?	❏
Does your business have significant repeat customers that you invoice?	❏
Does your business provide a product or service that qualifies it for an industry cluster in your region?	❏
Does your business provide jobs in your community or otherwise contribute to the economic development of your community?	❏
Are you considering or open to purchasing a franchise?	❏
Does a woman own the business?	❏
Does a military veteran own the business?	❏
Does a person with a disability own the business?	❏

	YES
Does the business owner belong to a minority group (African-American, Asian-American, Hispanic, Native American)?	❏
Does the business owner fit another "diversity" or "disadvantaged" variable (low-income, LGBTQ, immigrant, refugee, over age 50)?	❏
Is your business growing at a fast pace, or does it have significant growth potential?	❏
Is your business scalable?	❏

As you continue reading this book, you'll be able to identify the funding solutions that align with each yes you've checked on this questionnaire.

PART TWO

Diversity Funding

Funding for Veteran-Owned Businesses

Almost 2.5 million American businesses, one in nine, are owned by veterans of the United States military. Collectively, these businesses generate more than $1.1 trillion in sales, employ nearly 6 million people, and pay over $210 billion in payroll each year. Located in all parts of the country, vet-owned businesses span a wide range of industries, from retail to manufacturing, technology, construction, energy, transportation, real estate, agriculture, healthcare, education, and the list goes on. Upward of 250,000 service members return to civilian life each year, many of whom have the skill sets and desire to become business owners. In fact, veterans are 45 times more likely than nonveterans to be self-employed business owners.

Veterans who wish to start, buy, improve, or expand a business face the same funding challenges as their nonveteran counterparts. In addition, some veterans are eligible for funding that is targeted specifically for veterans, such as the sources featured in this chapter.

If you have served your country, you deserve to know about funding that has been set aside for veterans. Armed with that information, you can then decide whether it is advantageous for you to target one or more of the vet-specific funding opportunities available to you.

VETERANS AFFAIRS BUSINESS GRANTS
FOR SERVICE-DISABLED VETERANS

The Vocational Rehabilitation and Employment (VR&E) program of the US Department of Veterans Affairs (VA) offers self-employment and business ownership grants for service-disabled veterans. The VR&E self-employment grant, also known as the Chapter 31 program (Title 38 of the United States Code, Chapter 31) is a disability benefit through the Veterans Benefits Administration (VBA). It is available to all veterans who qualify and apply for a Chapter 31 grant. VR&E grants are used primarily to provide self-employment that is possible given the applicant's disabilities. Candidates for the VR&E self-employment track are assigned to either a Category I or Category II grant, based on the "severity of the disability and the limitations to employability."

A service-disabled veteran who owns an existing business may be entitled to a VR&E grant (Category I or II) if that vocation is unsuitable due to the vet's disability. In that case, funding may be provided for services to help the veteran overcome his or her impairments to employment in the existing business. Funding is *not* provided for expenditures relating solely to improving, updating, or expanding an existing suitable business unless the expenditure is related to disability accommodations.

VR&E grants of up to $25,000 can be approved by the veteran's local Vocational Rehabilitation Officer. Amounts greater than $25,000 require approval from the local Vocational Rehabilitation Director. Grant awards may be used for vocational training, rehabilitative services relating to the veteran's VR&E training and rehabilitation plan, business training, inventory, supplies, equipment, and/or business licenses and insurance.

Meet with your local Veterans Administration vocational rehabilitation counselor (VRC) to inquire about and begin the application process for a VR&E self-employment grant. Come prepared with facts and figures demonstrating the viability of your business idea, your capabilities to launch and run the business, and verification of your service-related disability.

Ask your VRC about "fast tracking" your self-employment plan. Fast track planning may be used if self-employment is the primary focus of your vocational rehabilitation goals.

If you previously participated in either the VA's Chapter 31 self-employment program or a state vocational rehabilitation program and don't currently meet Chapter 31 criteria, ask your VA counselor about "limited and specifically defined" self-employment assistance under program 38 U.S.C. 3117.

A GUN SHOP OF HIS OWN

Eric Landon (an alias) proudly served in the US Air Force. His 20-year military career included management and supervisory experience, training instructor, firearms/weapons inspector, ammunition and supply accountability, records management, and several other areas of responsibility. After Eric was honorably discharged from the military, he set his sights on starting a gunsmith business that focused on selling and servicing firearms and accessories and on teaching and promoting firearm safety practices. His target markets were civilian defense contractors, government agencies, and consumer firearm enthusiasts.

Eric applied for VR&E self-employment benefits and was assigned a Category I. Although it took almost five years for the VA to approve his grant and release the funds, that $70,000 enabled him to acquire the training, equipment, and supplies to open his gun shop. The business successfully launched and continues to thrive.

PRIVATE GRANTS FOR VETERAN-OWNED BUSINESSES

Private grants for veteran-owned businesses are hard to come by, but they're usually easier to qualify and apply for than government grants. So it might be worthwhile to spend a few hours searching the Internet for nonprofit organizations offering business grants to veteran-owned businesses. Two such grant programs for veteran entrepreneurs are briefly described here.

Farmer Veteran Fellowship Fund

The Farmer Vet Coalition accepts applications for Farmer Veteran Fellowship grants during a limited period once a year. Grant recipients are required to participate in the Farmer Veteran Fellowship Program, which includes periodic progress reports and mentoring of other farmer veterans.

Eligibility	Honorably discharged veteran or active service member with an agricultural or ranching startup.
Grant	Monetary grant of $1,000–$5,000, for which funds go to the third-party vendor, rather than directly to the veteran, for the purchase of items needed to launch the business.

StreetShares Veteran Small Business Awards

This initiative of StreetShares Foundation (the nonprofit arm of StreetShares) in partnership with Samuel Adams Brewing Company is a cross between a business grant, pitch competition, and mini-accelerator.

Eligibility	Veteran, reservist, and active-duty member of the US military (or spouses of), who are US residents, at least 21 years of age, and a majority owner of a for-profit legal business in the United States.
Grants	Three monetary grants per month: $15,000 first prize; $6,000 second prize; $4,000 third prize. Plus in-kind business coaching and mentoring.

COMPETITION-BASED FUNDING FOR VETERAN-OWNED BUSINESSES

Various state and local government agencies, nonprofit organizations, and industry associations sponsor or cosponsor business competitions for veteran-owned startups. Some of these competitions are open to veteran-owned businesses nationwide, while others are open to veteran-owned businesses in a specific geographic area. Competition winners typically receive cash awards and business coaching and/or assistance.

Veteran Shark Tank

This annual business-pitch competition is an initiative of the Greater Philadelphia Veterans Network (GPVN), backed by corporate sponsors, and hosted by the Urban League of Philadelphia, Pennsylvania.

| Eligibility | Greater Philadelphia-based startup or early-stage business that is majority-owned by a US veteran or service member who is a US resident. |
| Awards | Cash prize (grant) of up to $20,000, plus in-kind services and support. |

Veteran's Business Battle

A joint initiative of the Houston chapter of Entrepreneurs' Organization (a global peer-to-peer nonprofit organization) and the Veterans in Business Association (VIBA) at Rice University's Graduate School of Business, Veterans Business Battle (VBB) is a two-day event of workshops and networking opportunities that culminates in a business-pitch competition.

| Eligibility | Idea-stage or early-stage companies that are majority (51 percent) owned and controlled by honorably discharged US veterans. |
| Awards | Applicants selected to compete in VBB receive free admittance to the two-day event, space to exhibit business materials, and the opportunity to pitch their venture to a panel of potential investors, lenders, and corporate partners. VIBA awards a $1,000 cash prize (grant) to a voted-upon "crowd favorite." VBB competitors typically receive debt and/or equity financing as a result of their participation in the event. |

INCUBATOR/ACCELERATOR-BASED FUNDING FOR VETERAN-OWNED BUSINESSES

A few incubators and accelerators, such as Bunker Labs and Vet-Tech, target veteran-led ventures throughout the country. Other incubators and accelerators target veteran-led startups in specific geographic areas—such as Future Lab's Veteran Entrepreneurship Training (New York City); Military Entrepreneur Development Center (San Diego, California); The Armory Incubator (Phoenix, Arizona); Venture Hive (Fort Walton Beach, Florida); Washington University's Veteran's Incubator for Better

Entrepreneurship, VIBE (Tacoma, Washington); and VetLaunch (New Orleans).

Bunker Labs

Founded by veteran entrepreneur Todd Connor, Bunker Labs is a national nonprofit membership organization supported through corporate sponsorships. During its first three years, Bunker Labs ran a 12-week in-house accelerator program at its Chicago headquarters, while local Bunker Labs chapters offering entrepreneurial training and networking opportunities sprang up around the country. Today, Bunker Labs provides accelerator services at a national level through Launch Lab Online while continuing to provide local networking and other resources through chapters in several US cities.

Eligibility	Startup, early-stage, or growth-stage companies that are majority owned and led by US veterans, active service members, and/or their spouses.
Program	10-mission online course providing over 1,000 hours of entrepreneurial education, thought leadership, tools, and resources. Includes weekly check-ins with veteran founders.
Cost	Local and national meetups, pitch competitions (with cash prizes), and access to a network of veteran entrepreneurs and veteran-focused investors.

Vet-Tech

Vet-Tech is a nonprofit organization that focuses exclusively on accelerating the nation's veteran-led startups. Headquartered at the Plug and Play Tech Center in Silicon Valley, Vet-Tech connects US veterans and service members with an expansive support network, including Plug and Play, one of the world's largest incubators and accelerators, and Founder's Institute, one of the world's largest idea-stage and startup-launch accelerators.

Eligibility	Idea- or early-stage technology-related startups; majority owned and led by US veterans or active service members; located anywhere in the United

	States; with a team, minimum viable product (MVP), traction, and scalability.
Program	14-week program tailored to the individual startup. Hands-on guidance from advisors and mentors; startup resources; access to corporate partnerships and funding opportunities.
Cost	No application or program fees. Vet-Tech seeks an equity stake (usually, single digit) in the "most promising companies" in its accelerator.
Perks	Free and discounted professional services. Ongoing access to the Vet-Tech network. Access to 100Vets, an initiative of Vet-Tech and Funder's Institute (FI), that enables veteran founders to apply for a Funder's Institute Fellowship, which provides a full refund to FI's startup launch program.

GOVERNMENT LOAN PROGRAMS FOR VETERAN-OWNED BUSINESSES

Various state, county, and city governments around the country offer loan programs for veteran business owners, which typically offer more flexible terms than most conventional lenders. Two such lending programs are briefly described here, to give you an idea of what might be available in your area.

Colorado: Veteran Access Loan Opportunity Resource

Veteran Access Loan Opportunity Resource (VALOR) is an initiative of the Colorado Enterprise Fund (CEF), a nonprofit organization and community development financial institution (CDFI), in referrals and business counseling from local SBA Small Business Development Centers.

Eligibility	Small businesses located in the State of Colorado that are majority owned by veterans who do not qualify for a business loan from a bank.
Loan	Term loan of up to $500,000. Zero interest for up to six months, then discounted 2 percent from

standard CEF interest rate. Up to 10 years repayment terms. 1.3 percent loan initiation fee.

Uses   Working capital, equipment, inventory, property improvements, business purchases, purchases of commercial real estate.

New York: Veteran Loan Program

This program is administered by the New York Business Development Center (NYBDC) and supported by the New York State Common Retirement Fund, the New York State Comptroller, and partnering banks.

Eligibility   Small businesses located in the State of New York, majority owned by New York residents who are current or former members of the US military.

Loan   Term loan of $50,000–$100,000. Below-market fixed interest rate. Repayment terms vary based on need and use.

Uses   Working capital, business acquisition, purchase of real estate, machinery, equipment.

ONLINE LENDING PLATFORMS SUPPORTING VETERAN-OWNED BUSINESSES

At this time, StreetShares is the only online lending platform focused solely on veteran-owned businesses. However, some online business lending platforms—such as Connect2Capital—give special consideration and sometimes more flexible terms to veteran-owned businesses.

Connect2Capital

C2C is the online lending platform of Community Reinvestment Fund (CRF) USA, a national nonprofit community development financial institution (CDFI).

Eligibility   Small businesses majority-owned by veterans and headquartered in the United States that qualify for an SBA Advantage Loan.

Loan	Term loan of $50,000–$4 million. Prime plus 2.75 percent interest rate. Up to 25 years repayment terms. Down payment as low as 10 percent.
Uses	Business acquisition, owner-occupied commercial real estate, leasehold improvements, equipment, working capital, debt refinancing.

StreetShares

Cofounder and CEO Mark L. Rockefeller, an Air Force veteran who served in Iraq, has described StreetShares as "*Shark Tank* meets eBay." StreetShares pledges the first 5 percent of the requested loan amount, and investor members compete in online auctions to bid any portion (up to 90 percent per bidder) of the requested loan amount. StreetShares combines the lowest bids into a single loan, which ensures the lowest possible interest rate. StreetShares collects the funds from lenders, takes its 10 percent fee off the top, and disperses the remaining funds to the borrower.

Eligibility	Incorporated or limited liability corporations, in operation at least one year, with at least $25,000 in revenues and growing, majority-owned by a US resident who is a US veteran.
Loans	Term loan: $2,000–$100,000; maximum 20 percent of annual revenue. Line of credit: $5,000–$100,000; maximum 20 percent of annual revenue. Contract financing (term loan) up to $500,000. 6–14 percent interest on a term loan; 2.95 percent interest per draw on a line of credit. 3–36 months repayment terms; installments paid weekly via automatic electronic withdrawal from borrower's account. 3.9–4.95 percent closing fee; comes out of principal. Guarantor but no collateral required.

AN ILLUMINATING BUSINESS RISES UP AND SHINES

Zachary Green enlisted in the US Marine Corps at the age of 18. After serving as an infantryman and completing the Officer Candidate Program at Quantico, he transitioned out of the service and into the corporate world, working in brand development, marketing, and sales. Then came the 9/11 terrorist attacks on the United States, which inspired Zach to become a volunteer firefighter. Working in smoke-darkened buildings motivated him to wrap his fire helmet and tools with glow-in-the-dark tape. He soon began making and selling more sophisticated versions of his photo-luminescent firefighting gear to fire stations in the Cincinnati, Ohio area. Six months later, he left his job and started his own company, MN8 Foxfire.

The business took off and grew quickly, which required hiring people and building inventory. To address constant cash-flow challenges, Zach drained his savings, refinanced his home, and maxed out his business credit cards. When a large contract was paying slowly and a few big new orders unexpectedly came in, Zach didn't have the funds to produce the needed inventory or to make payroll, bringing his heroic business to its knees. MN8 needed an infusion of cash pronto. Zach requested and got a loan from StreetShares, which he promptly paid back. He later received additional funding from StreetShares, including its Patriot Express Line of Credit.

Today, more than 6,000 firefighters in 25 countries use MN8 products—including the New York Fire Department. One of Zach's proudest moments was watching a national news clip of FDNY firefighters wearing MN8 products rescuing a window washer from high up the new World Trade Center tower.

ANGEL INVESTOR GROUPS TARGETING VETERAN-OWNED VENTURES

Most angel investors invest in businesses in which they have a personal interest. That is precisely why some angel investors focus exclusively or inclusively on veteran-owned businesses—such as the two angel groups featured here.

Hivers & Strivers

Focus   Early-stage startups with high-growth and high-yield potential that are owned and led by military veteran entrepreneurs.

Deals   Equity investment of $250,000–$1 million equity, although an amount of less than $250,000 may be invested. When larger rounds of investment capital are needed, Hivers & Strivers seeks syndicate deals with other investment groups in its network.

Cost   The firm's partners, all US veterans, remain "actively involved" in the companies in which they invest, serving as board members and advisors, helping to open doors, and providing expertise.

Vet-Biz Network

Focus   Early-stage startups owned and/or led by US veterans.

Deals   Equity investment of $100,000–$10 million, although a lesser amount (minimum $25,000) may be invested. When greater amounts of funding are needed, Vet-Biz Network may seek syndicate deals with other investment groups.

Perks   Provides guidance and support to the ventures in which it invests.

Cost   No application fees. Vet-Biz Network charges a "success fee" to each funded venture, based on the amount of equity funding raised: 5 percent on the first $1 million, 3 percent on the second $1 million, and 2 percent on funding in excess of $2 million.

VENTURE CAPITAL GROUPS TARGETING VETERAN-OWNED VENTURES

If your business is VC-ready, you'll increase your odds of landing a deal by targeting venture capital firms that are veteran-focused or veteran-friendly, the best of which are led by entrepreneurs and investors who are themselves US veterans—like the two firms featured here.

1836

Founded by a group of veterans and business leaders, 1836 invests solely in veteran-owned businesses.

Focus	Veteran owned and/or led startups in the lower-middle market (less than $100 million annual revenue), located in Texas and the Gulf Coast region (preferably, greater Houston area), and with commercialized products, an established customer base, strong returns, and high-growth potential.
Deals	Equity investments "aligned with the needs of the business."
Cost	One-on-one guidance, technical assistance, and execution resources.

Task Force X Capital

Task Force X Capital (TFX) is a veteran-led advisory and venture capital firm.

Focus	Technology and technology-enabled startups with an innovative initiative in an existing industry and growing marketplace, with at least one US veteran on the founding leadership team.
Deals	Multistage investment capital with focus on seed, startup, and early-stage venture capital. TFX takes an equity stake in each company in which it invests.
Cost	Provides its portfolio companies with resources and support designed for long-term partnership and

growth—including assistance with strategic planning, access to a network of strategic partners, and advice on proven business practices and tactics.

RAISING FUNDS TO RAISE THE BAR IN ACADEMIC TESTING

ProctorFree is an educational technology company cofounded by Mike Murphy, an army veteran who served in Iraq and a former marketing director for Everblue Training Institute, and by Velvet Nelson, who holds a master's in education and previously worked 10 years in education. ProctorFree is an on-demand, automated student authentication and online proctoring service that deters cheating on tests and exams.

After a successful startup, the founders sought venture capital to expand their business and enhance their technology. The successful investment round was led by Real Ventures with participation by Task Force X Capital (TFX), a vet-led venture capital firm focused on veteran-owned businesses.

Mike reports that TFX provided "more than just working capital"; they also imparted valuable guidance. "Working with TFX allowed us to combine the best of military ethos with civilian business practices in order to achieve growth."

RESOURCES FOR VETERAN-OWNED BUSINESSES

The following organizations provide information and services to help veterans fund, launch, grow, manage, and operate their businesses.

US Small Business Administration (SBA)

Center for Veterans Institute for Procurement (VIP). Provides free training workshops on procuring federal government contracts. VIP Start is for vet-led companies wishing to enter or expand the federal market; VIP Grow is for established companies already contracting with the government that wish to accelerate their success in the federal market.

Operation Boots to Business. This free entrepreneurship preparation program for veterans is held on military installations around the world in collaboration with the Institute for Veterans and Military Families (IVMF) at Syracuse University.

Veteran Women Igniting the Spirit of Entrepreneurship (V-WISE). Funded in part by SBA and provided through IVMF, V-Wise offers online training, annual conference, networking, and mentoring for female veterans and female military spouses.

Veterans Business Outreach Program (VBOP). VBOP offers free entrepreneurial-development services, such as business plan development, feasibility analysis, business practice training, and mentorship, provided through 20 Veterans Business Outreach Centers (VBOCs) around the country.

Franchise Incentives and Support for Veteran Entrepreneurs

VetFran. The Veterans Transition Franchise Initiative, an initiative of the International Franchise Association (IFA), offers free franchise training, information, financial assistance (including scholarships), access to vet-friendly franchise opportunities, and support to veterans. More than 600 IFA members also offer financial incentives—such as reduced franchise fees, advertising fees, and royalties—to veteran franchisees through the VetFran program.

Veterans Business Services (VBS). This franchise accelerator for veterans and service-disabled veterans offers franchise consulting and training, access to franchises with the "most advantageous acquisitions terms" to veterans, and links to funding sources. VBS is a private business consulting firm that charges for its services, but partners with Veteranscorp, a nonprofit organization that offers free business advice and assistance to veteran-owned businesses.

Procurement Support for Veteran-Owned Businesses

Federal, state, and some local governments have laws and programs in place that either require or encourage public entities to award a portion of certain government agency procurement contracts to veteran-owned businesses. Some private-sector organizations, institutions, and corporations also have initiatives to contract with veteran-owned businesses. The following organizations offer veterans assistance in preparing, certifying, and/or connecting with procurement opportunities.

National Veteran Business Development Council (NVBDC). NVBDC is the only third-party Veteran Owned Business (VOB) certification program in the United States. NVBDC's eMarketplace also connects major corporations with NVBDC-certified veteran businesses.

National Veteran-Owned Business Association (NaVOBA). NaVOBA is a membership organization that provides advocacy, training, mentoring, "insider" information, and an online VetBiz Directory designed to "open doors" to corporate supplier contracts for veteran-owned businesses.

VetBiz Network (VBN). VBN is a membership organization that provides information, education, and training to help veteran-owned businesses secure procurement contracts with government agencies and corporate America. (*Note:* VBN is not affiliated with the angel investor group Vet-Biz Network.)

Vets First Contracting Program. This initiative of the US federal government gives veteran-owned small businesses (VOSB) and service-disabled veteran–owned small business (SDVOSB) the highest priority for open-market procurements of the US Department of Veterans Affairs (VA). The Vets First Verification Program provides training and assistance to prepare and guide the veteran business owner through VOSB/SDVOSB certification and the federal contracting process. In conjunction with the Vet's First Contracting Program, the VA's Direct Access Program connects certified VOSBs and SVOSBs with procurement opportunities via a multiple-agency event (National Veterans Small Business Engagement) and industry-specific events (Business Opportunity Showcases).

Information, Networking, and Other Resources for Veteran Business Owners

American Corporate Partners. This free 12-month small business development program provides post 9/11 veterans and transitioning/

retiring service members with one-on-one mentoring from professionals of Fortune 500 companies.

Institute for Veterans and Military Families (IVMF). Syracuse University's IVMF offers several programs supporting veteran-owned businesses, including:

- VetNet (free entrepreneurship webinars and networking tools)
- Entrepreneurship Bootcamp for Veterans with Disabilities (EBV)
- EBV Accelerate—a two-week online course, a three-day residency at one of 10 universities to create a personalized action plan for a business, and 12 months of mentorship
- Entrepreneurship Bootcamp for Families (EBV-F)
- Coalition for Veteran Owned Businesses (COVB; facilitates private-sector procurement opportunities for VOBs)
- Boots to Business
- V-WISE Ignite and V-WISE training

Patriot Boot Camp. This intensive, three-day educational and mentoring program is designed to empower active duty service members, veterans, and military spouses to start technology-focused businesses. Patriot Boot Camp is an initiative of Techstars Foundation, a philanthropic organization of Techstars, a technology startup accelerator.

Startup Veterans. This intensive 16-week, mentor-based entrepreneurial training course is "by vetrepreneurs for vetrepreneurs." The $1,800 fee for the course is often covered in whole or part by donors; payment programs are also available to qualified applicants.

Vet to CEO. This program offers free online courses for transitioning military members and veterans, including a seven-week core program, Entrepreneurship for Transitioning Warriors.

VetCon. This annual conference for veteran entrepreneurs offers three days of workshops, speakers, and networking opportunities with mentors and investors. Cost: $200–$500.

Veterans and Military Business Owners Association (VAMBOA). VAMBOA is a nonprofit trade association offering free membership and resources to veteran and active military businesses owners. Benefits include training, VOB certification, conferences, and discounts; networking opportunities with government and private-sector procurement agents; advertising and promotional opportunities.

TARGET FUNDING VARIABLES FOR VETERAN-OWNED BUSINESS

Use any combination of the following keywords to search the Internet for each type of funding you want to investigate. For each search, specify one or two variables per each keyword position—for example: small business (keyword #1), disabled veteran, veteran owned (keyword #2), business loan, microloan (keyword #3), government (keyword #4), Boston, Massachusetts (keyword #5).

Keyword #1	small business | startup | business owner | entrepreneur
Keyword #2	veteran | disabled veteran | veteran owned | disadvantaged | underrepresented.
Keyword #3	vocational rehabilitation grant | business grant | business competition | incubator | accelerator | business loan | microloan | loan program | loan fund | lending program
Keyword #4	government | CDFI | economic development | community development | name of industry sector
Keyword #5	United States| name of city | name of state | name of county

Funding for Businesses Owned by People with Disabilities

Employed people with disabilities are nearly twice as likely to be self-employed than are employed people without disabilities (15 percent versus 8 percent). Many are business owners who just happen to have a disability. Others are self-employed because they could not find a job due to the barriers to employment that people with disabilities often face.

As Ted Kennedy Jr., a disability civil rights attorney and board chair of the American Association of People with Disabilities, has stated, hiring managers often disregard people with disabilities, seemingly on the presumption that people with disabilities can't do the job or it would cost too much to accommodate them.[1]

In the United States, less than 20 percent of people with disabilities were in the workforce in 2016, compared with about 70 percent of the nondisabled population. What's more, a larger percentage of workers with disabilities are employed in low-paying jobs.

For people with disabilities, business ownership can be a way to engage in employment that is more than just a low-wage, part-time job to supplement their disability benefits. It can be a way to pursue an occupation of their choice that both accommodates their disabilities and offers greater financial independence. It can be a way to thrive, not merely survive.

I have been helping people with disabilities to start, stabilize, and expand their own businesses for more than 20 years. And I want you to know this: if you have a disability and are self-employed or want to be, funding is available to help you achieve your entrepreneurial goals.

The funding options and resources featured in this chapter are specifically for businesses owned by people with disabilities. I encourage you to read the other chapters in this book, too, to uncover additional funding that might be right for you and your venture.

SOCIAL SECURITY PROGRAMS FOR SELF-EMPLOYMENT

The Social Security Administration (SSA) has two work-incentive programs—*Plan to Achieve Self-Support (PASS)* and *Ticket to Work*—that can be used to help start a business or return to self-employment.

PASS Program

A Plan to Achieve Self-Support (PASS) is a written plan of action for achieving an employment goal—either to secure a specified type of job or to start a specified business. With an approved PASS, the earnings and resources you set aside for your work goal don't count as personal income when determining your Supplemental Security Insurance (SSI) eligibility and payment amount. So, if you already receive SSI, a PASS may entitle you to a higher SSI payment. If you're currently ineligible for SSI, a PASS may qualify you for SSI benefits.

To ensure that your Plan to Achieve Self-Support and business plan meet all requirements of the Social Security Administration, check with your vocational counselor about enlisting the help of a PASS plan specialist and a business counselor. Several regional Social Security offices have PASS specialists on staff; for a list of those locations, go to the SSA website and search for "passcadre." Free business plan assistance is available at your local Small Business Development Center (SBDC) or SCORE (Counselors to America's Small Business) office. You can also hire a private business counselor to help with your business plan, the cost of which can be included in your PASS.

Eligibility   You must meet *all* of the following criteria:

- Receive Social Security Disability Insurance (SSDI).

- Receive Supplemental Security Income (SSI) and have income that reduces your SSI payment amount, or would be eligible for SSI if not for your income and other assets.

- Have no more than $2,000 ($3,000 if married) worth of personal resources that won't be used for your Plan to Achieve Self-Support.

- Using a PASS to reach your self-employment goal would help reduce or eliminate your reliance on SSI, SSDI, or both.

Amount   Your state's maximum monthly SSI benefit is the maximum amount of income you can set aside for business expenses without those earnings being counted as income for the purpose of determining your SSI eligibility and payment amount.

Uses   With a PASS, you can earn and save money to purchase services and items needed to start a business, including:

- Education and training to prepare for self-employment

- Special transportation to and from school or work

- Childcare while you work to secure money to start your business

- Specialized impairment-related equipment (wheelchair, assistive technology, modifications to workplace or vehicle)

- Certain medical expenses (attendant care, physical therapy)

- Employment and/or vocational rehabilitation counseling

- Business counseling

- Equipment, tools, and supplies for your business

Ticket to Work and Self-Sufficiency Program

If you receive Social Security disability benefits (SSDI and/or SSI), you can use a Ticket to Work, issued by the Social Security Administration, to earn the income to pay for services and support needed to achieve your specified work goal, including starting a business.

SSA will also pay an approved service provider (*employment network*, or EN) to help you establish and reach the "milestones" and "outcomes" required to your self-supporting employment. You can work with a service provider of your choice, provided that person or organization is an approved Ticket to Work EN. Most state vocational rehabilitation (VR) agencies are preapproved ENs for the Ticket to Work Program. I strongly recommend working with an EN, who will know the somewhat complicated ropes and rules of the Ticket to Work Program.

Two important Ticket to Work Program rules to know up front are:

- Your Ticket to Work self-employment goal could, if achieved, help reduce or eliminate your reliance on SSI, SSDI, or both.

- You must make "timely progress" toward achieving specified milestones and outcomes.

VOCATIONAL REHABILITATION BUSINESS GRANTS FOR PEOPLE WITH DISABILITIES

Every state vocational rehabilitation agency in the United States provides services that support the employment goals of people with disabilities, including self-employment. This assistance includes monetary grants to help pay for the costs of starting a business or establishing self-employment. Each state sets its own policies regarding the use of voc-rehab grants for self-employment. (Two programs are described below.)

In addition, your VR counselor may refer you to business development specialists—such as a local Small Business Development Center (SBDC), SCORE office, or approved Community Rehabilitation Provider (CRP). These organizations can often provide nonmonetary support, such as free or reduced-cost services (i.e., business plan development) and items (i.e., a computer).

If you're interested in applying for a voc-rehab business grant, contact the vocational rehabilitation agency or department in your state and ask to speak to a VR counselor regarding funding and assistance to achieve self-employment or to start a small business. Some states have a separate VR division for residents who are blind or sight-impaired. To find the VR office in your state, go to the Job Accommodation Network (JAN) website, navigate to the Accommodation Search portal, and type "State Vocational Rehabilitation Agencies" into the Searchable Online Accommodations Resource (SOAR) database.

Eligibility	Must have a documented disability and must require vocational rehabilitation services to attain or regain self-employment. The assessment phase of the grant application process will determine VR eligibility. In most cases, recipients of Social Security disability benefits (SSDI and/or SSI) are automatically eligible for VR services.
Amount	$5,000–$10,000 monetary grant.
Uses	Items and services required to prepare you for business ownership and/or to start the business. Does *not* cover real estate construction/purchase, vehicles, taxes, wages, ongoing support (after initial startup). Does *not* fund existing businesses, speculative businesses, businesses trafficking in illegal goods/services. Most state voc-rehab programs do *not* fund franchises, businesses that do not pay minimum wage, nonprofit organizations.

Summaries of two state voc-rehab self-employment grant programs follow.

Alaska Division of Vocational Rehabilitation

Tier I Grant	$5,000 for allowable startup expenses.
Tier II Grant	First $5,000 of allowable startup expenses plus 50 percent of allowable expenses in excess of $5,000,

up to $10,000, and 5 percent of allowable expenses in excess of $10,000.

Connecticut Bureau of Rehabilitative Services

The state's maximum contribution toward eligible costs associated with establishing an eligible small business (excluding training costs and costs for vehicle or work site modifications necessitated by the individual's disability) are:

- $5,000 if the projected net income of the proposed business after two or more years in operation (following anticipated completion of services) is less than the SGA amount specified by the Social Security Administration.

- $10,000 if the projected net income of the proposed business after two or more years of operation (following anticipated completion of services) is at or above the amount the Social Security Administration considers "substantial gainful activity" (SGA).

OUT OF THE BUBBLE AND INTO ENTREPRENEURSHIP

Jonathan Chase, who was diagnosed with Asperger's syndrome at age 14, describes his school experience as "an absolute nightmare." At 16 he dropped out to become a musician, and by age 18 he was playing bass guitar in a blues band several nights a week. His music career unexpectedly led to his first public speaking experience, on the topic of being "different" in the "different" world of working musicians. That spurred a second career as a motivational speaker focused on helping others better understand autism and helping young people on the spectrum learn the life skills necessary to reach their maximum level of independence.

Then, in 2013, with the help of a state vocational rehabilitation grant, he launched Jonathan Chase Consulting. His services include mentoring teens and young adults with autism; consulting with families, schools, and nonprofit organizations; and public speaking. The $8,000 voc-rehab grant covered the startup costs of professional services to develop the business plan, logo and branding, business cards, flyers, website, a slide presentation, and "a new shirt for a [promotional] video shoot."

In 2016, Jonathan launched a crowdfunding campaign to fund phase two of his business plan: the launch of Out of the Bubble Publishing and publication of his book *From Surviving to Thriving: Classroom Accommodations for Students on the Autism Spectrum*. The $8,500 raised on Kickstarter was used for professional services to develop, edit, design, and publish the book.

Through his business, music, and advocacy, Jonathan Chase continues to empower people on the autism spectrum in his hometown of Portland, Oregon, and nationwide.

MATCHED SAVINGS GRANTS
FOR ENTREPRENEURS WITH DISABILITIES

Some nonprofit organizations, government agencies, and community-based lenders that serve disadvantaged individuals offer individual development account (IDA) programs, also known as matched savings grants. With an IDA, the organization contributes one or more dollars for every dollar the accountholder saves. The contribution ratio varies with the IDA provider, and rarely exceeds more than $4 contributed per $1 saved. Most, but not all, IDA programs allow funds to be saved and used to start or expand a business. Some IDA programs aimed at aspiring small business owners target disadvantaged individuals, including those with disabilities.

If you're working with a state vocational rehabilitation agency or local Small Business Development Center, your voc-rehab counselor or SBDC counselor should be able to refer you to an IDA program for entrepreneurs with disabilities. Another way to find potential IDA program(s) near you is to go to the website of Prosperity Now (a national nonprofit organization focused on helping disadvantaged people achieve financial stability) and navigate to the Find an IDA Program portal. There, you click on an interactive map of the United States for the names and contact information of IDA programs in your state. You will need to contact the IDA provider directly to learn more about and apply for an IDA program.

Following are some representative IDA programs for entrepreneurs with disabilities.

Northwest Access Fund

This nonprofit community development financial institution (CDFI) provides both loans and IDAs for the purchase of assistive technology to enable people with disabilities to achieve greater independence, including self-employment and small business ownership. The loan program is available at Northwest Access Fund locations in both Oregon and Washington; the IDA program is available only in Washington.

The IDA is a dollar-for-dollar (1:1) match, up to $2,000 accountholder savings and up to $2,000 match. To be eligible for the IDA program, the accountholder must be an adult resident of Washington who has a disability or is caring for a minor or other family member with a disability. The household income can be no more than 80 percent of the county median income, and household assets can be no more than $20,000.

Startup New York Inclusive Entrepreneurship Program

This collaborative initiative of Syracuse University's Burton Blatt Institute, Whitman School of Management's South Side Innovation Center (SSIC), and Onondaga County helps people with disabilities and/or economic disadvantages obtain the training and business development resources needed to establish, grow, and sustain successful small businesses. Participants in the Inclusive Entrepreneurship program can enroll in an IDA with a 1:1 match, up to $1,000 saved and $1,000 matched.

($) **Consult with a Social Security Disability benefits counselor before opening an IDA.** If you receive Supplemental Security Income (SSI), especially if it's your only supplemental income to Social Security Disability Insurance (SSDI), it is important to follow the SSI asset limit rules so you don't risk losing your SSI benefits. Two factors may affect that: (1) Many IDA programs require the accountholder's IDA deposits to come from *earned income*. Because Social Security Disability benefits are considered *unearned income*, the IDA accountholder's contributions to the IDA must come from a source other than SSDI or SSI. (2) If the financial organization receives federal funding for its IDA program, the Social Security

Administration's asset limits of $2,000 ($3,000 per couple) do not apply. Otherwise, all funds in an IDA (including the match) will count toward the $2,000 limit.

GOVERNMENT LOANS FOR BUSINESSES OWNED BY PEOPLE WITH DISABILITIES

Some commerce and/or economic development agencies of state governments have business loan programs established specifically for businesses owned by people with disabilities. These lending programs provide access to reduced-interest financing by way of loan guarantees and/or direct loans. Some of the lending programs cover various business-related expenses. Others cover expenses unique to entrepreneurs and business owners with disabilities—such as for assistive technology, adaptive office equipment, and modifications to the place of business (including home-based businesses).

State-funded lending programs for people with disabilities may also help the business owner apply for the loan at no cost. Most also offer free business counseling and/or training.

Some states have business financing programs specifically for small businesses owned by people with disabilities. Summaries of two such programs follow.

Illinois: Minority/Business/Disabled/Veteran Participation Loan Program

The MBDV PLP is administered by the Illinois Department of Commerce and Economic Opportunity (DCEO), which goes by the trade name Advantage Illinois.

Eligibility	Illinois-based small or midsize businesses that is majority-owned by an eligible individual with a disability.
Loan	Term loan of $10,000–$200,000. (Interest rate not available.) Up to 7 years repayment terms.
Uses	Business procurement, startup, expansion.

New Mexico: Self-Employment for Entrepreneurs with Disabilities (SEED) Loan

The SEED loan program is administered by the New Mexico Technology Assistance Program (NM TAP).

Eligibility	New Mexico resident with a disability who needs home modification in order to telecommute from an existing job, become self-employed, start a business, or expand a business.
Loan	Term loan of $1,000–$30,000. (Interest rate not available.) 12–60 months repayment terms.
Uses	Tools, computers, business equipment, supplies, home office/work modifications, portable buildings.

($) **Tap into business development and funding assistance from organizations focused on your disability.** State government agencies and nonprofit organizations that focus on a particular disability sometimes provide access to funding and resources geared toward entrepreneurs with that disability. Check for self-employment and small business counseling, training, technical assistance, and funding support offered by (or through) national and state organizations such as American Federation for the Blind, Autism Speaks, Brain Injury Association of America, Multiple Sclerosis Foundation, National Association for the Deaf, Oregon Commission for the Blind, and United Cerebral Palsy Association.

CDFI LOANS FOR BUSINESSES OWNED BY PEOPLE WITH DISABILITIES

Some community development financial institutions (CDFIs) offer business lending programs aimed at entrepreneurs with disabilities. Brief descriptions of two such CDFIs follow. For more information on CDFIs, please see Chapter 11, "Community Development Financial Institutions."

Accion

Accion US, the nation's largest nonprofit online lending network, operates four community development financial institutions (CDFIs) that serve small businesses throughout the country—including, as a priority objective, businesses owned by people with disabilities. Qualification requirements, loan amounts ($300 to $1 million), loan uses, repayment terms, interest rates, collateral requirements, and other terms and conditions depend upon the loan products offered by the individual CDFI. For more information, including which Accion location serves your state, visit the US Accion website.

Iowa Able Foundation

This statewide nonprofit lender and CDFI provides financial education, credit-building assistance, microloans, and term loans to help individuals with disabilities establish self-employment or start or grow a small business. Allowable funding uses include the purchase of assistive technology, home or workplace modifications, vehicle modifications, and business startup and growth expenses.

A GRANT, AN IDA, AND A WEALTH OF TALENT BUILD A SUCCESSFUL ONLINE BUSINESS

When Salvatore Apodaca, a graphic designer and former systems analyst, first launched Old West Poker Supplies, LLC, an online retailer/reseller of poker and casino products, his main goal was to own a business he enjoyed and that would accommodate his disability. Then, Sal began to design and print customized ceramic poker chips, which enabled him to apply his artistry and for which his Portland, Oregon–based business received national acclaim.

As initial startup funding, Sal received a grant of $4,500 from the Oregon Vocational Rehabilitation Department. Those funds went toward the purchase of a computer, professional editing software, an office printer, inventory and supplies, and accessibility equipment. To expand the custom poker chip side of his business, Sal opened a matched savings account through CASA of Oregon, a nonprofit community development financial institution (CDFI). He used the IDA cash-out of $2,600 to help pay for a high-end printer and a printing press.

Salvatore Apodaca filled tens of thousands of orders to casinos, poker enthusiasts, and collectors for more than 15 years, until his untimely death in February 2018. A gifted artist and gracious human being, Sal is sorely missed

> by his customers, his family, and me, one of his biggest fans and his business counselor.

($) **Tap into business development and funding assistance from organizations serving individuals with your disabling conditions.** Government agencies and nonprofit organizations that focus on a particular disability—such as autism, hearing impairment, visual impairment, and traumatic brain injury—often provide access to resources geared toward entrepreneurs with those disabilities. Check for such organizations at the federal, state, and local levels, such as Autism Speaks, Brain Injury Association of America, National Institute for the Blind, and Washington State Department of Services for the Blind.

RESOURCES FOR ENTREPRENEURS AND BUSINESS OWNERS WITH DISABILITIES

The following organizations support entrepreneurs and business owners with disabilities through advocacy, information, education and training, mentoring, and networking. Most also provide advice and direction on obtaining the resources and capital to start, buy, or grow a business.

Procurement Support for Businesses Owned by Individuals with Disabilities

Many state and local government agencies and institutions throughout the United States have "preferred source" programs for procuring certain goods and services from businesses that are majority-owned by individuals with disabilities—such as the state procurement preference programs profiled here.

Connecticut: Small Contractors Set-Aside Procurement Program. Under this program, full or portions of contracts for certain goods and services purchased by public agencies in Connecticut are reserved for exclusive bidding from targeted disadvantaged small businesses. The bidding company must be: (1) 51 percent owned, controlled, and operated by individual(s) with a disability (or other minority); (2) certified by the state of Connecticut as a Minority Business Enterprise (MBE); (3) based and operating in Connecticut; (4) a for-profit enterprise with annual gross revenues not exceeding $15 million.

Minnesota: TG/ED/VO Small Business Procurement Program. The Minnesota Office of State Procurement (OSP) operates a price-preference program for targeted group (TG), economically disadvantaged (ED), and veteran-owned (VO) small contractors. Target groups are small businesses owned by minorities, women, and people with disabilities. Eligible TG businesses receive up to a 6 percent price preference; if the TG business is awarded the contract, the original tendered price is paid. The bidding TG contractor must be: (1) at least 51 percent owned by an individual with a disability, racial minority, or woman; (2) certified as a Target Group by the Minnesota Office of Procurement; (3) operated and controlled by the TG-qualifying business owner; (4) independent of any other company; (5) based and operating in Minnesota; and (6) a disadvantaged business enterprise (DBE), as defined by the US Department of Transportation.

Education/Information/Networking
for Business Owners with Disabilities

Disabled Businessperson's Association (DBA). DBA is a nonprofit membership organization providing business ownership guidance to people with disabilities throughout the United States. Volunteer entrepreneurs, executives, and professionals with disabilities support aspiring and existing business owners with disabilities through educational programs and mentoring. Collaborates with vocational rehabilitation specialists, educators, and business advisors to guide people with disabilities toward their self-employment goals.

Griffin-Hammis Associates. This private consulting firm specializes in the development of employment opportunities for people with disabilities. Offers training and technical assistance for customized self-employment, the cost of which can often be covered by state vocational rehabilitation grants and other resources.

Job Accommodation Network (JAN). JAN is a service of the US Department of Labor's Office of Disability Employment Policy (ODEP), offering free technical assistance, consulting, and mentoring to support the self-employment and small business ownership goals of people with disabilities. Provides ongoing support throughout all stages of the business startup process.

United States Business Leadership Network (USBLN). USBLN is a nationwide nonprofit organization dedicated to facilitating the inclusion of people with disabilities in the work force. Offers two programs for business owners with disabilities: (1) Disability Supplier Diversity Program (DSDP), the leading third-party certifier of disability-owned business enterprises (DOBE) in the United States, offering certification, education, and business matchmaking (procurement) services. (2) Supplier Mentoring Program, offering education and information in the areas of accessing capital, business planning, business management, branding/marketing, strategic collaboration, supply chain management, and more.

TARGET FUNDING VARIABLES FOR ENTREPRENEURS WITH DISABILITIES

Use any combination of the following keywords to search the Internet for the type of funding you want to investigate. For each search, specify one or two variables per each applicable keyword position—for example: startup, business owner (keyword #1); disabilities, blind (keyword #2); business grant, self employment grant (keyword #3); (keyword #4); United States, Georgia (keyword #5).

Keyword #1	business | small business | startup | business owner | founder | entrepreneur
Keyword #2	disabled | disabilities | disadvantaged | underrepresented
Keyword #3	blind | deaf | visually impaired | hearing impaired | brain injury | autism | cerebral palsy | multiple sclerosis | name of other disability
Keyword #4	vocational rehabilitation grant | assistive technology | business grant | self-employment grant | individual development account | matched savings | business loan | microloan | loan program | loan fund | lending program

Keyword #5	community development | economic development | business development | CDFI | government | name of industry sector
Keyword #6	United States | name of city | name of state | name of county

Funding for Minority-Owned Businesses

The number of minority business enterprises (MBEs) in the United States increased 39 percent from 2007 to 2012 and continues to rise. Minority-owned businesses are also twice as likely to export and three times as likely to have international operations as are non-minority-owned enterprises and are leading exporters in 14 key industry sectors.

At the same time, minority-owned businesses are more likely to be rejected for a loan, receive smaller loans, and pay higher borrowing costs than their nonminority counterparts. In keeping with these disparities, minority entrepreneurs are also less likely than their non-minority counterparts to apply for small business loans, primarily because they fear rejection. They're also less likely to receive investment capital.[1] Although more minority-owned enterprises are securing conventional business loans and venture capital than in the past, the struggle for parity continues for many minority entrepreneurs. Funding opportunities that specifically target minority entrepreneurs are usually more accessible and more suitable sources of funding with which to start, grow, or stabilize a minority-owned business.

GRANTS FOR MINORITY-OWNED BUSINESSES

Minority business grants, like grants for all for-profit enterprises, are limited. But if you can find a grant aimed at ventures like yours, it will bring an infusion of money with no interest or equity strings attached. The best place to search for a small business grant for minority-owned businesses is with your state and local government agencies—such as the programs featured here.

Peoria, Illinois: Minority-Business Implementation Grants (M-BIG)

M-BIG is an initiative of Grow Peoria, the economic development agency of the City of Peoria.

Eligibility	Small business with no more than 50 employees; located in Peoria; majority owned by individual(s) in any federally recognized minority group. If an existing business, the funded project must be for a new product, service, or market. If it is a startup, the funded business should be in an emerging or untapped market. Preference is given to enterprises with high growth and job creation potential.
Award	Monetary grant of $2,500–$5,000.
Uses	Equipment, machinery, professional services, inventory, working capital.

Southeast Michigan: NEIdeas Growth Grants

The Rewarding Ideas for Business Growth grant program is an initiative of New Economy Initiative (NEI), a philanthropic economic development project of the Community Foundation for Southeast Michigan (CFSEM), operated with assistance from Global Detroit and other community partners. Although NEIdeas growth grants are not solely for minority-owned businesses, the program focuses on a region with a large minority population, economically depressed neighborhoods, and numerous businesses owned by minorities.

Eligibility	Existing businesses in operation at least three years; in any industry; located in the cities of Detroit, Hamtramck, or Highland Park.
Awards	Monetary grant of $10,000 to each of 26 businesses annually. Plus access to the NEIdeas network, an entrepreneurial ecosystem that includes business

advising, training, mentoring, lenders, investors, and other business resources.

Uses The funded project must enable the business to grow in a way that not only sustains and strengthens the business but also benefits the cities and neighborhoods that need the business the most.

HOW $10,000 GRANTS HELP 26 NEIGHBORHOOD BUSINESSES GROW EVERY YEAR

NEIdeas, an annual business competition sponsored by New Economy Initiative (NEI), awards 26 grants of $10,000 each to small businesses in the Detroit, Michigan area. Year after year, the majority of those grants go to minority-owned businesses located in the very neighborhoods they serve. For example, 77 percent of the 2018 NEIdeas challenge were minority-owned and 65 percent were women-owned businesses. Here is how five 2018 NEIdeas winners used their grants to grow their businesses.

- **Detroit Marshall Arts Institute**, founded and owned by George Reynolds, an African American martial arts expert and electrical engineer, a martial arts training facility for children and young adults and a licensed after-school childcare program. *Ideas funded*: Purchase used van and create STEM program and instructional materials.
- **EnACT Your Future, Inc.**, owned by Justine Sheu, an Asian-American urban educator and serial entrepreneur, provides engaging standardized test prep classes to students in low-income communities in the Detroit greater metro area. *Idea funded*: Create a video marketing campaign to raise awareness of ACT test prep courses.
- **La Cuscatleca, Inc.**, an immigrant-owned grocery store and café selling imported Latin American food products and prepared foods. *Ideas funded*: Ravamp interior and expand current product offerings to turn store/café into a community hub.
- **Nail Rite Construction, Inc.**, founded and owned by Kimle Nailer, is a black woman–owned drywall construction company that contracts to general contractors in commercial and residential markets throughout

> Detroit. *Ideas funded:* Hire and train an estimator to utilize new bidding software and purchase a used vehicle for the company's mobile trade school.
>
> - **Source Bookseller**, owned by Janet Webster Jones, an African American retired educator, is an independent bookstore in Midtown Detroit specializing in nonfiction books and complementary products. *Ideas funded:* Revamp the interior of the store and create marketing materials to promote the bookshop's thirtieth anniversary.

COMPETITION-BASED FUNDING FOR MINORITY-OWNED BUSINESSES

Some business pitch and business plan competitions target minority-owned enterprises. These competitions, many of which offer cash awards and in-kind services, tend to be short-lived (one- to five-year) initiatives of a business incubator or accelerator, college or university, state or local government agency, or nonprofit organization. The following competitions are currently in force and are representative of business competitions for minority-owned businesses.

Black Business Pitch Competition

This regional business pitch challenge was created and is presented by the LA Black Investors Club (LABIC), a nonprofit organization "serving as a conduit to venture creation, capitalization, and capacity-building for diverse communities."

Eligibility	Minority-owned startup less than two years in operation and having no direct or indirect operating relationship with an existing large corporation, investment firm, or government agency.
Awards	In-kind products and services, such as free consulting with a venture capital fund manager, free subscription to *Entrepreneur* magazine, AMEX gift cards, etc.

Latino Perfect Pitch

This nationwide business pitch competition is sponsored by Wells Fargo and was created in 2015 by Hispanicize Media Group, LLC, as part of Hispanicize Week, an annual (since 2009) four-day event for Latino "trendsetters and newsmakers" in digital content creation, journalism, marketing, entertainment, and tech entrepreneurship.

Eligibility	Latina- or Latino-founded companies less than five years in operation and planning to attend the Hispanicize event.
Awards	Monetary grant of $5,000, plus in-kind services (e.g., branding, promotional) and connections to other resources, including mentoring and business accelerator opportunities.

NABIN Innovation Challenge

Held annually, the Innovation Challenge is a business-plan competition sponsored by the Native American Business Incubator Network (NABIN), a virtual business incubator for Native American–owned businesses.

Eligibility	Start-up and early-stage companies founded and led by members of federally recognized Native American tribes.
Awards	Cash prize (grant) of $5,000–$15,000 and a spot in a NABIN cohort.

INCUBATOR- AND ACCELERATOR-BASED FUNDING FOR MINORITY-OWNED BUSINESSES

Since the 2005 launch of the nation's first business accelerator, Y Combinator, accelerators and incubators have become an important part of startup ecosystems in the United States. Unfortunately, multiple sources indicate that the rate at which minority (and female) founders participate in high-tech incubators and accelerators has lagged behind that of their white (and male) counterparts.[2] But efforts have been and continue to be made to make startup ecosystems more inclusive, and today, several incubators and accelerators target minority-led ventures on either an exclusive or inclusive basis.

Camelback Ventures Fellowship (CVF)

Eligibility   Early-stage education and social impact ventures; located in low-income US communities; founded by Black, Latino, East Asian, South Asian, Native American, or other underrepresented entrepreneurs.

Program   Six-month virtual accelerator and three 4-day in-person summits. One cohort of 12 fellows per year. Each fellow is assigned a personal coach and participates in workshops, peer mentoring, and specialized counseling. Final summit includes a pitch session before potential investors and partners. Each CVF fellow receives $40,000 in seed equity funding.

Cost   No application or program fees. Camelback receives a 0.5 to 5 percent equity stake in each CVF startup in which it invests.

Perks   Facilitates resource- and relationship-building during and after the fellowship, including networking opportunities with potential investors and partners.

Manos Accelerator

Eligibility   Early-stage high-tech companies in the consumer Internet, mobile, or cloud computing space; located in the United States; founded and led by Latino/Hispanic entrepreneurs.

Programs   One-week, on-site (Silicon Valley) accelerator, held monthly. Five or six startup teams per cohort. Education, guidance, mentoring, guest speakers, and networking. Demo Day, one-on-one meetings with potential investors. Three-month virtual accelerator with weekly curriculum (podcasts), mentorship (teleconferencing), and homework sessions.

Cost   Startup teams accepted into the on-site accelerator pay program fees as well as their travel, room, and board during the program.

Perks   Ongoing access to free and discounted resources.

GOVERNMENT LOAN PROGRAMS FOR MINORITY-OWNED BUSINESSES

Some state government agencies offer financial assistance to minority-owned businesses, usually in the form of direct loans and/or loan guarantees—such as Mississippi's and Ohio's programs, summarized below. In many cases, state funding for minority-owned businesses is part of a program aimed at "disadvantaged" business owners (minorities, veterans, women).

Mississippi Minority Business Assistance

The state of Mississippi offers three business loan programs for socially and economically disadvantaged businesses owners, including minorities.

MS Minority Business Enterprise Loan Program

Eligibility   Mississippi state-certified minority-owned or women-owned business.

Loan   Term loan of up to $250,000; 50 percent of eligible project costs. 4.75 percent fixed interest rate. Repayment terms of up to 7 years (working capital), 10 years (equipment/machinery), and 15 years (buildings/land).

Uses   Fixed assets, inventory, working capital.

MS Minority Business Micro Loan Program

Eligibility	Mississippi state-certified minority-owned or women-owned business.
Loan	Term loan of up to $35,000. 6.75 percent fixed interest rate. Up to 7 years repayment terms.
Uses	Fixed assets, inventory, working capital.

MS Minority Capital Fund

Eligibility	Mississippi state-certified minority-owned start-up or existing business.
Loan	Term loan of $5,000–$250,000; 100 percent of eligible projects costs. (Interest rate not available.) Up to 15 years repayment terms.
Uses	Fixed assets, inventory, machinery/equipment, working capital, alteration and renovation (A&R), construction loan financing, real estate financing.

Ohio Minority Business Direct Loan Program

The Ohio Development Services Agency offers a state-funded *take-out financing* loan program.

Eligibility	Operating business certified (by State of Ohio) as a minority business enterprise (MBE), for which the financed project will create or retain jobs for Ohioans. Business owner(s) contribute 10 percent of project cost and secures interim financing for remaining 90 percent (reduced to 50 percent upon completion of project and release of state's direct loan funds).
Loan	Term loan of $45,000–$450,000; 40 percent of eligible project costs. 3 percent fixed interest rate. Repayment terms of up to 10 years for equipment/machinery and up to 20 years for real estate.

Uses	Acquisition, renovation, or construction of land and/or buildings; acquisition of machinery and equipment; soft costs related directly to the fixed asset expenditure (such as architectural/engineering costs, installation costs for machinery, financing costs for bank loans).

COMMUNITY-BASED ECONOMIC DEVELOPMENT FUNDING FOR MINORITY-OWNED BUSINESSES

Funding programs designed to facilitate the development of successful minority-owned businesses exist in many municipalities and regions having large minority populations. Most community-based economic development initiatives for minority-owned businesses are collaborations between state or local government agencies and nonprofit organizations, colleges and universities, and/or community development financial institutions (CDFIs). These programs typically include education, advisory, and funding components.

JumpStart

JumpStart is a nonprofit organization providing an inclusive economic ecosystem for startups and small businesses in Ohio, primarily Northeast Ohio. More than one-third of the companies supported by JumpStart are owned and/or led by minorities and/or women. JumpStart in collaboration with Northeast Ohio Entrepreneurial Services Program (ESP) provides a suite of services, including outreach, education and training, technical assistance, mentoring, networking, and scale-up assistance. In partnership with Ohio Third Frontier, JumpStart makes equity investments in eligible startups through its Evergreen Fund, Focus Fund, and Next Fund.

Evergreen Fund

Focus	Seed-stage tech startups that can validate product feasibility and market need; located in any of the 21 counties of Northeast Ohio or willing to locate to Cleveland's Health-Tech Corridor (HTC).

	Companies with diverse teams highly desirable and actively sought, but not required.
Deals	Initial investment of $250,000; follow-up round of $500,000–$1 million. Equity investment or convertible note.

Focus Fund

Focus	Seed-stage tech startups that can validate product feasibility and market need. Minority- and/or woman-led startups located anywhere in Ohio.
Deals	Initial investment of $250,000; follow-up round of $500,000–$1 million. Equity investment or convertible note.

Next Fund

Focus	Early-stage tech startups that have significant market traction and can attract Series A capital; located anywhere in Ohio. Companies with diverse teams highly desirable and actively sought, but not required.
Deals	Initial investment of $500,000–$1.5 million; follow-up round of $2.5 million–$5 million. Equity investment.

Washington Area Community Investment Fund (Wacif)

Wacif is a regional, nonprofit community development financial institution (CDFI) that provides disadvantaged businesses located in underserved communities in the Washington, DC, metropolitan area with access to capital and technical assistance. About 80 percent of Wacif loans go to minority- and women-owned businesses. Wacif offers the following loans, all of which require collateral, a nonrefundable application fee, and a closing fee. No minimum credit score is required.

Opportunity Loan

Eligibility	Less than 12 months in operation.
Loan	Term loan of $5,000–$25,000. Up to 18 percent interest rate. Up to 36 months repayment terms.

Microloan

Eligibility	Minimum 12 months in operation.
Loan	Term loan of $5,000–$50,000. Up to 10 percent interest rate. Up to 72 months repayment terms.
Uses	Equipment, inventory, working capital.

Equipment Financing

Eligibility	Minimum 12 months in operation.
Loan	Term loan of $5,000–$50,000. Interest rate of up to 10 percent. Repayment terms of up to 72 months.

Working Capital Term Loan

Eligibility	Minimum 12 months in operation.
Loan	Term loan of $50,001–$150,000. Up to 18 percent interest rate. Up to 72 months repayment terms.

Contract Term Loan

Eligibility	Minimum 12 months in operation.
Loan	Term loan of $50,001–$150,000. Up to 18 percent interest rate. Up to 72 months repayment terms.
Uses	Equipment, inventory, working capital.

Contract Line of Credit

Eligibility	Minimum 12 months in operation.
Loan	Credit line of $5,000–$50,000. Up to 10 percent interest rate. Up to 72 months repayment terms.
Uses	Equipment, inventory, working capital.

HOW A REFUGEE COUPLE TURNED A FOOD CART BUSINESS INTO A POPULAR RESTAURANT

When Mohamed Yousef fled his war-torn homeland, Ethiopia, as a teenager in the 1980s, he surely could not have imagined he'd one day own an award-winning restaurant in Portland, Oregon. The first seeds to a brighter future were planted while Mohamed was living in a Sudanese refugee camp when he received a United Nations scholarship to an American college in Cairo, Egypt. There, he met and married his wife, Khadija. After earning a degree in business, Mohamed was offered residency in one of three countries: Australia, Canada, or the United States. He chose the United States, leaving Khadija in Cairo, where she worked as a chef for foreign diplomats. Mohamed worked and saved, eventually enabling his wife to join him in America. The couple moved to Portland, Oregon, where they had relatives.

In 1994, the Yousufs founded Horn of Africa, a food cart serving regional cuisine from the coast of Northeast African, which they operated at the downtown Portland Saturday Market and at local festivals. Soon, they also began catering special events. Then, in 2007, they expanded their business by opening a full-service restaurant. To help fund the purchase of the building and equipment and the cost of improving the facility, the Yousufs worked with Prosper Portland, the City of Portland's economic/urban development agency. They received a subsidized loan with a fixed interest rate of .04 percent as well as a $536,000 New Market Tax Credit.

After 20 successful years, the Horn of Africa restaurant closed its doors in 2018 so that Mohamed and Khadija could semi-retire. The couple's Horn of Africa catering business and Horn of Africa food cart at Portland Saturday Market continue to thrive.

LENDERS TARGETING MINORITY-OWNED BUSINESSES

Many banks and other conventional financial institutions have outreach campaigns promoting their services to minority business owners, but few offer lending programs specifically for minority-owned businesses. Some online lending platforms and private finance companies do have lending programs aimed at minority-owned small businesses. Just beware of high interest rates, hidden fees, and other predatory practices employed by some (not all) finance companies and online lenders. Community-based lenders usually offer less stringent qualification criteria, fair interest rates and terms, and transparency.

By way of example, here are the minority business loan programs of a finance company and a community development financial institution (CDFI).

Balboa Capital Minority Small Business Loans

Balboa Capital Corporation is a private finance company business bureau headquartered in Southern California, with satellite offices in Northern California, Arizona, and Washington. The firm's Minority Small Business Loan is available only through the Balboa Capital online lending platform.

Eligibility	Minority-owned businesses in operation more than one year, with at least $300,000 in annual revenues. Considers all credit scores.
Loan	Term loan of up to $250,000; unsecured. "Competitive" interest rate based on the borrower's financial standing. 3–24 months repayment terms.

Business Consortium Fund

Business Consortium Fund, Inc. (BCF) is a nonprofit CDFI and a non-profit business development program of the National Minority Supplier Development Council (NMSDC). BCF provides financing and business advisory services exclusively to ethnic minority–owned businesses through a national network of partners that include the NMSDC and its affiliated regional councils as well as major corporations, commercial lenders, and business support organizations. BCF offers the following business financing programs, which are available to qualifying NMSDC-certified minority-owned business enterprises (MBEs).

BCF Direct Lending Program

Loans	Term loan or line of credit of $75,000–$500,000. Term loan amounts of up to $1.125 million may be

considered on a case-by-case basis. Prime plus up
to 3 percent interest rate. Up to 7 years.

Loan Participation Program (LPP)

LPP loans are made by BCF-certified lenders and are guaranteed by BCF.
This reduces the risk to lenders, enabling them to provide financing that
would otherwise be unavailable based on the lender's normal underwriting standards.

Loans Line of credit, equipment term loan, working capital term loan, or intermediate term loan of up to
$1.125 million. Prime plus up to 3 percent interest
rate. Up to 7 years repayment terms.

Specialized Financing

BCF provides access to accounts receivable financing through its alliances
with a national bank and a specialty finance company, enabling certified
small businesses to accelerate cash flow through the sale of their corporate or government receivables to BCF alliance partners.

Loans Commercial/government contracts financing;
accounts receivable factoring; commercial real
estate loans; USDA business/industry loans (and
loan packaging services). Loan amounts are
determined by individual lenders based on type of
financing, contract/receivables variables, and borrower's credit risk. Under certain circumstances,
BCF participates in accounts receivables loans
made by alliance partners.

Long-Term Debt/Equity Financing

These loans are made through Triad Investments LP, a federally licensed
specialized small business investment company (SSBIC) and wholly
owned subsidiary of BCF. Triad also provides long-term mezzanine type
equity funding to disadvantaged small businesses that meet the eligibility requirements for an SSBIC investment, as defined by the US Small
Business Administration (SBA).

Triad funding is available for expansion capital, permanent working capital, and long-term working capital. Financing options are: (1) subordinated debt with a minimum repayment term of five years; (2) subordinated debt with a minimum repayment term of five years and an equity warrant enabling Triad to acquire a percentage of the company; or (3) straight equity investment by Triad.

VENTURE CAPITAL GROUPS TARGETING MINORITY-OWNED BUSINESSES

It will come as no surprise to any entrepreneur of color that minorities are underrepresented in the venture capital arena. Only a single-digit percentage of investors employed by VC firms are minorities, and only a single-digit percentage of venture capital goes to minority-founded startups. But that is changing. The number of VC groups founded by and staffed with minority investors is on the rise, as is the volume of VC going to minority-founded companies. Following are a few of the growing number of VC groups targeting minority-owned ventures.

Harlem Capital Partners

HBCP is a New York-based, minority-owned, early-stage venture capital firm with a mission to "change the face of entrepreneurship by investing in 1,000 diverse founders" (minorities and women). Makes seed and Series A investments in revenue-generating ($100,000+ revenue) companies in any industry, located in the United States, with tech-enabled products for underserved markets, and led by founders of "all ethnicities, genders, and walks of life."

Kapor Capital

Headquartered in Oakland, California, Kapor Capital is the venture capital group affiliated with the Kapor Center for Social Impact, a nonprofit organization dedicated to facilitating diversity and inclusion in education, the workplace, business ownership, and communities. Invests in seed-stage, tech-driven, diversity-led companies across all sectors that are dedicated to closing gaps of access, opportunity, or outcome for low-income communities and/or communities of color in the United States.

$ **If you're a minority founder in search of angel investors, cast a wide net.**
Two of the few angel groups that exclusively target minority-owned ventures
are Black Angel Tech Fund (tech) and Harriet Angels Syndicate (black and
Latina women founders). So you may need to look for minority angel investors and
for angel investment networks that have track records investing in minority-led
companies.

RESOURCES FOR MINORITY-OWNED BUSINESSES

Following are some of the many sources of free advice, information, training, mentoring, networking, and/or technical assistance to help minority
entrepreneurs start, expand, and sustain successful businesses.

Procurement Support for Minority-Owned Businesses

National Association of Minority Contractors (NAMC). Leading construction trade association providing minority-owned contractors with access
to business development training and contracting opportunities with
major corporate partners and public agencies.

National Minority Business Council (NMBD). Nonprofit membership association for minority business enterprises (MBEs) providing access to procurement events and opportunities, supplier readiness education (federal,
corporate, export), networking with corporations, and more. Does not
provide MBE certification.

US Small Business Administration (SBA). SBA's 8(a) Business Development
program enables certified 8(a) companies to bid on federal contracts set
aside for disadvantaged business enterprises (DBEs), including minority-
owned businesses. Program 8(a) certification, training, technical assistance, and supplier database are offered free at Procurement Technical
Assistance Centers (PTACs) throughout the country.

$ **Check whether your state has a minority-owned supplier initiative and
certification program.** The National Conference of State Legislatures (NCSL)
maintains a list of state government diversity procurement programs on its
website, with hyperlinks to each state program.

Information and Networking for Minority Entrepreneurs and Businesses

The following are a few of the top resources for minority entrepreneurs and minority-owned businesses throughout the nation. Additional resources for minority-owned business are also available at the local and state levels.

Association for Enterprise Opportunity (AEO). National research and advocacy nonprofit organization that facilitates the flow of capital and professional services to underserved Main Street businesses, including minority-owned businesses. My Way to Credit, AEO's online lending referral marketplace for small businesses, focuses on underserved enterprises.

Black & Brown Founders. National nonprofit organization offering community support and access to education, mentoring, and funding, opportunities to technology and tech-enabled businesses founded by black and Latinx entrepreneurs with modest resources.

Latinas Startup Alliance (LSA). Silicon Valley–based nonprofit organization with a mission to empower Latino innovators and Latino-led technology startups in the United States by providing a support network of fellow entrepreneurs/innovators, mentors, and investors.

Minority Business Development Agency (MBDA). Program of the US Department of Commerce, serving large, medium, and small businesses owned and operated by African Americans, Asian Americans, Hispanic Americans, Native Americans, Pacific Islanders, and Hasidic Jews. Provides technical assistance and access to capital, supplier contracts, and marketing opportunities to minority-owned businesses through a nationwide network of MBDA Business Centers and strategic partners.

Minority Chamber of Commerce (MCC). National nonprofit membership organization that advocates for minority-owned business development and procurement inclusion. Members have access to business education, marketing services, referral services, networking opportunities, state and corporate procurement opportunities, and potential investors.

National Urban League Entrepreneurship Centers. Signature program of the National Urban League, providing business counseling, mentoring, and training geared toward enabling minority entrepreneurs to obtain financing and procurement contracts that support job creation and preservation.

US Black Chamber of Commerce (USBC). Nonprofit advocacy and membership association of more than 100 self-sustaining local/regional Black Chambers and small business associations nationwide. Collaborates with strategic partners to provide members with training, networking, contracting opportunities, and access to capital.

US Hispanic Chamber of Commerce (UHCC). Nonprofit organization of more than 200 Hispanic Chambers across the country, providing Hispanic entrepreneurs and business owners with business development education, guidance, and technical assistance as well as access to networking and financial resources.

US Pan-Asian American Chamber of Commerce (PAAAC). Nonprofit membership organization providing business development and procurement support (domestic and Pan-Asian markets) to US businesses owned by East Asian, South Asians, Southeast Asians, and Pacific Islanders. Programs include business education/training, a business-pitch competition with cash prizes, Asian American–owned business certification, business matching (procurement).

Venture Funding Network Alliance (VFNA). National nonprofit organization that engages in strategic partnerships with major corporations, government agencies, and nonprofit organizations to help build and sustain financially strong diverse business enterprises (DBEs). Connects minority owners of small and medium-sized businesses to advisors, business experts, investors, and other funding resources across the country.

TARGET FUNDING VARIABLES FOR MINORITY-OWNED BUSINESSES

Use any combination of the following keywords to search the Internet for the type of funding you want to investigate. For each search, specify one or two variables per each applicable keyword position—for example: startup (keyword #1); minority owned, Latinx (keyword #2); accelerator (keyword #3); technology, edtech (keyword #4); United States, Oregon (keyword #5).

Keyword #1 business | small business | startup | founder | entrepreneur

Keyword #2 minority owned | minorities | African American | Asian American | black | Hispanic | Latinx | disadvantaged | underrepresented

Keyword #3 business grant | business competition | incubator | accelerator | business loan | microloan | loan program | loan fund | lending program | venture capital | angel investor | investment capital

Keyword #4 community development | economic development | business development | CDFI | government | name of industry sector

Keyword #5 United States | name of city | name of state | name of county

Funding for Women-
Owned Businesses

Female entrepreneurship has been on a steady rise in the United States, with the number of women-owned businesses nearly doubling between 1997 and 2017. Today, almost 40 percent of the nation's privately held companies are owned by women, and women launch an average of 1,000 businesses per day. Not only are women-owned businesses increasing at two and a half times the rate of all US businesses combined, but both the revenue growth and employment growth of women-owned businesses have also outpaced the national averages for all businesses. What's more, startups founded by women are 20 percent more likely to be revenue-generating and bring 35 percent higher returns to investors than all start-ups combined.

This extraordinary progress has been made despite the historic funding disparity between women-owned and men-owned businesses. Women-owned businesses receive less than 5 percent of the total dollar volume lent to businesses. Less than 3 percent of VC funding goes to woman-led companies, and 12 percent goes to mixed-gender leader teams.

Fortunately, the business funding gender gap is narrowing, and larger shares of debt and equity capital are going to women-owned ventures, in part because more women are in lending and investing decision-making positions. Female entrepreneurs are also successfully tapping into alternative funding options—such as accelerators, competitions, crowdfunding, grants, and specialized lending programs.

Targeting funding opportunities aimed specifically at women-owned businesses should be a priority funding strategy of any women-led startup or small business. Not only do such funding sources focus on women-owned businesses, they also tend to offer more favorable terms.

PRIVATE GRANTS FOR WOMEN-OWNED BUSINESSES

Like all business grants, those aimed at women-owned small businesses are in relatively short supply, usually available for a limited period of time, and competitive. But if you can find a grant for which you might qualify, the opportunity to receive free money can be worth the time spent searching and applying for grants. By way of example, the following are a few private grants for women-owned businesses that are in force at this time.

Cartier Women's Initiative Awards

Eligibility	Innovative, socially responsible, early-stage business owned by English-speaking women anywhere in the world.
Awards	Monetary grant of $100,000 to each of six laureates and monetary grant of $30,000 to each of 12 finalists annually. Grantees also receive business coaching, entrepreneurship training, networking opportunities, and participation in the INSEAD Social Entrepreneurship 6-Day Executive Program.

GIRLBOSS Foundation

Eligibility	Adult female creative (individual, not business) pursuing an entrepreneurial venture in design, fashion, music, or the arts.
Awards	Two $15,000 monetary grants per year (biannually).

COMPETITION-BASED FUNDING FOR FEMALE ENTREPRENEURS

Winning a business pitch or business plan competition is a great way to get a relatively small but no-cost infusion of cash for your startup or existing small business. Winners and often finalists usually also receive in-kind business counseling and sometimes other professional services. The following business competitions are representative of the many such events targeting women-owned and/or women-led businesses in the United States.

Entrepreneur YOU Business Plan and Pitch Competition

Sponsored by the Michigan Women's Foundation (MIWF) in partnership with Springboard Enterprises and held annually, Entrepreneur YOU is a Dolphin Tank event in which contestants pitch their businesses and receive feedback from a panel of experts.

Eligibility	Women-led small business enterprise in the state of Michigan.
Awards	Nine grants per competition, with three recipients per each of three regions. Cash prizes (grants) of $10,000, $5,000, $2,500, and $1,000. Grant recipients also receive free postcompetition assistance.

Women Founders Network Fast Pitch Competition

The Women's Founders Network sponsors and holds the Fast Pitch competition annually.

Eligibility	Women-led companies with high growth potential located in the United States.
Awards	Three monetary grants: $20,000 first prize; $7,500 second prize; $2,500 third prize. Top 10 contestants receive free coaching, mentoring, professional services, and networking opportunities with investors.

INCUBATOR- AND ACCELERATOR-BASED FUNDING FOR WOMEN-OWNED BUSINESSES

Twenty years ago, I would have been hard-pressed to come up with a handful of business incubators and accelerators that explicitly targeted female-led companies. Today, dozens of incubators/accelerators focus exclusively or primarily on women-owned businesses, and many of the nation's top incubators/accelerators have made it a priority to include women's ventures in their programs. Some incubators/accelerators are restricted to business ventures in a certain city, state, or region. Others are open to women-led ventures throughout the United States or around the world. Following are two of the top accelerators for women-led enterprises.

MergeLane Funderator

Eligibility	High-growth US startup with at least one female leader.
Program	Eight-day intensive accelerator providing coaching, leadership training, mentoring. Held 4 to 6 times per year with 8 to 10 participants per cohort.
Costs	No charge to participants.
Perks	All cohort fellows are candidates for investment capital from MergeLane Venture Fund. MergeLane receives an equity stake in and provides ongoing support to each alumnae company in which it invests.

Springboard Accelerator

Springboard Enterprises, a nonprofit organization dedicated to advancing women-led, technology-focused companies, currently runs three accelerators in the United States: Health Innovation Hub, Tech Innovation Hub, and Fashion Tech Lab.

Health Innovation Hub

Eligibility	High-growth, technology-focused life science or digital health startup with at least one woman

in senior management who has a significant equity stake.

Program   Two tracks annually, Digital Health and Life Science, each with a cohort of 10 to 15 participants. Each participant works with a personal advisory team, participates in virtual workshops, and has access to investors and corporate decision makers. Each track includes a one-week boot camp, a four-month advisory period, and presentations to active investors and potential strategic partners.

Costs $5,000 program fee per each company selected for a cohort. Small warrant contribution encouraged.

Perks   Continuing access to a network of vetted influencers, investors, and corporate decision makers. Lifelong access to the global alumnae network, visibility opportunities, and discounted services.

Tech Innovation Hub

Eligibility   Technology startup that is or will be raising capital to develop a scalable technology for the enterprise or healthcare market and has at least one woman in senior management with a significant equity stake.

Program   One accelerator per year; 12 to 15 companies per cohort. Four-month program consisting of a three-day boot camp, a personal advisory period that includes virtual workshops and one-on-one meetings with relevant experts, and presentations to relevant investors or corporate partners.

Costs $100 application fee. $5,000 program fee per each company selected for a cohort. Warrant contribution of 1–2 percent encouraged.

Perks   Continuing access to an extensive and growing network of vetted influencers, investors, and corporate decision makers. Lifelong access to the global alumnae network, visibility opportunities, and discounted services.

Fashion Tech Lab

Cofounded by the Partnership Fund for New York City and Springboard Enterprises, the Fashion Tech Lab is produced by Springboard Enterprises.

Eligibility	Early and growth stage, fashion-focused technology startup headquartered in the United States (or team is eligible to work in the United States and has visas), with at least a working beta version of its technology, at least one technical team member, and at least one female founder or female senior executive with a significant equity stake.
Program	One accelerator per year; 6 to 10 companies per cohort. Twelve-week program held in New York City consisting of workshops, panel discussions, mentoring, and collaboration led by experienced entrepreneurs, senior business executives, industry experts, retailers, and investors. Culminates in a Demo Day of founder presentations to retailers, investors, and media.
Costs	$250 application fee. $2,500 program fee per each company selected for a cohort. Warrant contribution of 1 percent also encouraged.
Perks	Ongoing exposure, networking, and investment opportunities.

STATE GOVERNMENT FUNDING FOR WOMEN-OWNED BUSINESSES

Many state governments offer funding programs for women-owned businesses or for disadvantaged businesses including female-led enterprises. The funding may be a grant (rare), loan, loan guarantee, or reduced-interest loan. Summaries of two such programs follow.

New York: Empire State Development

Empire State Development New York (ESDNY) offers both a microloan program and a revolving loan program targeting minority entrepreneurs, including women.

Micro Enterprise Loan Fund Program

Eligibility   High-risk, for-profit, small business with up to $100,000 in gross revenues, certified by the State of New York as a minority-owned business enterprise (MBE) and located in a targeted area of the state.

Loan   Term loan of up to $7,000.

Uses   Acquisition or improvement of real property; purchase of equipment/machinery; working capital.

Revolving Loan Trust Fund Program

Eligibility   High-risk, for-profit small business with up to $100,000 in gross revenues, located in New York, and certified by the State of New York as a minority-owned enterprise (MBE).

Loans   Working capital loan of up to $35,000. Fixed-asset loan of up to $50,000.

Washington: Linked Deposit Program

A portion of the state's short-term surplus funds is used to purchase certificates of deposit from qualified banks that make loans to women-owned (and minority-owned) businesses. The state transfers 2 percent of the interest earned on the CDs to cover the reduced interest rate that participating banks provide to qualified borrowers.

Eligibility   Small business located in the state of Washington that is certified a woman's business enterprise by the Washington State Office of Minority and Women.

Loan	Term loan of up to $1 million. No limit on number of loans per business. 2 percent below market interest rate. Up to 10 years repayment terms.
Uses	Accounts receivables financing, equipment purchases, lines of credit, real property acquisition, working capital, other business-related financing.

CROWDFUNDING FOR WOMEN-OWNED BUSINESSES

Women entrepreneurs have been more successful at online crowdfunding, especially rewards-based seed crowdfunding, than their male counterparts. That is due, in part, to the "crowd" being populated with as many female funders as male funders. If crowdfunding is a funding option for you, I encourage you to look into crowdfunding platforms that target female entrepreneurs—such as those described below.

SheEO

Eligibility	Woman-owned and woman-led company based in a country in which SheEO operates (including the United States) that is revenue-generating ($50,000–$1.5 million in annual revenue), has export potential, and is creating a better world through its business model, product, or services.
Platform	Debt-based crowdfunding with curated backers (*activators*). Recruits 500 activators (all women) per regional cohort, per year. Each activator contributes $1,100 per cohort, $100 of which goes to operating costs. The remaining $1,000 is pooled and loaned to five ventures selected by the activators. The low-interest loans are paid back in 20 quarterly payments over five years. All 25 semifinalists receive feedback from the Activators in their cohort, have access to all 500 Activators in the online SheEO community, and participate in the SheEO Venture Retreat and SheEO Summit.

Fees   No application or participation fees.

Support   Activators provide monthly coaching and leverage their expertise, networks, and buying power to help grow their cohort businesses.

Women You Should Fund

Eligibility   Woman-led venture located in the United States and seeking funding for a project, product, or business

Platform   Rewards-based crowdfunding. Entrepreneur/founder sets funding goal, reward(s), start date, and end date of campaign. Contributors (*backers*) pledge dollar amounts of their choice. Campaign creator is paid and rewards are distributed only if funding goal reached. Potential backers include entrepreneur's network as well as the social media network of Women You Should Know (WYSK), a digital hub of female empowerment with more than 4 million members.

Fees   5 percent of funds raised goes to WYSF. 2.9 percent + $.30 of each transaction goes to a third-party credit card processor.

Support   Free booklet, *Women You Should Fund Campaign Guide*. Personalized branding/marketing consulting and crowdfunding/marketing video creation/production services available for purchase.

LOAN PROGRAMS FOR WOMEN-OWNED BUSINESSES

Most lending programs aimed specifically at female-owned enterprises are offered by community development financial institutions (CDFIs), often in partnership with a nonprofit organization or government agency. Some nonprofit organizations lend directly to women-owned businesses, in which case the nonprofit itself may be a CDFI. Other nonprofit organizations offer lending programs for women-owned businesses in partnership with a lender other than a CDFI. Online lenders that focus on women-owned businesses, such as Accion US, are another option and typically offer more flexible loan qualification criteria and credit terms than conventional lenders.

Following are representative loan programs for women-owned businesses from a microlender, a state government agency, and a nonprofit organization.

Grameen America

This nonprofit organization provides microloans, no-fee savings accounts, and financial training to economically disadvantaged women entrepreneurs in several regions of the United States.

Eligibility	Woman living below the federal poverty level who wants to start or expand her micro or small business, agrees to follow the Grameen lending model, and lives near one of Grameen America's branches in major cities across the country.
Loan	Term loan of up to $1,500. Amounts of subsequent loans may be higher. About 5 percent interest. 26 months repayment terms; weekly payments. No loan or late fees.
Uses	Startup or growth expenses.

Wisconsin Women's Business Initiative Corporation

WWBIC is both an economic development corporation (nonprofit organization) and a certified CDFI that provides business education, technical support, and access to capital to economically and socially disadvantaged small businesses throughout Wisconsin.

Eligibility	Startup or small business located in Wisconsin and majority-owned by a woman, person of color, and/or low-income Wisconsin resident.
Loan	Term loan of $1,000–$100,000 (up to $250,000 with SBA Community Advantage Guarantee). Fixed interest based on prime market rate. $75 application fee. Up to 72 months (up to 120 months with

SBA Community Advantage Guarantee) repayment terms.

Uses   Equipment, machinery, fixtures, leasehold
improvements, supplies, inventory, working capital.

Women's Business Loans

This initiative of the US Women's Chamber of Commerce (USWCC) provides eligible firms with access to "quick, easy, affordable" loans through
the program's partner, Lending Club, a leading small business lending
platform. UWSCC also gifts a $250 reward to each business that secures a
loan through Women's Business Loans program.

Eligibility   Small business in the United States (some states
exempt) with at least $75,000 in annual reve-
nue, 20 percent owned for at least two years by a
female resident of the United States (or on a long-
term visa).

Loan   Term loan of up to $300,000. From 5.9 percent
fixed interest rate. 1 to 5 years repayment terms.

Uses   Expenses related to growing an existing business.

FROM STRUGGLING BAKERY TO THRIVING ENTERPRISE—ONE MICROLOAN AT A TIME

Lourin, a dedicated businesswoman and mother of four, loves baking her
favorite Mexican pastries. But she was struggling financially to support herself
and her children with only the earnings from her small bakery. She wanted to
expand but knew she wouldn't qualify for a bank loan. A friend introduced her
to Grameen America, a leading microfinance lender, and in 2010, Lourin joined
Grameen America and received her first microloan of $1,500 to help increase
her bakery production.

Over the course of the next eight years, Grameen America invested more
than $80,000 in Lourin—helping her expand her bakery, open an electronics
shop, and set a long-term goal of opening her own restaurant. This series of
microloans and the business counseling provided by Grameen America has

> enabled Lourin to increase her earnings and provide a stable future for her family.

ANGEL INVESTOR GROUPS TARGETING WOMEN-OWNED BUSINESSES

The number of angel investor groups that actively invest in women-owned companies has been growing, and many are being founded and populated with female investors. This is an exciting development because one of the main reasons women-founded ventures have historically received a single-digit portion of equity funding is that the investment world has been dominated by male decision-makers who have often underestimated, undervalued, and misunderstood female entrepreneurs and the businesses they create and build. That, too, is changing, as more men join the ranks of angel investors that focus on women-led ventures.[1]

Angels are selective about which entrepreneurs and businesses they invest in. You should be equally discerning in seeking and selecting angel investment capital. Start by targeting angel investment groups that support women entrepreneurs like you and ventures like yours.

Here are two of the many angel investment groups focused on women-led ventures.

Golden Seeds

Founded and led by women, Golden Seeds is one of the largest angel investor networks in the United States, with six chapters and hundreds of female and male investors. It is dedicated to collaboratively assessing, funding, and supporting women-led companies.

Focus   Scalable B2B or B2C business domiciled in the United States, with at least one woman in a position of equity, influence, and power. Typically invests in companies that support gender diversity; are "doing truly exciting things" in consumer, healthcare, and technology products or services; and have a plausible exit strategy five to eight years out.

Deals	Equity investment of $250,000–$2 million.
Perks	Ongoing guidance to portfolio companies and access to venture capital.

Pipeline Angels

Founded by renowned Latina entrepreneur Natalia Oberti Noguera, Pipeline Angels is a network of female investors dedicated to helping female social entrepreneurs of diverse ethnicities, backgrounds, and ages.

Focus	Early-stage startup registered in a US state, engaged in a social or environmental mission, with a woman or nonbinary femme founder or cofounder.
Deals	Total equity investment of $40,000 to $14 million per company. Angel round, funding round, seed round, Series A round, convertible note. Each investor makes an equity investment of at least $5,000 in a company showcased at a Pipeline Angels Pitch Summit.
Perks	Ongoing access to growing network of entrepreneurs, investors, and thought leaders.

VENTURE CAPITAL GROUPS TARGETING WOMEN-OWNED BUSINESSES

Recent and emerging data validates what female entrepreneurs and venture capitalists have long known or suspected: women investors tend to better understand women-led ventures, and women-led ventures funded by women investors perform better.[2] Fortunately, increasingly more women are joining and leading VC firms—such as the two featured here. Investing in women-led startups is also now part of the investment strategy of more male-led VC firms.

Female Founders Fund

Led by two female founding partners, Female Founders Fund (F^3) is a network of female and male investors who back "talented female founders with disruptive and innovative ideas that better serve their consumers."

Focus	Early-stage, technology-driven, women-owned startup engaged in e-commerce, web-enabled products and services, marketplaces, and platforms.
Deals	Equity investment of $1 million–$20 million. Seed, Series A, venture rounds.
Perks	Mentoring and support from a community of founders, CEOs, senior executives, and other industry experts.

SoGal Ventures

The world's first female-led, millennial investment group, SoGal backs future-focused, human-centric, diversity-led companies in the United States and Asia Pacific.

Focus	Early-stage startup with a female founder or gender-diverse founding team and/or a primarily female customer base. Interested in ventures that impact "how we live, work, and stay healthy." Portfolio includes consumer, health, and SaaS companies.
Deals	Equity investment of $10,000–$3 million. Pre-seed through Series A. SoGal usually seeks to be the first institutional investor.
Perks	Access to curated information and resources, peer-to-peer support system, and events sponsored by SoGal and its partners.

MOMPRENEUR TURNS PAIN INTO PROFIT

Rachel Jackson was a busy working mom when the magic and discomfort of breastfeeding her first child inspired her to find a better way to relieve the pain of mastitis. She put her law career to the side, developed Rachel's Remedy Breastfeeding Relief Packs, the only FDA-cleared (patent pending) moist heat and cooling packs for nursing moms, and in 2015 launched Rachel's Remedies,

LLC. She went on to develop Rachel's Remedy washable antimicrobial breast pads and is developing other all-natural women's health remedies. In 2017, Rachel's Remedies entered into a three-year licensing partnership with Dr. Brown's, a leading brand of healthful baby products.

To date, Rachel has raised $700,000 for her venture, most of which came from Launch New York, Inc., a nonprofit venture development organization (VDO) investing in high-growth companies in Upstate New York, and Z80Labs, a business incubator/accelerator focused on Internet-tech, green-tech, and health-tech startups. Jackson has also received equity funding from private investors and won $5,000 in The Pitch, a business pitch competition for women-owned and minority-owned businesses in the Buffalo, New York area.

RESOURCES FOR WOMEN ENTREPRENEURS AND BUSINESSES OWNERS

Following are sources of free information, training, counseling, and/or technical assistance to help women entrepreneurs start, expand, and sustain their own businesses.

US Small Business Administration (SBA)

The SBA's Office of Women's Business Ownership (OWBO) collaborates with myriad agencies and organizations to make business ownership and business development resources available to women. Programs include the following.

Women's Business Centers (WBC). A nationwide network of more than 100 Women's Business Centers (WBCs) works with local SBA offices and community partners to provide women entrepreneurs with free business counseling and assistance as well as access to other SBA programs and funding resources.

Women-Owned Business Federal Procurement Program. This SBA-funded program helps certified women-owned businesses (WOBs) compete for federal contracts and works with federal agencies to achieve the government's goal of awarding 5 percent of contracting dollars to women-owned small businesses.

Procurement Support for Women-Owned Businesses

Most government agencies and many large corporations have procurement programs that allot a percentage of their contracts to women-owned small businesses. To qualify for these programs, the company must be certified as a woman-owned small business. Federal government agencies require SBA-approved certification as a Women-Owned Small Business (WOSB). State governments often have their own certification protocol, but many accept WOSB-certified contractors. Some corporations require or accept WOSB certification; others require or prefer certification as a Women's Business Enterprise (WBE). The following organizations support women-owned businesses seeking government and/or commercial contracts.

Procurement Technical Assistance Centers (PTACs). A network of 100 PTACs, with more than 300 local offices across the United States, provides free assistance in self-certifying as an WOSB or EDWOSB as well as federal and state government-contracting training and counseling.

National Association of Women Business Owners (NAWBO). NAWBO is a fee-based, third-party SBA-approved WOSB (government) certifier and WBE (private sector) certifier. Offers fee-based training, mentoring, and networking opportunities with commercial and government purchasing agents.

United States Women's Chamber of Commerce (USWCC). USWCC is a fee-based, third-party SBA-approved WOSB and EDWOSB certifier (government) and National Women Business Enterprise (NWBE) and International Women Business Enterprises (IWBE) third-party certifier (private sector).

Women's Business Enterprise National Council (WBENC). WBENC is a fee-based, third-party SBA-approved WOSB certifier (government) and WBE certifier (private sector). Offers fee-based procurement training and free access to an online database connecting WBENC-certified women-owned businesses with commercial and government contracting opportunities.

Information, Networking, and Other Resources for Women Business Owners

Following are a few of the many organizations that provide services and resources to help women fund, launch, and grow their businesses. Other national and local organizations provide similar support to women-owned startups and small businesses.

Black Female Founders. This nonprofit membership association advocates for and supports black female entrepreneurs worldwide. Offers free workshops and webinars, networking opportunities, and funding connections (investor referrals, introductions).

Dell Women's Entrepreneur Network (DWEN). DWEN, an initiative of Dell Technologies, connecting women entrepreneurs around the globe with networking opportunities, funding connections, information, and technology. Annual summit brings together Dell executives and 200 selected DWEN-member entrepreneurs for collaboration, thought leadership, and networking.

EBW2020: Empowering a Billion Women by 2020. EBW2020 connects women to financial, education, networking, and other resources to launch, build, or scale their businesses. Offers annual summit, accelerator, and free e-newsletter.

EnrichHER. This diversity-centric, women-led membership organization connects female entrepreneurs with funders, mentors, and other resources through its virtual community and live events. Website features a running list of funding opportunities, updated weekly.

National Association of Women Business Owners (NAWBO). NAWBO is a nonprofit membership organization with 60 chapters and more than 5,000 members. Offers dues-paying members free education, information, mentoring, networking, and access to capital.

National Women's Business Council (NAWBC). This nonpartisan federal advisory of prominent female business leaders serves as independent counsel to the federal government. The Grow Her Business portal of the NAWBC website lists more than 200 resources for women-owned businesses, including accelerators, business competitions, education/ training, funding, and contracting opportunities.

United States Women's Chamber of Commerce (USWCC). USWCC is a nonprofit membership organization that uses a platform of influence, innovation, and opportunity to work with and on behalf of members, helping them to start and build successful businesses and gain access to government contracts.

TARGET FUNDING VARIABLES FOR WOMEN-OWNED BUSINESSES

Use any combination of the following keywords to search the Internet for the type of funding you want to investigate. For each search, specify one or two variables per each applicable keyword position—for example: small business (keyword #1); woman owned, female founder (keyword #2); angel investor, investment capital (keyword #3); (keyword #4); United States, (keyword #5).

Keyword #1	business | small business | startup | business owner | founder | entrepreneur
Keyword #2	woman owned | female founder | women | black women | Latina women | disadvantaged | underrepresented
Keyword #3	business grant | business competition | incubator | accelerator | business loan | microloan | loan program | loan fund | lending program | venture capital | angel investor | investment capital
Keyword #4	community development | economic development | business development | CDFI | government | name of industry sector
Keyword #5	United States | name of city | name of state | name of county

Funding for Other Diversity Groups

Most diversity funding programs for startups and small businesses target companies owned by minorities and/or women. Usually, *minority* is defined as business owners whose ethnicity (25 percent+) is Asian-Indian, Asian-Pacific, Black, Hispanic, or Native American. Other diversity funding targets entrepreneurs who are *economically or socially disadvantaged,* such as veterans and people with disabilities. Some business funding programs aimed at minority and/or disadvantaged business owners encompass businesses owned by members of other diversity groups, such as individuals who identify as lesbian, gay, bisexual, transgender, or queer (LGBTQ); people over age 50; immigrants and refugees; and people of various faiths. This chapter explores some of the funding opportunities designated for businesses owned by these "other" diversity groups.

FUNDING FOR LGBTQ-OWNED BUSINESSES

LGBTQ-owned enterprises have been on the rise, and upward of 1.4 million LGBTQ-owned companies currently exist in the United States, including some of the most successful, such as Calvin Klein, Facebook, and PayPal. Nevertheless, LGBTQ+ entrepreneurs report having experienced bias from investors and lenders or do not disclose their sexual orientation to deter bias. That said, funding opportunities that are either exclusive or inclusive to LGBTQ-owned enterprises do exist and are increasing. Several examples of LGBTQ-focused business funding options follow.

Awards and Competitions for LGBTQ-Owned Businesses

The best place to start your search for LGBTQ-focused and LGBTQ-inclusive business competitions is in your own backyard, especially if you live in an urban area with a large LGBTQ population. Following are two examples of local LGBTQ business competitions.

LGBTQ Biz Pitch. Sponsored by the National Gay and Lesbian Chamber of Commerce (NGLCC), this pitch competition is held at the annual NGLCC Business & Leadership Conference. The competition is open to NLGCC-certified LGBTQ Business Enterprises nationwide as well as US businesses that are eligible for and intend to secure LGBTQ Business Enterprise certification through NLGCC. Three finalists pitch their businesses for a chance to win a $50,000 prize package—$25,000 cash and $25,000 worth of in-kind business consulting.

PNC Bank's LGBT Business Award. This award, which includes a $10,000 cash prize, is presented at the annual business luncheon of the Independence Business Alliance (IBA), Greater Philadelphia's LGBT Chamber of Commerce. It is awarded to a local LGBTQ or ally company that is an IBA member and "poised to grow, innovate, and give back to the community."

LGBTQ CHAMBER SUPPORT HELPS MOVE A DISRUPTIVE E-RETAILER FORWARD

Established in 2015 by business and hospitality leaders Keith Schiesz, CEO, and Matthew Wilson, president, eParel, LLC, is the parent company of Bib & Tucker, a disruptive retail platform that lets hospitality companies design and manage their own employee-driven uniform programs online. Bib & Tucker's Signature Collection bears the prestigious Made in NYC label, and its marketplace includes famous retail brands such as Calvin Klein, Levi's, Van Heusen, Vans, and others. The clothing and accessories (hats to shoes) are carefully selected with an eye toward style, comfort, variety, functionality, durability, and looking fresh throughout the workday.

As fabulous as the uniforms are, they almost (*almost*) play second fiddle to the Bib & Tucker business model and the proprietary technology enabling it. The platform allows hospitality companies to set up their own online uniform boutique, stocked with a selection of customized (with company logo, for example), ready-to-wear uniform apparel. Employees choose and order their own uniforms, shipped directly to the employee. The hospitality company has the option of prepaying for all, certain, or none of the uniform pieces, and Bib & Tucker also offers credit and financing options for employees. Employees get a choice in what they wear and the convenience of shopping at home. Hospitality companies are relieved of the burden and expense of ordering, reordering, distributing, and laundering uniforms, saving considerable money and time.

Impressive! Innovation at its best.

When one of my colleagues who is affiliated with the National LGBT Chamber of Commerce (NLGCC) shared eParel's story and told me they'd won the 2018 NLGCC Biz Pitch, I wasn't surprised. But Keith and Matthew were.

At the close of the competition, Keith remarked, "We were up against two great companies. We're overwhelmed, but elated, that we won.

"The prize—$25,000 cash and a $25,000 business products and consulting came—at a critical stage in the business. The cash went toward starting to build a sales team, the first employees hired in the two-person operation. The Apple products were needed and put to good use, and the marketing support provided by the media company Chatterbox helped to move the business forward. But the value of winning the competition went beyond the awards.

"The Biz Pitch competition built our confidence, helped us further refine our idea, expanded our network, and gave us additional exposure," Keith said. "The Chamber also introduced us to potential customers who are NGLCC members in purchasing roles and who own businesses."

That's what Chambers are for—guiding, helping, and connecting members.

Incubator- and Accelerator-Based Funding Targeting LGBTQ-Owned Businesses

StartOut Growth Lab is distinct from most business incubators in its "explicit focus" on LGBTQ-founded startups. However, several diversity-inclusive incubators and accelerators either have LGBTQ-specific programs or seek to include LGBTQ founders in their cohorts—such as those 500 Startups, featured here.

500 Startups Unity & Inclusion Summit. This annual one-day event isn't a business incubator or accelerator, per se, but serves a similar purpose in that it features workshops on topics such as raising capital and growth marketing and gives attending LGBTQ founders access to industry experts and investors. Although the Unity & Inclusion Summit is exclusively for LGBTQ-led technology startups, 500 Startups, one of the most active seed venture capital firms in the world, invests in companies led by founders of diverse ethnicity, culture, and gender.

StartOut Growth Labs. StartOut, the largest national nonprofit organization for LGBTQ entrepreneurs, in partnership with Nixon Peabody, a nationwide law firm, runs two on-site (San Francisco), six-month Growth Labs per year, each with a cohort of seven founders. The program provides office space, mentoring, education, and networking opportunities. StartOut takes no equity in SGL participating companies; instead, each founder pays StartOut a onetime fee (currently $750). Cohort members also cover their living expenses during the six-month program.

($) **Look for LGBTQ "inclusive business" incubators and accelerators in your area.** Two examples: Tampa Bay Wave's TechDiversity Program, a business accelerator for local high-potential technology startups that are majority owned or operated by a member of the LGBTQ community, woman, minority, and/or veteran. Propeller, a nonprofit incubator and accelerator that supports "diverse" entrepreneurs, including LGBTQ individuals, whose startups address social and environmental disparities.

Community-Based Lending for LGBTQ-Owned Businesses

Most financial institutions recognize the benefits of lending to LGBTQ-owned businesses. That is why so many banks and other financial institutions market to LGBTQ entrepreneurs. If you qualify for a bank business loan, it can be a viable funding source for your business. However, I encourage you to also check into community-based lenders that target LGBTQ-owned businesses, such as the two examples cited here. Community lenders typically offer less restrictive qualification requirements and more flexible terms than conventional lenders. Examples follow.

Coast Community Capital. This nonprofit certified community development financial institution (CDFI) promotes small business growth throughout the state of Massachusetts via free business counseling and workshops and various funding options, including SBA loans, loan guarantees, and direct loans. For several years, Coast Community Capital has had an initiative to "empower" local LGBTQ businesses by providing funding and resources.

Opportunity Fund. This certified CDFI is one of the largest small business lenders in the United States. Based and originally operating only in California, Opportunity Fund now serves 12 additional states through its partnership with Lending Club. Opportunity Fund specializes in lending to underserved businesses—including those owned by LGBTQ entrepreneurs—that don't qualify for bank loans.

Investment Groups Targeting LGBTQ-Owned Businesses

A small but growing number of angel investor networks and venture capital groups have "diversity" or "inclusion" investment strategies that encompass LGBTQ companies, among them Astia Angels, Backstage Capital, and Pipeline Angels. Two of the few investor networks dedicated solely to LGBTQ ventures are Gaingels and StartOut Investor Portal.

Backstage Capital. As articulated by the firm's founder and managing partner, Arlan Hamilton, Backstage Capital invests in the "very best founders who identify as women, people of color, or LGBTQ. I personally identify with all three." Any underrepresented founder of a technology or technology-enabled company in the United States seeking early-stage or seed venture capital is welcome to apply for angel or micro-VC investment consideration with Backstage Capital.

Gaingels. This global affinity network of LGBTQ and ally investors (angel and venture capital) connects LGBTQ entrepreneurs with access to capital, mentors, business acumen, and other resources. A selection committee chooses which companies are given the opportunity to present to investors at Gaingels hubs in Los Angeles, New York, San Francisco, Toronto, and London. Each member of the Gaingels syndicate decides independently whether and how much they wish to invest in a company.

Procurement Support for LGBTQ-Owned Businesses

Although the SBA's LGBT inclusion program encourages federal government agencies to contract with LGBTQ business enterprises (LGBTBE), at this writing the federal government has no set goal for awarding a portion of its contracts to LGBTQ suppliers. Several state and local governments also have LGBTQ-supplier diversity/inclusion initiatives, as do many public institutions and nonprofit organizations. Likewise, many corporations, including more than a third of Fortune 500 companies, actively seek to contract with LGBTQ-owned companies. Most (if not all) of these programs require LGBTBE certification from a recognized source, such as the two most prominent LGBTBE certifiers cited below.

Golden Gate Business Association. GGBA, the world's first LGBTQ Chamber of Commerce, serves LGBTQ-owned businesses in the San Francisco Bay Area. GGBA works in partnership with the National Gay and Lesbian Chamber of Commerce (NGLCC) to help prepare LGBTQ companies for NGLCC's *LGBT business enterprise* (LGBTBE) certification and to connect with purchasing agents for corporations, nonprofit organizations, and government agencies in the region.

National Gay and Lesbian Chamber of Commerce. NGLCC is a nonprofit LGBTI (lesbian, gay, bisexual, transsexual, intersex) business advocacy and membership organization with numerous affiliate chambers throughout the United States. NGLCC provides *LGBT business enterprise* (LGBTBE) certification, business resources, and procurement connections to corporate partners. NGLCC also has an international division, which facilitates global procurement opportunities for LGBTI businesses.

In 2016, Equator Coffees & Teas became the first LGBTQ-owned company to win the SBA National Small Business of the Year Award. The venture was launched in 1995 by life partners Brook McDonnell and Helen Russell—on a shoestring and in their garage. Headquartered in the San Francisco Bay Area, Equator Coffee & Teas is now a renowned social impact company focused on sustainability, with more than 500 wholesale accounts, seven retail cafes, and 100+ employees.

Resources for LGBTQ-Owned Businesses

The resources cited in this section are aimed specifically at LGBTQ entrepreneurs and business owners throughout the United States. Many other national, state, and local resources aimed at "socially disadvantaged" groups also encompass LGBTQ entrepreneurs and business owners.

Lesbian Business Community (LBC). Free online searchable directory of lesbian-owned and LGBTQ-friendly businesses throughout the United States. Provides free access to informative and inspiring articles on a wide range of LGBTQ business–related topics.

Lesbians Who Tech. Worldwide community of lesbian entrepreneurs and professionals and their allies in technology, promoting the inclusion and visibility of women, LGBTQ people, and people from diverse backgrounds who are underrepresented in technology. Offers content-rich website and sponsors leadership conferences, networking events, and a coding scholarship.

National Gay and Lesbian Chamber of Commerce (NGLCC). In addition to facilitation and support of LGBTQ procurement inclusion, advocates for and supports inclusion of LGBTQ individuals in business and the marketplace. Members are eligible for discounts from participating companies and organizations.

OutBüro. Free and premium membership organization for the LGBTQ business, entrepreneur, startup, and professional global community. Website features free access to online LGBTQ business directory, online job portal, networking platform, and blog (filled with leads to resources, including funding).

Out in Tech. Nonprofit membership organization with chapters in several major US cities and London seeks to empower LGBTQ technology entrepreneurs and professionals by offering education, networking, and publicity opportunities to its 20,000+ members.

StartOut. Nonprofit membership organization that "connects and educates LGBTQ entrepreneurs to empower great leaders and businesses." Free membership includes access to expert advice and networking tools;

premium membership includes access to free services as well as to mentoring, an online investor platform, and an online business directory. Runs Growth Labs, an incubator/accelerator for LGBTQ-owned startups.

Trans*H4CK. Nonprofit organization that produces a hackathon and a speaker series for trans technologists and as a "hub" and "mini-incubator" has helped launch numerous trans startups and social enterprises.

US Small Business Administration. Works in partnership with the National Gay and Lesbian Chamber of Commerce to increase SBA's outreach to and inclusion of the LGBTQ business community, with the objective of ensuring that LGBTQ business owners have greater access to SBA educational and loan programs and federal government contracting opportunities.

FUNDING FOR ENCORE ENTREPRENEURS

Today, the highest rate of entrepreneurial activity in the United States is among people between the ages of 55 and 64. In recent years, boomer founders and millennial founders each account for almost a quarter (23–25 percent) of startups in the United States.

Although the funding options available to *encore* (or *silver*) entrepreneurs are essentially the same as those available to younger entrepreneurs, elder founders tend to fund their new businesses differently than do more junior founders. The most widely used forms of business financing for older entrepreneurs are:

- Cash, primarily from personal savings (55 percent)
- Tax-deferred retirement plans, such as 401(k)s and IRAs (28 percent)
- Gifts and loans from family and friends, including inheritances (19 percent)

Those, however, are not the only funding methods used by encore entrepreneurs. If starting a successful business is a goal for the second or even third act of your life, consider the following funding options, too.

Business Competitions for Encore Entrepreneurs

Any encore entrepreneur can enter a "best" business, business pitch, or business plan competition that is not age-specific but for which the business is otherwise eligible. Many such business competitions award cash prizes and/or in-kind business products and services. (For more information, please check out the free, downloadable bonus chapter "Competition Based Funding" at kedmaough.com.)

One business competition aimed solely at startups and small businesses owned by silver entrepreneurs is the Purpose Prize. Sponsored and produced by AARP since 2016, the Purpose Prize is a national award that recognizes encore social entrepreneurs.

Purpose Prize nominees are US citizens aged 50+ whose innovative and impactful work (paid or unpaid, for-profit or nonprofit) is of substantial benefit to society. Each year, the Purpose Prize is awarded annually to five individuals, with each winner receiving a cash prize ($60,000 in 2018) as well as free publicity and networking opportunities. One of the five annual Purpose Prize winners is also awarded the Andrus Prize for Intergenerational Excellence in recognition of a social impact venture that "brings multiple generations together for a better community." In addition, AARP selects 5 to 10 Purpose Prize fellows, each of whom receives a cash prize ($5,000 in 2018) as well as educational, publicity, and networking opportunities.

For more information and to nominate yourself or someone else for the AARP Purpose Prize, visit the AARP (.org) website and search for "Purpose Prize."

Team up with a younger cofounder. *Intergenerational entrepreneurship*—in which, for example, a sixty-something entrepreneur and a thirty-something entrepreneur team up to launch a business—is a trending strategy that is yielding successful companies. It may also open doors to business funding opportunities. Case in point: Housecalls for the Homebound, a New York City business founded by a retired physician in his seventies, his middle-aged son (a software engineer), and his twenty-something grandson (an accountant). Housecalls for the Homebound is a 2015 AARP Purpose Prize winner, for which it received a cash prize of $100,000.

Rollovers for Business Startups (ROBS) for Encore Entrepreneurs

Many 50+ entrepreneurs cash out their 401(k) or other tax-deferred retirement plan to help fund their business ventures, which often means they pay income taxes and early withdrawal penalties on the cashed-out funds. ROBS is essentially a tax procedure that enables you to invest a portion (not all) of your personal 401(k) in your business without cashing out your retirement account. If you have at least $50,000 in a 401(k) or other tax-deferred account and are at least 59½ years old, you might be able to use a Rollover for Business Startup (ROBS) to help buy, start, or grow your business.

Here's how it works:

1. Form a C corporation, a business structure that enables a company to have shareholders, for your new (or existing) business.

2. Create a tax-deferred retirement plan, such as a 401(k) or IRA, for the newly-formed C corporation. *Note:* Roth 401(k) and Roth IRAs are ineligible for ROBS.

3. Roll over your personal 401(k) to your company's new 401(k).

4. Use funds from the new 401(k) to purchase stock in your business. With this step, your company's new retirement plan becomes a shareholder in your newly formed C corporation.

5. Use the proceeds from the sale of the stock (to the retirement plan) toward either acquiring a business or franchise, starting a business, or growing your existing business. (To learn more about using ROBS to purchase a franchise, please see Chapter 16, "Funding for a Franchise.")

One benefit of using a ROBS is that you pay no taxes and no early withdrawal penalties on the rolled-over funds. Another is that ROBS is not a loan, so you pay no interest and do not repay the funds invested in your business. Additionally, the funds are usually available within three to four weeks. Finally, you can return the percentage of profits owned by your company's retirement plan to the retirement plan.

Using ROBS to fund a business does have downsides, however. Setting up and running a C corporation and enrolling in a ROBS are complicated and costly processes. Both a C corporation and a ROBS come with a host of rules, regulations, and restrictions as well as ongoing administrative and reporting requirements. You will need to hire a ROBS provider to set up a C corporation and a ROBS as well as to administer the retirement plan and IRS filings on an ongoing basis. The initial setup costs can be $5,000 or more, which must come out of your pocket. You cannot use funds from either your personal 401(k) or your new business 401(k) to pay for those expenses. Perhaps the biggest drawback to a ROBS is the inherent risk of diminishing your retirement funds should your business fail or should you exit the business without returning all or most of the funds to the retirement plan.

ROBS is not for everyone, but it is a viable funding option for encore entrepreneurs who are willing and able to take on the challenges and risks involved in a Rollover for Business Startup. If you are considering a ROBS, do some research to learn the basics of ROBS and C corporations, consult with your attorney and/or accountant, and weigh the pros and cons to determine whether a ROBS is right for you.

If you decide a Rollover for Business Startup is a funding option for you, hire a qualified and reputable ROBS provider to assist you. Three of the country's leading ROBS consultants are Benetrends, FranFund, and Guidant Financial.

A ROBS LAUNCHES A REWARDING NEXT CHAPTER FOR A CORPORATE RETIREE

At age 59, Skip Sheppard decided to retire from a long corporate career and buy a small business near his home in Ipswich, Massachusetts. He looked into convenience stores, pizza shops, and other enterprises before he found the perfect match: a marine and fishing supply store in nearby Gloucester. Skip had grown up in a fishing village on the coast of Maine, and he'd been an avid tuna fisherman and recreational boater for decades. With a Rollover for Business Startup (ROBS) transacted through Guidant Financial's 401(k) Business Financing services, Skip used $200,000 of his retirement funds to buy and expand Three Lantern Marine & Fishing Store.

It was a gamble, as all new businesses are, that paid off handsomely. Within a few years Skip transformed the neighborhood store with $275,000 in annual sales into a $3 million business selling both commercial and recreational fishing supplies, tackle, gear, and bait. Skip continues to add both product lines and customers, and to enjoy his silver entrepreneurship.

Debt Funding for Encore Entrepreneurs

The fourth and fifth most common forms of business funding for encore entrepreneurs are lines of credit (17 percent) and unsecured loans (13 percent)—both of which typically require excellent credit scores. Secured business loans, including SBA-guaranteed loans, are among the least common business funding options used by encore entrepreneurs. Although nearly half of aspiring business owners age 50+ have considered obtaining an SBA-guaranteed loan, only 9 percent of them received an SBA loan, either because they didn't meet the requirements or they didn't meet the business owners' requirements.

Older business owners in good financial standing are more apt to secure the loan type, amount, and terms they want from a bank or credit union with which they've done business for a long time. Another potential debt-funding option for encore entrepreneurs is a community development financial institution (CDFI). CDFI loans are usually easier to get and offer better terms than conventional business loans. (Please see Chapter 11, "Community Development Financial Institutions.")

As a general rule, encore entrepreneurs are wise to not take on a heavy debt load to start or grow a business.

$ **Give your business a kick start with crowdfunding.** For all the adventurous spiritedness of their youth, aging baby boomers tend to be leery of using crowdfunding for a business venture. Don't be! Crowdfunding can be, and has been, a viable funding option for encore entrepreneurs—provided you choose the right crowdfunding platform and the right format (for example, rewards- or donor-based, if you don't want to take on debt or share equity), and provided you create and run an effective crowdfunding campaign. (For more information, check out the free, downloadable bonus chapter "Crowdfunding" at kedmaough.com.)

Equity Funding for Encore Entrepreneurs

Securing investment capital can be a challenge for encore entrepreneurs. But it's not impossible—provided the startup is the type of high-growth enterprise that angel investors and venture capitalists seek. If that's the case, pitch to investors who specialize in your industry niche. All the better if that happens to be the longevity sector (innovative products and services for seniors), one of the largest and fastest-growing markets in the United States. When seeking equity funding, leverage your past experience, knowledge of the market, and financial strength.

Resources for Encore Entrepreneurs

Following are several of the most helpful resources for people 50+ years who are launching or growing a business.

AARP. National nonprofit membership organization, providing research, advocacy, information, and resources aimed at facilitating the economic opportunity (including business ownership), social connectedness, and legal rights of aging Americans. AARP's media content (magazine, e-bulletin, blog, podcasts, videos, TV) routinely covers a wide range of topics around encore entrepreneurship and silver business ownership. AARP Foundation's Work for Yourself@50+ program offers workshops, webinars, tools, and other resources. AARP also sponsors the Purpose Prize, recognizing 50+ social entrepreneurs, and runs The Hatchery, a business incubator for startups with innovations that enhance the quality of life for people 50+.

Boomer Venture Summit. Annual conference of angel investors, venture capitalists, entrepreneurs, corporate executives, and media that focuses on technology-enabled innovations for the longevity economy. Held in Silicon Valley, the summit also includes two business competitions with cash and in-kind prizes.

Next Avenue. "Public media's first and only national journalism service for America's booming older population" delivers daily content on ideas and issues that are vital to the aging population. Various aspects of encore entrepreneurship and silver business ownership are regularly featured in Next Avenue's online portal, newsletters, and social media platforms as well as through partnerships with other PBS programs, such as Think TV, Local Talk, and Healthy Balance.

US Small Business Administration. Offers an online Checklist for Encore Entrepreneurs and the online course "Encore Entrepreneurs: An Introduction to Starting Your Own Business." Older entrepreneurs and business owners have access to business counseling through local Small Business Development Centers and to SBA-guaranteed loans.

BUSINESS FUNDING FOR IMMIGRANTS AND REFUGEES

According to the Americas Society and Council of the Americas (AS/COA), one of every four new businesses in the United States is owned by a foreign-born entrepreneur, and almost a third (28 percent) of Main Street businesses are immigrant-owned. In metropolitan areas with large immigrant populations, an even larger proportion of Main Street businesses are owned by "new Americans." It is not surprising, then, that most funding for immigrant-owned businesses comes from local and state sources, such as those cited below.

> Immigrants and their children have founded more than two-fifths of all Fortune 500 companies, according to the Center for American Entrepreneurship.

Incubators and Accelerators for Immigrant-Owned Businesses

Several business incubators and accelerators in the United States, especially those focused on technology startups, accept immigrant-founded companies. Many national incubators/accelerators, such as Techstars and Y Combinator, actively seek to incubate/accelerate immigrant-led startups. Following are examples of a local incubator and a local accelerator for immigrant-owned companies.

Philadelphia Immigration Innovation. Joint program of the community lender FINANTA and the nonprofit organizations Mt. Airy USA and the Welcoming Center for New Pennsylvanians, Philly I-Hub provides aspiring and established small business owners, both new immigrants and long-term residents, in the Northwest Philadelphia community of

Mt. Airy with the resources needed to develop their businesses. Services are free to eligible participants and include training, coaching, co-work space, networking, and access to funding opportunities.

Startup52. New York City's first (and currently only) business accelerator focused solely on accelerating the growth of innovative tech-enabled startups that have at least one founder who is a new immigrant, person of color, woman, or veteran; or identifies as LGBTQ; or has a disability.

Community-Based Funding for Immigrant-Owned Businesses

Following are a few of the many community development financial institutions (CDFIs), community banks and credit unions, local government agencies, and nonprofit organizations across the United States that offer business funding opportunities to immigrants, asylees, and refugees.

Arch Grants. Through its Global Startup Competition, this nonprofit, local economic development organization awards $50,000 equity-free grants and pro bono support services to entrepreneurs who locate their early-stage businesses in St. Louis. Arch Grants proactively seeks immigrant applicants, and more than 30 percent of active Arch Grant portfolio companies have at least one immigrant founder.

Business Center for New Americans (BCNA). This CDFI and SBA-certified microlender provides immigrant entrepreneurs in New York City with access to affordable credit, match-savings accounts, and business training.

California FarmLink. This CDFI supports immigrant, limited-resource, first-time, and other underserved farmers in California, primarily in the Central Coast, North Coast, Sacramento Valley, and San Joaquin Valley regions. Provides access to capital, financial and business management training, and assistance with acquiring or leasing land.

International Rescue Committee. The Microenterprise Program of the IRC's Center for Economic Opportunity (CEO) offers business training, technical assistance, low-interest loans, and matched savings accounts to immigrant business owners. IRC is a nonprofit organization and CDFI with 26 locations throughout the United States.

Opportunities Credit Union (OCU). This "grassroots community development" network provides small business loans, asset-building resources, training, and other resources to low-income and other underserved business owners in Vermont—including immigrants, people of color, and women.

Refugee Resettlement Office. The JumpStart Fund of King County, Washington's Refugee Resettlement Office provides affordable loans, business counseling, and technical assistance to eligible refugees, asylees, and other new immigrants who wish to start a business in the greater Seattle area.

Equity Funding for Immigrant-Owned Businesses

Angel investment networks and venture capital groups whose investment strategy focuses on startups founded by "minority" or "disadvantaged" entrepreneurs, such as Kapor Capital, sometimes include immigrant-owned businesses in that investment strategy. Some angels and venture capitalists specifically target immigrant-owned companies—such as the two featured here.

One Way Ventures. This Boston-based firm makes seed and Series A investments solely in immigrant-founded, US-based tech companies "covering all spectrums of the digital world." The firm's two cofounders and managing partners, both immigrants, each have 20 years of angel investing experience and 20 years of business leadership and operations.

Unshackled Ventures. This venture fund focuses exclusively on immigrant-founded startups in the United States, primarily high-growth, early-stage startups. Unshackled Ventures invests up to $300,000 in pre-seed and seed capital in exchange for 8–15 percent equity ownership. The firm also makes convertible loans. Unshackled Ventures offers an Innovator-in-Residence program and provides immigration/visa support to founders selected for participation in its programs.

 Tap into free community support for immigrant business owners. Areas of the country with large or growing immigrant populations typically have local and/or state government and nonprofit programs offering a variety of resources to help "new Americans" (legal asylees, refugees, and immigrants) start and grow small businesses. For example: Louisville, Kentucky's Refugees and Immigrants Succeeding in Entrepreneurship (RISE) program; New York City's Immigrant Business Initiative; Portland, Oregon's Immigrant and Refugee Community Organization (IRCO); Illinois Business Immigration Coalition; Massachusetts Immigration, Refugee, and Asylee (MIRA) Coalition; and Washington State's Ethnic Business Coalition.

FAITH-BASED BUSINESS FUNDING

Numerous community-based lenders, such as community development financial institutions (CDFIs), throughout the United States as well as online crowdfunding platforms focus on members of a specific religious faith. Likewise, some business incubators and accelerators, angel investor and venture capital groups, and business development organizations target entrepreneurs of a specified faith. To give you an idea of the type of business funding and resources that might be aimed at people of your faith, several examples follow.

Funding for Christian Entrepreneurs and Business Owners

California Adventist Federal Credit Union (CAFCU). Offers equipment loans, business term loans, and business lines of credit to credit union members, who must be Seventh Day Adventist church members residing in the state of California.

Center for Faith & Work/Entrepreneurship & Innovation Program. This Gospel-centered business development initiative of Redeemer Presbyterian Church of New York City offers a six-week Faith & Entrepreneurship course, a three-month Entrepreneurship Intensive course, and a Startup Pitch Night with cash prizes up to $7,500.

Christian Angel Investors. This online angel investment platform by Christian investors for Christian founders in the United States charges no fees for connecting Christian founders with Christian angel investors in its network. Christian Angel Investors also offers access to venture capital, lending sources, and professional (for pay) business consulting and technical services.

Christian Financial Credit Union. Through its partnership with Michigan Business Connection (MBC), Christian Financial Credit Union offers commercial real estate loans, accounts receivable loans, inventory/equipment loans, and business lines of credit to Christian business owners in the state of Michigan.

Telos Ventures. Headquartered in Silicon Valley, Telos Ventures Capital is an early-stage venture capital group that invests in Gospel-centered, for-profit ventures globally, primarily in technology-enabled solutions for the healthcare, education, and lifestyle sectors. Telos Ventures also offers co-working space and runs a business accelerator.

World Evangelical Alliance (WEA) Business Coalition. Headquartered in New York City, the WEA Business Coalition is an online hub providing information and resources (including incubators and funders) to founders and leaders of evangelical Christian businesses, ministries, and churches in 129 countries, including the United States.

Funding for Jewish Entrepreneurs and Business Owners

Duman Entrepreneurship Center. Housed at Jewish Vocational Services (JVS) in Chicago, the Duman Entrepreneurship Center supports Jewish entrepreneurs and business owners in the Chicago area with training, mentoring, and low-cost business loans.

Hebrew Free Loan of Detroit. This nonprofit community lender offers interest-free business loans of $20,000 to $100,000 to help start or expand a Jewish majority-owned business located in the state of Michigan. A member of the International Association of Jewish Free Loans, Hebrew Free Loan also offers personal loans of up to $20,000 for small business financing.

Jews for Entrepreneurship (JFE). Since its launch in 2009, this nonprofit organization has become a leading network of Jewish founders, investors, and technologists in Silicon Valley and New York City. JFE hosts entrepreneurship training workshops and demo events, runs an accelerator program, and offers networking and mentoring opportunities.

Tribe of Angels. Founded in 1999, Tribe of Angels is the oldest and largest network of accredited Jewish technology investors, entrepreneurs, researchers, executives, and graduate students. Members include Nobel Laureates, CEOs of Fortune 100 companies, and top international technology researchers.

Upstart Lab. Headquartered in the San Francisco Bay Area with hubs in Chicago and Southern California, Upstart Lab runs a national three-year accelerator for innovative, scalable Jewish startups. Upstart Incubator, a pilot program currently available only at the Chicago hub, provides technical assistance to innovative, early-stage Jewish startups.

Funding for Muslim Entrepreneurs and Business Owners

Affinis Labs. An award-winning social innovation firm, Affinis Labs partners with Elixir Capital, 500 Startups, Google, Facebook, the United Nations, and other organizations to provide seed funding, startup acceleration, capacity building, design sprints, software/app development, hackathons, prize competitions, and other resources to startups and growth companies led by Islamic entrepreneurs in Muslim communities worldwide.

African Development Center (ADC) of Minnesota. This nonprofit community development organization offers microloans, small business loans, and Sharia-compliant asset-based funding as well as entrepreneurship training, business technical assistance, and financial literacy workshops to businesses in African immigrant and refugee communities in Minnesota.

Lariba American Finance House. Headquartered in Southern California, Lariba offers RIBA-free business and commercial financing to Muslim entrepreneurs and business owners throughout the United States.

Minneapolis Alternative Financing Program. This initiative of the city's Community Planning and Economic Development department provides small businesses (neighborhood retail, service, or light manufacturing) in Minneapolis with loans that comply with Islamic law (Sharia) for the purchase of equipment and/or to make building improvements.

TARGET FUNDING VARIABLES FOR DIVERSITY BUSINESSES

Use any combination of the following keywords to search the Internet for the type of funding you want to investigate. For each search, specify one or two variables per each applicable keyword position—for example: small business (keyword #1); LGBTQ, entrepreneur (keyword #2); business grant (keyword #3); (keyword #4); United States (keyword #5).

Keyword #1   business | startup | small business | entrepreneur

Keyword #2   diversity | inclusion | LGBTQ | encore entrepreneur | 50+ entrepreneur | immigrant | refugee | Christian | Jewish | Muslim

Keyword #3   business grant | business competition | incubator | accelerator | individual development account | matched savings | rollover for business startup | business loan | microloan | CDFI | loan fund | loan program | lending program | venture capital | angel investor | investment capital

Keyword #4   name of city | name of county | name of state | federal | national

PART THREE

Community-Based Funding

Economic Development Funding

Every state, many counties, and most municipal governments have an economic development plan to help create and sustain a thriving business community within their respective domains. Attracting and retaining large corporations and high-growth startups is a priority objective of most economic development plans. Likewise, the establishment and retention of small businesses is a priority objective of *all* state and local economic development plans. Many state and local economic development agencies offer financial incentives and/or financial assistance to startups and small businesses, often in partnership with other government agencies, non-profit organizations, financial institutions, and investment firms.

The most common types of financial incentives and assistance provided by state and local government economic development agencies (or corporations, if so structured) are tax exemptions, tax credits, grants, matched savings plans, loan guarantees, loan subsidies, loans (usually no-interest or low-interest, flexible-term or forgivable), and investment capital as well as free or discounted business resources, such as training, consulting, and technical assistance.

VARIABLES OF ECONOMIC DEVELOPMENT FUNDING

Target funding is about identifying and investigating those funding opportunities for which the qualification variables match the variables associated with your business. With economic development funding, that encompasses a broad range of diverse variables that vary from one funding opportunity to another, depending on the current economic development plan and initiatives for that area. Those qualifying variables may include (but are not limited to):

- Business owner's ethnicity
- Whether the business owner meets that plan's socioeconomically "disadvantaged" criteria (i.e., disability, low-income, minority, woman, veteran, LGBTQ, immigrant/refugee)
- Location of business—particular state, county, region, city, neighborhood, or even street
- Whether the business is located in or locating to an urban renewal area, rural development area, historic district, enterprise zone, or opportunity zone (economically disadvantaged)
- Industry sector—i.e., retail, manufacturing, technology, agriculture, green, social impact
- Business size—based on revenues, number of employees, growth rate
- Business stage—seed, startup, existing, expanding, etc.
- Purpose for which funds will be or have been used—i.e., purchase or construction of real property; improvements to existing building; storefront (facade) improvements; purchase of equipment, materials, or inventory; adding jobs; employment of disadvantaged person (i.e., welfare recipient, ex-felon); relocating, stabilizing, or expanding business

As a hypothetical example of a targeted search for economic development funding, let's say I'm a Mexican American female and the owner of Cut Color & Curl, a four-station family hair salon located in an historic building in the Old Town district of San Diego. I'm seeking funding to expand my business and transform it into an upscale day spa with 10 full-service hair styling stations and also offering manicures, pedicures, facials, massages, and beauty products for sale to clients. I need financial assistance to help pay for the following:

- Hire a freelance designer to create a new logo, signage, and business cards

- Lease the retail space adjoining my existing business
- Make improvements to the expanded interior space
- Make storefront improvements
- Purchase additional equipment and furnishings
- Purchase materials and inventory
- Hire and train a full-time receptionist/cashier (a new position)
- Update my website
- Promote my expanded and rebranded business

My search for economic development agencies and programs that might offer funding for my business expansion would include the following variables:

Old Town San Diego | City of San Diego | San Diego County | Southern California | State of California | economic development | community development | small business | woman owned | minority owned | Hispanic | Latinx

I would do a few Internet searches using different combinations of four or five of those variables to identify every economic development agency and community development organization servicing my enterprise zone (Old Town), my city (San Diego), my county (San Diego), my region (Southern California), and my state (California). I'd go to the website of each agency and organization—one by one, starting with the nearest to me—and search the site for any funding opportunities that align with my funding needs and for which I might qualify.

As a test, I used those variables and that process to search online for economic development funding for my hypothetical business expansion. Doing several searches using different combinations of variables, I identified the following potential funding sources and resources.

1. **Online directory of Old Town San Diego businesses.** Free advertising for my expanded and rebranded business as a member of the Old Town San Diego Chamber of Commerce.
   Source: Old Town San Diego Chamber of Commerce website

2. **List of hyperlinked "business assistance organizations,"** including:

   - **City of San Diego Economic Development Department**
   - **California Southern Small Business Development Corporation**
   - **Acción San Diego.** Nonprofit CDFI offering low-interest, flexible-term microloans of $300–$300,000 as well as free business and financial counseling to low- to moderate-income business owners throughout San Diego County.
   - **Clearinghouse Community Development Financial Institution.** CDFI network offering flexible credit terms and fair interest rates to small business throughout California.
   - **National Association of Women Business Owners**, San Diego chapter. Free resources, marketing opportunities, discounts on business products and services, and other support.
   - **SDBizGuide.** Online directory of businesses in San Diego; free advertising for my expanded and rebranded business.
   - **San Diego Hispanic Chamber of Commerce.** Free business counseling and an online business directory (more free advertising!) to chamber members.

   Source: Old Town San Diego Chamber of Commerce website

3. **Storefront Improvement Program.** Available to qualifying small businesses in San Diego, including Old Town. Provides free professional facade design services and a grant equal to one-half of approved construction costs (up to $12,000 for historic buildings).

   Source: City of San Diego Economic Development Office

4. **Business Finance Loan Program.** A local government loan initiative offering low-interest gap loans to small and medium-sized businesses in the cities of San Diego and Chula Vista that do not meet traditional banking requirements. Finances up to 50 percent of costs for construction, equipment, or soft costs like training or salaries.

   Source: City of San Diego Economic Development Office

5. **California Competes Tax Credit.** An income tax credit available to businesses relocating to California or to existing California businesses that are growing. (Remember: Money saved is money earned—for use in funding your business.)
   Source: California State Government Business Portal

6. **California Small Business Loan Guarantee Program.** Funded and administered by Small Business Finance Center (SBFC) of iBank (Infrastructure and Economic Development Bank) in partnership with Southern California Small Business Development Corporation. Guarantees 80 to 95 percent of loans up to $20 million, $2.5 million maximum guarantee, up to seven-year term, negotiated "fair" interest rate.
   Source: California State Government Business Portal

LOCAL ECONOMIC-DEVELOPMENT FUNDING FOR STARTUPS AND SMALL BUSINESSES

A local economic development (community development) program may target startups and/or small businesses in a specific region, county, municipality, or neighborhood. I love local economic development funding! In fact, I financed the purchase of my office building with 6 percent down and a fixed interest rate of .04 percent through a city government economic development loan program for small businesses. By way of example, following the financial assistance and incentives for startups and small businesses offered by a regional economic development organization and a local economic development agency.

Appalachian Partnership for Economic Growth (APEG)

APEG is a collaborative, economic development, nonprofit organization for the 32 counties in the Appalachian region of southern and eastern Ohio. APEG works with regional partners to provide these funding sources and resources to entrepreneurs and businesses in the region:

- **Business counseling, training, and networking.** Provided free through APEG's partnerships with government agencies, consultants, universities (e.g., Ohio University Innovation Center), and nonprofit organizations (e.g., Appalachian Center for Economic Networks, a business incubator).

- **Loan program.** Low-interest loans of $25,000–$100,000 with flexible terms for startup or expansion for small businesses that do not qualify for bank loans. Provided through Appalachian Growth Capital, a regional nonprofit community development financial institution (CDFI), an adjunct of Appalachian Partnership for Economic Growth Foundation.

- **Manufacturing technical assistance.** Provided by APEG members who are industry experts in Lean manufacturing, workforce skills development, quality improvement, etc.

- **Wood products manufacturing and marketing support.** Provided through APEG's Forest to Furniture program, supported by the SBA's Regional Innovation Cluster Initiative. (Please see Chapter 10, "Industry Cluster Funding.")

City of Philadelphia

The economic development agency of the City of Brotherly Love shows its *big* love for local businesses by offering myriad financial incentives and assistance—including (but not limited) to those cited below. Unless otherwise specified, the programs listed here are available to businesses throughout the Philadelphia area. Please note that a Philadelphia-based business may also qualify for additional funding through the state of Pennsylvania's economic development agency.

Tax Incentive Programs

- **Jump Start Philly.** Exempts new job-creating businesses in Philadelphia from paying net profits tax and business income and receipts tax during first two years of operation. Waives certain licensing and registration fees as well.

- **Keystone Innovation Zone (KIZ) Tax Credit.** Up to $100,000 annually for eligible innovation/technology companies less than eight years in business, located in designated KIZs.

- **Keystone Opportunity Zone (KOZ) Tax Exemption or Reduction.** For property owners and/or businesses that meet capital

investment or new employment targets and are located in a
designed KOZ site.

- **Real Estate Abatement.** For 10 years, on rehabilitation or
  replacement construction of certain deteriorating commercial/
  industrial buildings.

- **Employment of Returning Military Veterans Tax Credit.** Up to
  $15,000 per veteran hired to fill a full-time or part-time posi-
  tion at a business in Philadelphia.

- **Fair Chance Hiring Initiative Tax Credit.** $5 per hour for each
  ex-felon hired by a Philadelphia-based business and paid at least
  the minimum wage.

- **Green Roof Tax Credit.** 25 percent of costs, up to $100,000, to
  build a green roof on a building owned by a Philadelphia-based
  company.

- **Philadelphia Job Creation Tax Credit.** 5 percent per each new
  full-time job created and filled or 2 percent of annual wages
  paid by a business in Philadelphia.

- **Small Business Health Care Tax Credit.** Up to 35 percent of health
  insurance premiums paid for full-time employees by an eligible
  small business.

- **Sustainable Business Tax Credit.** $4,000 annually for certain
  sustainable businesses.

- **Welfare to Work Tax Credit.** Up to $8,500 per each long-term
  welfare recipient hired and employed for at least one year.

- **Work Opportunity Tax Credit.** 40 percent of first $6,000 of wages
  per short-term welfare recipient, SSI-recipient, or ex-felon hired
  and employed for at least one year.

Grant Programs

- **Business Security Camera Reimbursement.** Up to 50 percent of
  total cost of eligible safety camera installations per single commercial property, maximum $3,000.

- **Gateway Philly.** Building rent reimbursement, up to $30,000 to any qualifying company with 20 or more employees that relocates to Philadelphia, after one year of operation in the city.
- **Philadelphia Energy Authority Small Business.** Grants and rebates for energy audit and for purchase of energy-efficient lighting and equipment for nonfranchise food and drink businesses.
- **Storefront Improvement.** Reimbursement of up to 75 percent of cost of eligible improvements, up to $10,000 for single commercial property and $15,000 for multiple-address or corner business property, within designated commercial corridors.

Loan Programs

- **Capital Consortium.** This group of more than 35 local nonprofit and for-profit commercial lenders works with the Philadelphia Department of Commerce to provide startups and existing businesses located in or relocating to Philadelphia with several financing products—including zero-interest and low-interest loans and lines of credit.
- **Empowerment Zone (EZ).** Loan-pool lending opportunities for eligible startup or existing businesses in designated EZ urban renewal neighborhoods, in partnership with Financial and Technical Assistance Center (FINANTA) and North Philadelphia Financial Partnership/NFPD Financial Assistance.
- **InStore.** Forgivable loans of $15,000–$50,000 to eligible retail, food, and creative for-profit and nonprofit enterprises for the purchase of equipment and materials to establish a new location or expand an existing location in an eligible commercial corridor. No installment payments required, and loan is forgiven if recipient meets program guidelines for five years.
- **Kiva City Philadelphia.** This partnership of the City of Philadelphia, Kiva Zip Trustees, and local nonprofit community groups and microfinance lenders enables small businesses in Philadelphia to crowdfund 0 percent interest loans to start or expand their businesses.

- **Philadelphia Industrial Development Corporation (PIDC).** This public-private economic development corporation works in partnership with the city of Philadelphia to offer term loans, subordinate term loans, bridge loans, lines of credit, and loan guarantees to eligible Philadelphia-based businesses or businesses relocating to Philadelphia.

Training/Consulting/Technical Services

The city of Philadelphia works in partnership with numerous local non-profit organizations that offer a wide range of business-development resources to entrepreneurs and business owners in the Philadelphia region. Some of those organizations, including those listed below, provide both resources and offer financial assistance.

- **Entrepreneur Works.** Free business training, tools, and one-on-one counseling as well as affordable, flexible-term loans to entrepreneurs and small business owners.

- **FINATA.** Nonprofit lender offering financing (FIN) by way of affordable, flexible loans and technical assistance (TA) to entrepreneurs and small business owners.

- **The Expertise Center (TEC).** Providing education/training, economic development opportunities, and access to funding sources to high-potential minority entrepreneurs and business owners.

- **The Merchants Fund (TMF).** Philadelphia charity established in 1854 that provides grants to small businesses in the Philadelphia area who are facing financial hardship.

- **Women's Opportunities Resource Center of Greater Philadelphia (WORC).** Offers entrepreneurial training, business assistance, matched savings programs, and access to financing and other business resources to women entrepreneurs and business owners (primarily those who are economically disadvantaged).

A COMMUNITY DEVELOPMENT LOAN
ENABLES EXPANDED CARE TO SENIORS

Registered nurses Eshonda Blue and Jessica Wright are cofounders and co-owners of Innovative Senior Solutions (ISS), headquartered in Cordele, Georgia. In 2010, Eshonda and Jessica approached the River Valley Area Development Corporation (RVDC) of Columbus, Georgia, for a loan to finance an adult day health center in their hometown of Cordele. The business owners received an $18,750 loan through RVDC's Revolving Loan Fund (RLF), funded by the US Economic Development Administration (EDA), and contributed $6,250 of their own capital. The funds were used to lease and renovate a vacant house and to purchase furniture and fixtures for the ADCH.

The EDA-funded RLF loan allowed ISS to expand by financing the first of three Adult Health Care Centers—which provide seniors, individuals with disabilities, and those at risk of being placed in a nursing home with a safe and secure environment during the day while remaining in their homes and community. The loan also enabled ISS to grow from a two-person home care service to an award-winning small business employing more than 100 people and serving more than 100 clients in 19 counties.

STATE ECONOMIC DEVELOPMENT FUNDING FOR STARTUPS AND SMALL BUSINESSES

Economic development funding programs are a great option for startups and small businesses because their sole purpose is to help build and grow businesses that create jobs and bring tax revenues to the community. Every state government wants to have an Apple or NIKE or Lockheed in its backyard and to be the birthplace and headquarters of the next Fortune 500 company. Likewise, every state wants its small to midsize businesses to proliferate and thrive, because small businesses are the lifeblood of every community.

State governments spend billions of dollars on economic development initiatives, which always include financial incentives and assistance for startups and small businesses located in or locating to the state. These programs vary greatly from state to state and change along with the state's ever-evolving economic development priorities and budget.

Following is an example of a state economic development agency that offers multiple financial incentives and assistance to businesses.

Colorado Office of Economic Development and International Trade

The Colorado Office of Economic Development and International Trade (OEDIT) does indeed offer, per the agency's "Choose Colorado" website, a "wealth of funding support" to "businesses seeking financing" to launch, grow, or relocate in Colorado. Cited below are several OEDIT financial programs that are suited to startups and/or small businesses.

Financial Incentives

- **Advanced Industry Tax Credit.** Annual tax credit given to Colorado companies that invest in Colorado early-stage (less than 5 years in operation) small businesses (less than $5 million in annual revenues) in seven designated advanced industries. Investors must be precertified and investees preapproved for this equity investment program by the Colorado OEDIT.

- **Aviation Development Zone Tax Credit.** State income tax credit of $1,200 per each new full-time employee of a business involved in the maintenance and repair, completion, or modification of aircraft and located within approved Aviation Development Zone airports.

- **Enterprise Zone Tax Credits.** A suite of various tax incentives (investment, job training, new employee, sponsored health insurance, R&D, vacant commercial building rehab, commercial vehicle investment) for businesses in or locating to various Enterprise Zones throughout Colorado.

- **Job Growth Incentive Tax Credit.** Performance-based income tax credit for businesses pursuing job-creation projects that would not occur in Colorado without this support. To qualify, the company must create at least 20 new jobs with an average yearly wage of at least 100 percent the average for that location, and all new jobs must be maintained for at least one year from hire date.

- **Job Growth Incentive Tax Credit (JGICT) Higher Education Partnership (HEP).** Performance-based state income tax credit for businesses partnering with state higher education institutions (HEI) to support job growth (i.e., college grad new hires), academic development, and economic expansion.

- **Preservation of Historic Structures Tax Credit.** For owners and qualified tenants of designated commercial properties that commence a certified rehabilitation of their property. Jointly administered by OEDIT and History Colorado.

- **Rural Jump-Start Tax Credit.** This joint initiative of OEDIT and Colorado Department of Revenue provides state income tax credits, state sales and use tax credits, and county and municipality personal property tax credits to eligible new businesses that relocate to Jump-Start Zones. It also provides state income tax credits to new hires of those businesses.

Financial Assistance

- **Advanced Industries Early-Stage Capital and Retention Grant Program.** Grants for early-stage Colorado-based startups for proof of concept and/or for the commercialization of designated advanced industry products or services that meet a market need and can be created or manufactured in Colorado and exported globally.

- **Advanced Industries Export Accelerator Grant Program.** Grants for aspiring and existing small and medium-sized Colorado-based businesses to offset international business development and marketing costs.

- **Colorado FIRST and Existing Industry (CFEI) Job Training Grant Program.** FIRST grants reimburse companies relocating or expanding in Colorado for custom training of net new hires. CFEI grants reimburse existing Colorado companies for custom training of employees in order to remain competitive within their industry, adapt to new technology, and prevent layoffs.

- **Creative Career Advancement Grant Program.** Reimbursable matching grants up to $2,500 for creative entrepreneurs and artists (Colorado residents) to help stimulate their commercial creative business.

- **State Trade Expansion Grant Program (STEP).** Grants to aspiring and existing Colorado-based small and medium-sized exporting businesses to offset global business and export development activities.

- **Colorado Development Block Grant (CDBG) Business Loan Fund.** Loans and loan guarantees to Colorado residents to start, stabilize, or expand a business or microbusiness (fewer than five employees) in Colorado through 14 regional CDBG Business Loan Funding locations throughout the state.

- **Colorado Capital Access (CCA).** Low-cost loans from designated lenders, in collaboration with CHFI (Colorado Housing Financial Institute), a community development financial institution (CDFI), in partnership with Colorado Office of Economic Development and International Trade (OEDIT) and the State Small Business Credit Initiative (SSBCI).

- **Venture Capital Authority (VCA).** Makes seed and early-stage capital investments of $250,000–$3.4 million in eligible Colorado-based startups via two Colorado Funds established with an independently operated fund manager.

HOW SWEET THE GRANT OF MARKETING INSIGHT

Deborah Tuggle is the founder and owner of two all-natural cookie companies in Lakewood, Washington: Friday's Cookies, a gourmet line, and Bite Me! Inc., baked and frozen shortbread cookies. In 2016, Deborah entered Washington State's Economic Gardening program with the main goal of expanding and diversifying her customer base. The Economic Gardening team used market research, geographic information systems (GIS), and digital marketing analysis to produce solutions in three primary areas, as follows.

High-quality sales leads. One specialist built a profile of Deborah's consumer base, which was a more affluent group of consumers than she had thought. GIS tools were then used to identify areas throughout the nation where those affluent consumers and the retailers catering to them are located, resulting in a list of 253 groceries to target. Deborah also followed the team's suggestion to hire a food broker to help with prospecting.

Industry trends and intelligence. Another specialist researched the upscale specialty gourmet market to identify other segments in which to expand, such as meal delivery kits and organic food markets. Identification and analysis of key competitors yielded benchmarking and best practices in areas such as market positioning, social media, and charitable/community partnerships.

Digital marketing. A third specialist conducted an SEO analysis of Tuggle's website and identified ways to improve Bite Me!'s digital presence, with a particular focus on B2B development. He also investigated and suggested ways to leverage social media to get product into more retail stores and to connect with end consumers.

Within nine months, Deborah was making significant progress on expanding her client base, including the addition of 327 Safeway stores. To keep up with growing sales, she added 12 new jobs, including a production manager. Revenue increased from $1.6 million in 2016 to $1.8 million in 2017 and was set to reach $3 million in 2018.

"The information I have in my hands is priceless. It's something I can still use 10 years from now," she said. It was also inspirational. The competitive analysis revealed a competitor that was doing $35 million in annual revenue. "That gives me something to work toward. If they can do it, why can't I?"

($) **Identify and investigate *all* potential government funding opportunities in your state.** Go to website of your state's economic development agency to learn about the financial incentives, financial assistance, and business resources that the agency and its partnering organizations offer to small businesses in your state. Research the parameters, eligibility variables, and application process of each program to determine which ones align with your funding needs and how to tap into them.

TARGET FUNDING VARIABLES FOR ECONOMIC DEVELOPMENT FUNDING

Use any combination of the following keywords to search the Internet for potential community-based funding for your business. For each search, specify one or two variables per each applicable keyword position—for example: Houston, Texas (keyword #1); economic development, government (keyword #2); small business, retail (keyword #3); financing, storefront improvements (keyword #4); hub zone, immigrant (keyword #5).

Keyword #1	name of city | name of county | name of region | name of state
Keyword #2	economic development | community development | government | community development financial institution | CDFI
Keyword #3	business | small business | startup | name of industry sector
Keyword #4	financing | grant | loan | microloan | tax incentives | storefront improvements
Keyword #5	(applicable diversity variable) hub zone | low income | woman owned | minority owned | veteran owned | disabled | LGBTQ | immigrant | refugee

Industry Cluster Funding

Industry clusters are regional concentrations of interconnected industries. The cluster region can be a state, region within a state, county, or metropolitan or micropolitan area. A local cluster region can even be a geographic area within a municipality, such as a restaurant row or warehouse district. Three of the more famous industry clusters in the United States are Hollywood, Manhattan's Garment District, and Silicon Valley.

Typically, an industry cluster arises when several large corporations in related industries emerge or locate in a particular area, which then attracts other companies in related industries as well as suppliers and service providers for those industries to the area. Clusters also serve as hubs for education, research, financial, and other institutions and organizations that support cluster businesses.

The US Cluster Mapping Project, carried out by the Harvard University Institute for Strategy and Competitiveness and funded by the Economic Development Administration (EDA) of the US Department of Commerce, has classified America's "benchmark" industry clusters. Of those 67 broadly defined industry clusters, 51 are traded clusters and 16 are local clusters. *Traded clusters* are regional groups of enterprises that serve markets throughout and beyond the region, focusing primarily on national and/or international markets. *Local clusters* are regional groups of enterprises that serve primarily the local market. The clusters and subclusters defined by the US Cluster Mapping Project are used by the US Small Business Administration (SBA) and other federal, state, and local government agencies as well as most public institutions, organizations, and corporations throughout the United States.

Each region's clusters are unique to that area. One region may have several diverse traded clusters, while another region may have only a few closely related traded clusters. Every region also has local clusters that help fuel the economy in that area. A local industry cluster may be related or unrelated to one or more of the region's traded clusters.

Although large and midsize companies form the core of most industry clusters, startups and small businesses are integral components of every healthy cluster. Consequently, a cluster's supporting organizations often provide funding and other resources to help start and grow small businesses.

HOW TO FIND CLUSTER-BASED FUNDING

The first step in finding potential cluster funding for your venture is to determine whether your business fits any of the industry clusters in your region. To do that, go to the US Cluster Mapping Project Internet portal and search the online database for clusters in your region. You can search by any of four different region types: state, economic area, county, or metropolitan/micropolitan area. Search all traded and local clusters for your region.

Ideally, your business will fit in with one or more of the predominant traded and/or local clusters in your region. A thriving or growing cluster usually includes organizations that provide funding and other support to businesses in that cluster. Your next step, then, is to find those organizations—which is actually a multistep process of identifying and investigating interconnected organizations that are associated with a particular cluster.

To identify organizations associated with your cluster, I suggest using these three strategies:

1. Search the US Cluster Mapping Project's online registry of organizations for those that relate to regional clusters aligned with your business.

2. Check the Regional Innovation Clusters page on the US Small Business Administration (SBA) website to see whether your business fits any of the regional industry clusters supported by the SBA.

3. Search for state and local organizations that support the cluster industries associated with your business. This might include government agencies, universities, trade associations, business councils, innovation councils, economic development catalysts, entrepreneurship development organizations, business development corporations, business incubators, and accelerators.

US Cluster Mapping Project: Related Organizations

The Organization Registry on the US Cluster Mapping Project portal features profiles of numerous (but by no means all) organizations that support various regional industry clusters throughout the United States. Some of those organizations are added to the Registry by the US Cluster Mapping Project; others are added by the respective organization.

The Registry is searchable by 11 types of organizations: Chambers of Commerce & Industry Associations, Cluster Organizations & Initiatives, Companies, Federal Agencies, Federal Labs, Innovation & Entrepreneurship Organizations, Regional Partnerships & Initiatives, State & Local Government Agencies, Think Tanks & Research Organizations, Universities, and Other Organizations. An easier and faster way to search the US Cluster Mapping Project's online Organizations Registry is to go to the dashboard of each Region Type in your area and search for Related Organizations.

Following are brief profiles of organization supporting clusters in a particular state and a particular county.

South Carolina Council on Competitiveness

This nonpartisan, business-led, nonprofit organization, more commonly known as SC Competes, is tasked with advancing the long-term economic competitiveness of the state, industries, and citizens of South Carolina. Among the organization's initiatives is to provide statewide support to 2 of South Carolina's 10 strongest traded clusters, SC Aerospace Cluster and SC Logistic Cluster.

- **SC Aerospace Cluster.** Collaborative partnership of SC Competes, South Carolina Department of Commerce, and industry partners. Maintains online directories of SC

Aerospace companies and assets (universities, airports, military bases). Facilitates access to funding, financial/tax incentives, incubators/accelerators, workforce talent, site/building assistance, exporting assistance, research data/services, and other technical services.

- **SC Logistics Cluster.** Facilitated by SC Competes and conducted by the SC Executive Forum, consisting of business leaders from private sector and relevant state agencies, such as SC Department of Commerce, SC Department of Transportation, and SC Ports Authority. Maintains online directories of SC Logistics companies. Facilitates access to funding, financial/tax incentives, incubators/accelerators, workforce talent, site/building assistance, exporting assistance, research data/services, and other technical services.

Monterey County C² Competitive Clusters

This public-private economic development initiative of the Monterey County Business Council and the County of Monterey (California) seeks to support and further develop the county's six key industry clusters:

- Agriculture
- Tourism
- Education and Research
- Building and Design
- Wellness and Lifestyle
- Creative and Technology

The C² Competitive Clusters program supports cluster businesses primarily through advocacy, business education and training, technical services, promotional activities and opportunities, and access to affordable loans. Contributing partners include the Arts Council for Monterey County, California Coastal Rural Development Corporation, Monterey Peninsula Chamber of Commerce, Monterey County Convention and Visitors Bureau, Monterey County Farm Bureau, Monterey County Film Council, Monterey Bay Procurement Technical Assistance Center

(PTAC), and the SBA Central California Small Business Development Center (SBDC).

SBA-Supported Clusters

The Regional Innovation Cluster Initiative of the US Small Business Administration (SBA) provides services in support of select regional industry clusters throughout the country. These SBA designated and supported cluster service centers, each of which is operated by a contracting organization with expertise in the cluster industry, convene resources to help small businesses navigate funding, procurement, and supply chain opportunities. The centers also provide technical assistance to help cluster innovators commercialize promising technologies needed by government and industry buyers.

The SBA Innovative Economy Clusters initiative began in 2010 with 10 Regional Innovative Clusters, which has since grown to 14. As existing clusters mature and other high-priority clusters emerge, the regional clusters that SBA supports may change. All existing Regional Innovation Clusters are posted on the SBA website.

By way of example, following are brief descriptions of 3 of the 14 current Regional Innovation Clusters.

Appalachian Wood Products Cluster

Region	Southeastern Ohio, comprised of 32 primarily rural counties.
Provider	Appalachian Partnership for Economic Growth (APEG), which labels this cluster initiative *Forest to Furniture.*
Focus	Manufacturing of hardwood furniture, engineered wood products, veneer, plywood, and hardwood flooring. This cluster also participates in the interagency Partnerships for Opportunity and Workforce and Economic Revitalization (POWER) initiative, designed to assist communities impacted by changes in the coal economy.

Services   Provides loans and no-cost or low-cost training, education, and technical assistance.

St. Louis Bioscience Cluster

Region   St. Louis, Missouri, metropolitan area.

Provider   BioSTL.

Focus   Medical and plant biosciences, R&D manufacturing, marketing.

Services   Builds regional capacity in capital and entrepreneurship through training, recruiting, and increasing capital investment. Works collectively with partner organizations to provide cluster companies with access to incubators, technical services, research data, and funding.

San Diego Defense Industry Cluster

Region   San Diego County, California.

Provider   San Diego Defense Industry Cluster (SDRIC), hosted at San Diego State University.

Focus   Development, manufacturing, and marketing of products and services for C4ISR (command, control, communications, computers, intelligence, surveillance, reconnaissance), with particular attention to cybersecurity, autonomous systems, renewable energy, and other defense technologies.

Services   Technical assistance and connections to industry experts, research, funding, and other resources.

CLUSTER-BASED FUNDING BRINGS LIFESAVING BIOTECH TO REALITY

Based in St. Louis, Missouri, SentiAR is a biomedical engineering startup founded to commercialize technology that was originally developed at Washington University in St. Louis by founders Jennifer Silva, MD, SentiAR Chief Medical Officer, Assistant Professor of Pediatrics at Washington University, and Director of Pediatric Cardiac Electrophysiology at St. Louis Children's Hospital, and Jonathan Silva, PhD, SentiAR Chief Technology Officer and Assistant Professor of Biomedical Engineering at Washington University. SentiAR's Microsoft HoloLens-enabled intraprocedural 3D augmented reality platform provides real-time holographic visualization of the patent's actual anatomy during a clinical intervention.

The original visualization platform was created by Jon Silva, who secured more than $500,000 in grants to build the initial prototype. BioGenerator, the investment arm of BioSTL, an SBA-supported innovation cluster, helped launch SentiAR with a $48,000 pre-seed grant and technical assistance to further demonstrate the technology, understand regulatory requirements, conduct market research, develop an intellectual product strategy, and pursue non-dilutive grant funding.

BioGenerator subsequently co-led the $1.1 million seed round, investing $400,000. Additional seed capital came from Cultivation Capital (seed co-lead), Pinpoint Holding, and Oakland Capital Partners. BioGenerator and Cultivation Capital each followed up with additional $1 million investments. During that period, SentiAR also received a $50,000 Arch Grant, awarded by the City of St. Louis (a BioSTL cluster partner) to companies locating in downtown St. Louis. A few months later, with the help of BioGenerator, SentiAR received a $2.2 million federal grant from the National Institutes of Health (NIH) to advance SentiAR's augmented-reality hologram technology into clinical applications, initially for catheter ablation to treat cardiac arrhythmia.

Organizations Supporting Industry Clusters

The Organization Registry on the US Industry Cluster Mapping Project portal includes several (but far from all) of the organizations that provide support—including funding and no-cost and low-cost technical assistance—to startups and small businesses in regional industry clusters. Given the variety and sheer numbers of organizations engaged in developing and strengthening industry clusters, finding potential sources of funding for your cluster can seem daunting. The key is to search for organizations that serve as catalysts for cluster initiatives and programs in your region.

A catalyst organization for a particular industry might be a government agency, public-private economic development corporation, business council, trade association, innovation hub, or business or entrepreneur network. Typically, cluster catalysts work in partnership with other related organizations—such as universities, research labs, incubators/accelerators, industry research/advisory groups, investors, and financial institutions, which often provide services to cluster businesses.

As an example, when I searched the Internet for regional clusters in or near Fort Collins, Colorado, I found the following.

City of Fort Collins Cluster Initiative

This initiative, which is part of the Fort Collins Economic Health Office Strategic Plan and the City of Fort Collins Strategic Plan, supports the development of four local industry clusters.

- **Bioscience Cluster.** Companies and industry partners that research, develop, produce, and distribute medical devices, medical instruments, pharmaceuticals, and biofuels.

- **Hardware/Software Cluster.** Companies and industry partners that specialize in data mapping, computer programming, Internet service, software development, and computer facilities management.

- **Uniquely Fort Collins Cluster.** Companies that are unique, independent, and contribute to the area's quality of life—such as creative, cultural, tourism, breweries, and hospitality businesses—and organizations that support those businesses.

- **Water Innovation Cluster.** Companies and industry partners involved in researching, developing, and implementing water safety, water supply, and water management solutions.

The primary catalyst organization for the Bioscience, Hardware/Software, and Water Innovation clusters is Innosphere, a nonprofit incubator headquartered in Fort Collins. Innosphere accelerates the commercialization and growth of select high-impact technology startups and scale-ups. Core services include research support; entrepreneur education; technology validation; product iteration; supplier connections; advisory network; corporate partnerships; development of management team and business processes; funding, staffing, and marketing strategies; funding connections (investors, lenders, grantors). Other supporting organizations include the NoCo Health Partnership, NoCo Manufacturing Partnership, and Rocky Venture Institute.

The Uniquely Fort Collins cluster program is supported by the Downtown Creative District, Fort Collins Convention and Visitors Bureau, Fort Collins Downtown Business Association, Fort Collins Chamber of Commerce, NoCo Food Cluster, and Shop Fort Collins First.

SAMPLE CLUSTER-FUNDING SEARCH

The imaginary Bonny Hills Lavender & Aromatic Herbs is located on a popular bicycling and wine-touring byway in a rural community of Eugene, Oregon. The farm/nursery is owned by sisters Celeste (a master gardener), Mercedes (an artist), and Nola (a chemist specializing in personal care products), who inherited the property eight years earlier from their parents, retired second-generation hay farmers. Half of the farmland is planted in lavender, the rest in chamomile, fennel, rosemary, sage, thyme, lemon verbena, and other fragrant herbs. With the help of two full-time employees and seasonal workers, the three sisters produce live plants, essential oils, dried flowers, fresh-cut herbs, aromatherapy products, and personal care products, which are sold wholesale and on their e-commerce website.

The owners seek funding to expand their business. The first phase of the expansion is underway, the launch of two new product lines: culinary (honey, dried herbs, herbal tea) and arts/crafts (illustrations, greeting cards, pottery, dried wreaths). The second phase will transform the 30-acre family farm into an agritourism destination—with a retail gift shop (renovate existing vintage carriage house), gardening workshops, walking garden trails, wedding/event patio with gazebo and pavilion, meditation labyrinth, bed and breakfast inn (renovate existing vintage farmhouse), and tea house/wine bar (new building) serving locally produced teas, wines, and food products.

To identify regional clusters pertinent to the fictional Bonny Hills farm, I searched the US Cluster Mapping Project database by region, which yielded the following.

Regional Industry Clusters for Bonny Hills Lavender & Aromatic Herbs

Traded Clusters	Subclusters
Agricultural Input and Services	Agricultural Services
Distribution and eCommerce	Electronic and Catalog Shopping
Downstream Chemical Products	Personal Care and Cleaning Products
Food Processing	Specialty Foods and Ingredients, Coffee and Tea
Hospitality and Tourism	Accommodations and Related Services, Cultural and Educational Entertainment, Other Tourism Attractions
Local Clusters	**Local Subclusters**
Gifts and Souvenirs Retailing	
Hospitality Establishments	
Local Household Goods and Services	Gardening Products and Supplies
Personal Products Retailing	

Next, I checked the cluster-related organizations listed on the US Cluster Mapping Project website—which yielded the following potential funding and other resources for the Bonny Hills expansion.

- **Business Oregon.** The state of Oregon's economic development agency, also known as the Business Oregon Commission. Relevant offerings include:
  - **Business development loan.** For traded-sector manufacturing, processing, or distribution business with fewer than 100 employees, preferably in rural or distressed areas. To

purchase real estate, construct or improve buildings, buy
equipment and machinery, working capital.

- **Entrepreneurial development loan.** For startups, microenterprises, and expanding small businesses.
- **Agricultural bond program.** Low-interest loan for owners of
new and expanding farms with net worth of no more than
$750,000. To purchase farm land or depreciating farm prop-
erty (building construction, equipment).
- **Technical assistance.** From regional agribusiness development experts.

- **Oregon AgLink.** Nonprofit membership organization offering
information and promotional support, including an Agri-
Tourism Workbook.

- **Oregon Association of Nurseries.** Nonprofit membership organization hosting an online member directory for wholesale
buyers and an annual trade show attended by wholesale buyers.

- **Oregon Industry Cluster Network.** Initiative of the Oregon
Business Plan, administered by the Oregon Business Council,
a nonprofit association of Oregon business leaders. Connects
cluster industry leaders with researchers, educational institutions, media, venture capital, and other resources.

- **Northwest Farm Credit Services.** This government-sponsored
enterprise (GSE) is a financial institution regulated by the Farm
Service Administration and linked to the Oregon Farm Bureau.
Serves farms, ranches, nurseries, and other agribusinesses in
Idaho, Oregon, and Washington. Financing options include
real estate loans (purchase land and buildings; construction
or improvement of buildings and processing facilities); equity
and operating lines of credit; equipment financing. Supports
agribusiness development.

- **Travel Oregon.** Oregon Tourism Commission, doing business
as Travel Oregon, is a semi-independent agency of the Oregon
state government. Provides tourism businesses with networking, education and training, product development services, and

inclusion in a searchable online visitor guide. Special tourism development programs include bike-friendly businesses, culinary tourism, and agritourism.

Then, I went to the SBA website and checked the regional innovative clusters currently supported by the SBA—none of which were in Oregon.

Finally, I searched for and checked out state and local agencies and organizations that support regional industry clusters relative to the imaginary Bonny Hills farm and discovered several additional resources:

- **Oregon Department of Agriculture.** State government agency that connects Oregon agribusinesses to funding sources, trade associations, research institutions, marketing opportunities, and other resources, including the following.
  - **Craft3.** Regional nonprofit certified community development financial institution (CDFI) serving Oregon and Washington. Specialties include lending to small businesses owned by women, in rural communities, and in agribusiness, value-added processing, small retail, and hospitality clusters.
  - **Neighborhood Economic Development Corporation (NEDCO).** Regional nonprofit economic development corporation serving Clackamas, Lane, and Marion Counties. NEDCO's Community LendingWorks, a nonprofit CDFI offering fixed-interest term loans of up to $75,000 to small businesses in certain industry sectors, including agribusiness, arts, and retail.
  - **FoodHub.** Nonprofit membership organization with a searchable online hub that connects independent food-product producers, commercial buyers, regional distributors, industry suppliers, farmers' market managers, trade associations, and nonprofits in California, Oregon, Washington, Idaho, Montana, and Alaska.
  - **Oregon Lavender Association (OLA).** Nonprofit membership organization that "promotes lavender as a viable, thriving agribusiness in Oregon and supports members in their efforts to grow successful lavender-based businesses." Website features member profiles, events (festivals, photo

contest, Paint Out), farm tours, and online catalog of member products and services.

- **Travel Lane County.** Nonprofit membership organization marketed as Eugene, Cascades & Coast. Promotes regional tourism and special events, including farm tours, wine tours, bicycling tours, lavender festivals, and bed and breakfasts.

CREATIVE FINANCING FOR A CREATIVE CLUSTER STARTUP

As the founders of a startup, Kyle Lagendyk and Bill Ryan, owners of Bespoke Bee Supply in Portland, Oregon, were ineligible for conventional bank financing. Fortunately, their local banker referred them to Craft3, a nonprofit community development financial institution (CDFI) serving Oregon and Washington. Craft3 provided them with financial counseling and a loan within a month of submitting an application. The $60,000 loan was structured with interest-only payments throughout the startup phase, allowing the business to focus on manufacturing during the first six months, and accrued interest only on the drawn amount.

The business successfully launched and grew. In 2017, Bespoke Bee Supply moved into its shop in a shared building in an industrial district of Portland, Oregon, where they continue to create handcrafted, environmentally friendly hives for beekeepers.

TARGET FUNDING VARIABLES FOR INDUSTRY CLUSTER FUNDING

I encourage you to utilize the US Cluster Mapping Project's online searchable database and the Regional Innovation Clusters page on the SBA's website to determine whether your business aligns with any of those clusters and to track down potential funding for those clusters. Use any combination of the following keywords to search the Internet for potential state and local industry cluster funding for your business. For each search, specify one or two variables per each applicable keyword position—for example: United States, Illinois (keyword #1); small business (keyword #2); regional industry cluster, local industry cluster (keyword #3); construction, green building (keyword #4); economic development, gov, organization (keyword #5); urban, veteran owned.

Keyword #1   United States | name of city | name of state | name of county | name of region

Keyword #2   business | small business | startup | microenterprise

Keyword #3   industry cluster | regional industry cluster | local industry cluster

Keyword #4   name of industry sector | name of industry subsector

Keyword #5   (type of organization supporting industry cluster) agency | association | organization | economic development | gov | university | chamber of commerce

Keyword #6   (applicable diversity variable) hub zone | rural | urban | low income | woman owned | minority owned | veteran owned | disabled | LGBTQ | immigrant | refugee

Keyword #7   financing | grant | loan | microloan | matched savings | individual development account | venture capital | equity financing | training | technical support

Community Development Financial Institutions

Community development financial institutions, better known by the acronym *CDFIs*, are mission-driven, locally controlled, private-sector financial organizations that are certified by the US Department of the Treasury's CDFI Fund. Individual CDFIs raise capital from government agencies (including but not limited to the federal CDFI Fund), large banks, nonprofit foundations, nonfinancial institutions, and individual donors and investors. A CDFI uses the bulk of the capital it raises to provide financial products and services to the community it serves.

A CDFI may be a community development bank, community development credit union, community development corporation (CDC), community development loan fund, or community development venture fund. Many CDFIs are nonprofit; those that are for-profit direct profits toward financial stability rather than toward maximizing profits for shareholders. The shared mission of the more than 1,000 certified CDFIs across the nation is to spur economic growth in low-income, low-wealth communities by providing accessible, affordable financing to underserved residents, small businesses, and social-impact nonprofit organizations in their respective communities.

Many, but not all, CDFIs serve small businesses; some serve only individuals and/or community nonprofit organizations. Some CDFIs offer matched-savings grants (*individual development accounts*, or IDAs), and a small number offer equity financing to small businesses. Debt financing

is the core offering of all CDFIs, including those that target small businesses, which also provide business counseling to clients. In just five years
(2009–2016), CDFIs loaned more than $3.25 billion to more than 88,000
small businesses throughout the United States.

YOU MIGHT BE A CANDIDATE FOR CDFI FUNDING IF . . .

CDFIs are not ideal for every entrepreneur and enterprise, nor are CDFIs
available to all business owners and businesses. CDFI financing is reserved
for businesses located in economically distressed communities and
owned by economically or socially disadvantaged individuals who cannot
get financing from conventional sources. If your business fits that basic
eligibility criteria, CDFIs might be a funding option worth exploring.

Consider the upsides of CDFI business financing:

- **Deep knowledge of community.** CDFIs study local markets and
  work closely with community leaders to understand both the
  economic and sociocultural landscapes of their communities.
  They understand how your success will benefit both you and
  your community.

- **Low-income, low-wealth, no problem.** Unlike conventional lenders, an applicant's modest means are not a deal-breaker with
  CDFIs. In fact, the business being in a location or owned by
  an individual belonging to a demographic that is underserved
  by traditional financing sources is a requisite of CDFI business
  financing.

- **Diversity-friendly.** CDFIs don't merely "include" entrepreneurs
  of diverse backgrounds, they often target them. Many CDFIs
  have business financing programs aimed at one or more diversity groups, such as veterans, minorities, and women.

Nearly half (48 percent) of all CDFI borrowers (business and personal loans) are
persons of color, and the same proportion (48 percent) are women.

- **Open to businesses of varying shapes, sizes, and stages.**
  CDFI business lenders typically finance qualifying startup,

early-stage, and established microenterprises, home-based businesses, small businesses, and midsize businesses in almost every sector.

- **Flexible, individualized loan qualification criteria.** Although held to the same regulatory standards as other financial institutions, CDFIs consider more than credit scores, financial statements, and collateral. They also consider the feasibility and growth potential of the business, the capabilities and credentials of the founder/owner, and the value of the business to the community. CDFIs look at the business and business owner as a whole, and they're often willing and able to take on higher-risk loans than traditional business lenders.

The approval rate of CDFI loans and lines of credit for small businesses with less than $1 million in annual revenues is greater than 75 percent—higher than conventional banks, credit unions, and online lenders, according to Federal Reserve surveys.

- **Simple loan structure.** CDFI loans are self-amortizing (each payment applies to both interest and principal) and predominately fixed-rate. This enables a more predictable cash flow and minimizes the borrower's risks.

- **Low-to-moderate financing costs.** CDFI business lenders charge competitive interest rates, often below market rate, and charge no or low origination fees. CDFI interest rates average 4.75 to 9.38 percent. The average range of origination fees is 0.2 to 0.6 percent of loan value.

- **Flexible terms.** CDFIs typically give borrowers the option of a shorter-term loan with higher payments or a longer-term loan with lower payments. Collateral and/or a down payment may be required or requested, but most CDFIs can underwrite a loan to secure it by other means, and some CDFIs offer unsecured business loans.

- **Potential access to other financial products.** Many CDFI business lenders offer individual development accounts (IDAs), a form of grant in which the financial institution matches every dollar you save with a contribution of $1 to $5. A small percentage of CDFIs offer equity financing and/or equity-like financing (such as revenue-based financing).

- **Business development support.** Most CDFI business lenders offer free financial education, business training, business counseling, legal guidance, and sometimes technical assistance.

There are a few potential downsides of CDFIs to consider, too:

- **Narrowly defined eligibility criteria.** The business and/or the borrower's residence must be located within the CDFI's delineated community, and the business owner must provide evidence of the "disadvantage" variable(s) for which the CDFI targets its services. If you and your business have sufficient economic opportunity, sufficient income and assets, and access to conventional financing, you're unlikely to qualify for CDFI financing.

- **Lower loan caps than conventional lenders.** For some CDFI business loans, the maximum loan amount is $25,000 or $50,000. Others cap out at $100,000 or $250,000. CDFI business loan caps rarely go as high as $500,000 and even more rarely $1 million. However, some CDFI business lenders offer commercial real estate loans with higher maximum loan amounts.

> The majority (60 percent) of CDFI small-business loans are for less than $100,000.

- **The loan process is rarely simple and quick.** The flip side of the careful, individualized loan application process practiced by CDFI lenders—which typically includes financial and business counseling—is that it can take weeks or even a month or two. CDFI financing is designed to help you build a financially sound business over the long term, not to simply make a loan. A loan can also be delayed because the CDFI doesn't have the cash on hand to finance all the approved loans in its queue, as

CDFIs typically have fewer assets than conventional financial institutions. That said, the CDFI industry has been applying fintech and other measures to increase loan processing efficiency. In some cases, depending on the lender and the borrower, a CDFI loan can be approved and disbursed in as little as a week or two.

VARIABLES FOR IDENTIFYING POTENTIAL CDFI FUNDING SOURCES

Every community development financial institution has a designated target market. The financial products and technical assistance provided by a particular CDFI are based on the funding needs of that target market—which, in turn, are based on the economic development plan for that community and on the type of CDFI.

An individual CDFI's target market is delineated by both its *service area* variables and its *beneficiary* variables (clients). With CDFI business financing, the beneficiary variables of both the business and the business owner are typically specified.

A CDFI's target area is a designated geographic location, which may be any of the following:

- Municipality—such as a city, town, or township
- District, zone, neighborhood, or even street within a municipality
- Municipality and neighboring communities—such as a greater metropolitan area, "sister cities," or a central township and its surrounding rural areas
- Region within a state—counties or communities
- State or US territory
- Several states (not necessarily neighboring)
- Region of the country or US territory, encompassing two or more states or segments of two or more states
- United States

The beneficiary variables of a particular CDFI business loan may specify a certain:

- Number of employees—minimum and/or maximum
- Annual revenues—minimum and/or maximum
- Stage of business—i.e., seed, startup, early-stage, existing, high-growth
- Size of business—i.e., microenterprise, home-based, small, mid-size, Main Street
- Industry or social impact sector—i.e., education, healthcare, food/agriculture, retail, art/culture, technology
- Funding use(s)—i.e., acquire, lease, or renovate property; leasehold improvements; storefront improvements; purchase existing business; expand business; improve/stabilize business; purchase equipment or machinery; add jobs; purchase inventory; working capital

A CDFI's entrepreneur-related beneficiary variables may specify a certain:

- Personal income level—minimum and/or maximum
- Personal wealth—minimum and/or maximum
- Ethnicity—African American, Hispanic, Native American, or other ethnic group
- Military status—active duty, veteran, or spouse of
- Gender—woman, LGTBQ
- Individual with disabilities
- Immigrant, refugee, asylee
- Religious affiliation—i.e., Christian, Jewish, Muslim

As a hypothetical example, Josiah Abel is a Native American military veteran who plans to start an online artisan market to sell traditional artwork created by himself (a sculptor) and other members of the Little Traverse Bay Bands of Ottawa Indians of Michigan. The business will be based out of Josiah's home in the Village of Baraga, Michigan. He seeks funding to help pay for the following business expenses:

- Accounting, legal, and marketing services
- Conversion of a large metal barn on his personal property into office, warehouse, and packing/shipping space
- Freelance graphic design services to create a logo
- Equipment and machinery for office and warehouse/distribution
- E-commerce platform (software) for the online artisan market
- Inventory
- Freelance web design services
- Freelance web copywriting services
- Full-time assistant

To find CDFIs offering potential funding for his new enterprise, Josiah might search the Internet using the following variables:

CDFI | Native CDFI | small business | Michigan |
Native American | Ottawa Indians | Little Traverse
Bay Bands | veteran | art | artisan | home-based business |
microenterprise | web-based business

Using various combinations of a few of these variables at a time yielded the following five potential CDFIs for Josiah's new venture. A more extensive search might unearth additional potential CDFIs.

1. **Northern Shores Community Development, Inc.** Nonprofit community development corporation headquartered in Northern Michigan, offering:
   - Microloans, $500–$5,000. Michigan residents, with preference to Tribal Members.
   - Business loans, over $5,000. Michigan residents, with preference to Tribal Members.

- Artisan loans, up to $1,200 (but potential for larger loan
  with detailed business plan). For adult Little Traverse Bay
  Bands of Odawa Indians throughout Michigan who com-
  plete NSCD's free Native Artist Professional Development
  Training.
- Free technical support, including accounting principles and
  web-based marketing.
- Potential to receive free technical assistance from Michigan
  State University students, including marketing plans, web-
  site design, and accounting.

2. **Northern Initiatives.** Nonprofit community development loan
   fund, offering:
   - Regional Revolving Loan Fund, for startup or existing
     businesses in specified Northern Michigan communities
     (including Village of Baraga). For every $20,000 loaned out,
     an equivalent full-time job must be created.
   - Business loans (including SBA loans), $1,000 to $1 million,
     depending on borrower and purpose of loan (including
     equipment and working capital).
   - Free online videos on various business topics, including
     financial management, marketing, and record keeping.
   - Business coaching, available to borrowers only.

3. **Northland Area Credit Union.** Community development credit
   union, offering:
   - Wide range of business term loans, including for startup
     expenses, equipment purchases, and operating capital
   - Business lines of credit
   - Business credit cards

4. **Keweenaw Bay Ojibwa Housing & Community Development Corp.**
   Nonprofit community development corporation offering business loans and financial consulting to local small businesses.

5. **Opportunity Resource Fund.** Community development loan
   fund, offering business loans of $10,000 to $250,000 to small
   businesses in economically challenged areas throughout the
   state of Michigan. Lending purposes include startup capital,

equipment, inventory, working capital, build-out, business expansion, and short-term financing.

6. **Connect2Capital.** Nonprofit CDFI online lending platform offering veteran-owned small businesses nationwide loans of $50,000 to $4 million, terms up to 25 years, depending on borrower and purpose of loan (including startup capital, equipment purchases, inventory purchases, working capital).

THE VARIED SHADES OF CDFI SMALL BUSINESS FUNDING

CDFI business financing options range from matched savings accounts to microloans, commercial business loans, SBA loans, lines of credit, commercial real estate loans, debt refinancing, business credit cards, and other specialized loans, to equity-based investment capital. Which financing products an individual CDFI provides depends, in part, on whether the CDFI is a community development bank, a community development corporation, a community development credit union, a community development venture fund, or a community development microenterprise fund.

The eligibility requirements as well as the financeable uses, financed amounts, interest rates or equity share, terms, fees, and other features of a CDFI financial product are determined by the individual CDFI. So, too, are the educational and technical services offered by a CDFI (or a partnering organization) as well as whether those resources are provided at no cost or low cost.

The following profiles of a few different types of CDFIs will give you an idea of the variety of business funding opportunities offered by community development financial institutions.

Boston Community Venture Fund (BCVF)

CDFI Type   Community development venture fund; venture capital arm of Boston Community Capital (community development loan fund).

Service Area   Northeast—primarily Connecticut, Maine, Massachusetts, New Jersey, New Hampshire, New York, Pennsylvania, Rhode Island, Vermont.

Beneficiaries High-growth potential businesses that create financial, social, and environmental returns, particularly
those that enhance the stability of lower-income or
rural neighborhoods; are minority- or women-
owned; and/or produce products or services that
enhance the environment or reduce pollution.

Offerings Seed/startup, early, mid-, and late-venture growth
capital and emerging growth equity investments in
a broad range of industry sectors.

Carver Federal Savings Bank

CDFI Type Community development bank.

Service Area New York City.

Beneficiaries To support the economic development of residents,
businesses, and institutions in primarily African
American, low- to moderate-income communities with limited access to mainstream financial
services.

Offerings Business financing products include term loans
(leasehold improvements, equipment purchases,
working capital, business expansion); lines of credit
(working capital, receivables financing, seasonal
businesses); commercial real estate (mixed-use
properties and multifamily residences).

Center for Rural Affairs

CDFI Type Community development loan fund and community development microenterprise fund (Rural
Enterprise Assistance Project, REAP); community development corporation (Rural Investment
Corporation).

Service Area Distressed areas of Nebraska, primarily rural and
small towns.

Beneficiaries Family and independently owned farms and ranches, small businesses, private enterprises engaged in environment stewardship.

Offerings Business loan programs include:

- Microloans of up to $20,000, through REAP online lending platform

- Microloans of up to $10,000, in collaboration with GROW Nebraska, via Quick Grow Express online lending platform

- Direct business loans of up to $50,000, with pre-qualification via REAP online lending platform

- Small business loans of $50,001–$150,000, via the Rural Investment Corporation

WORKING CAPITAL AND FREE BUSINESS ADVICE LAUNCH A RURAL BUSINESS

Mary Jo and Don Longnecker of Indianola, Nebraska, are the owners of Odiss Enterprises, LLC, a small business that installs and services residential and commercial overhead doors. Before opening their first-ever business in June 2014, the Longneckers received business-planning assistance from the Center for Rural Affairs, a community development financial institution (CDFI). They'd also secured bank loan but needed a little more financing. The loan from the Center filled the gap, helping with the initial equipment investment, including the purchase of a truck-trailer and lift, as well as worker's comp insurance and other operating expenses.

The Center's assistance didn't stop after the business was up and running. Mary Jo attended a marketing workshop cosponsored by the organization's Women's Business Center, and their loan specialist provided technical assistance and business counseling along the way.

The Longneckers' have since expanded their service area, increased their product selection, and added another truck-trailer and lift. Odiss Enterprises now also employs two full-time workers and one part-time worker.

Connect2Capital

CDFI Type   CDFI online network, comprised primarily of community development loan funds and powered by Community Reinvestment Fund, USA (a national nonprofit organization).

Service Area   Nationwide, all 50 states.

Beneficiaries   Startups and small businesses, with specialized lending programs for manufacturers and for enterprises founded/owned by women, people of color, or veterans.

Offerings   Term loans (via online lending platform) and business development services (via webinars) for business acquisition (including franchises), equipment purchase, real estate purchase, refinance existing debt, permanent working capital. Core financing product is an SBA Advantage Loan of $50,000–$4 million; up to 25 years repayment terms; prime plus 2.75 percent interest rate. Applicants who are ineligible for an SBA Advantage Loan may be referred to a local nonprofit CDFI for financing.

Northwest Side Community Development Corporation (NWSCDC)

CDFI Type   Community development corporation.

Service Area   Northwest Side of Milwaukie, Wisconsin.

Beneficiaries   Midsize businesses expanding or locating in target areas. Currently focused exclusively on startup and expanding manufacturing companies. Past priorities have encompassed other industry sectors, such as grocery stores in neighborhoods that are "food deserts," as might future priorities.

Offerings   Commercial loans of $150,000–$700,000, typically layered into a larger financing package with other lenders.

Tongass Federal Credit Union

CDFI Type   Community development credit union.

Service Area   Southern Southeast Alaska.

Beneficiaries   New and established businesses owned by members of Tongass Federal Credit Union.

Offerings   Business financing products include:

- Term loans: purchase of equipment, inventory, business vehicles, commercial fishing and charter boats; for purchase or refinancing of aircraft.

- Business lines of credit: unsecured (working capital) and secured (by accounts receivable, equipment, inventory, real estate, or annual renewals).

- Commercial real estate: acquisition or refinancing; retail, warehouse, businesses condos, rural/remote property.

RESOURCES

The Federal CDFI Fund as well as numerous organizations that support community development financial institutions have online directories of the CDFIs each supports. My personal favorite is Opportunity Network's CDFI Locator.

CDFI Fund. Most of the content on the US Treasury's CDFI Fund website features is for CDFIs and partnering and organizations. However, the website includes an Awards Database of all certified CDFIs that is searchable by state.

Community Development Bankers Association (CDBA). The national trade association of community development bankers throughout the United States. CDBA's website has an online directory of CDBA's more than 75 members, searchable by state.

Community Development Venture Capital Alliance (CDVCA). National nonprofit advocacy and membership organization of CDFIs that offer equity financing. The CDVCA website includes a list of CDVCA members (45 at this writing); clicking on a hyperlinked listing activates a pop-up window providing information about that CDFI—including its target area, target industry(ies), and website.

National Federation of Community Development Credit Unions. National nonprofit membership organization of community development credit unions (CDCUs). The website features a member directory of its members, organized by state and providing the location, phone number, and a link to the website of each of its nearly 250 CDCU members.

Opportunity Finance Network (OFN). The largest national membership organization of CDFIs throughout the United States. The OFN website features a searchable CDFI Locator that provides key information about each of OFN's more than 240 members. You can search by CDFI name or by the state, area(s) served, organization type (i.e., CDFI loan fund, CDFI venture fund), and/or lending type (i.e., business, microenterprise). The OFN site also features profiles of some (not all) of its member CDFIs.

TARGET FUNDING VARIABLES FOR CDFI FUNDING

I encourage you to utilize the online directories of community development financial institutions (CDFI) provided on the websites of the organizations listed in the Resources section of this chapter. You can also use any combination of the following keywords to search the Internet for community development financial institutions (CDFI) for your business. For each search, specify one or two variables per each applicable keyword position—for example: CDFI, community development loan fund (keyword #1); nationwide, Michigan (keyword #2); small business, microenterprise (keyword #3); loan, microloan (keyword #4); minority owned, woman owned (keyword #5).

Keyword #1   community development financial institution | CDFI | community development loan fund | community development bank | community development credit union | community development corporation | community development venture fund

Keyword #2	name of city | name of state | nationwide
Keyword #3	business | small business | microenterprise
Keyword #4	loan | microloan | matched savings | individual development account | venture capital | equity financing
Keyword #5	(applicable diversity variable) hub zone | low income | woman owned | minority owned | veteran owned | disabled | LGBTQ | immigrant | refugee

PART FOUR

Funding for Inventions and Innovation

CHAPTER

Funding for Independent Inventors

Independent inventors tend to be masters at bootstrapping—at least during the concept development stages of the inventing process. When it's time to commercialize their ideas, most indie inventors need help covering the costs of transforming their idea into a commercially viable product and bringing it to market.

Funding an invention through conventional business financing, such as bank loans and venture capital, is virtually impossible—unless and until the product has been patented and has been selling well for at least a year or two. Consequently, many indie inventors use personal loans and personal assets to fund their inventions. All inventors, just like all entrepreneurs, need to put their own funds into their inventions, out of necessity and because future lenders, investors, licensees, and partners expect it. That said, I advise inventors (and entrepreneurs) to use personal assets sparingly and to use personal credit only as a last resort for their inventions.

As a business coach who's worked with numerous inventors over the years and as an inventor myself, I'm also here to tell you that you have other funding options. Remember, target funding isn't only about finding the right sources of capital for your venture. It's also about finding the resources you need at no cost or reduced cost.

IDEATION FUNDING

The early phase of the inventing process, when you're fleshing out and validating your concept, is ideally suited to inventing lean. This ideation stage typically involves producing preliminary drawings, preliminary realistic images, and preliminary models (rudimentary "looks-like" prototypes) of your idea as well as conducting preliminary patent searches for products similar to yours. The ideation process usually also involves preliminary market research, such as canvasing stores and product directories to identify and evaluate competitive products as well as conducting focus groups and user surveys to gauge interest in your idea.

You can save a lot of money during the ideation stage by doing much of that work yourself and by using free and low-cost resources for the stuff you don't have the expertise or time to do or to do well enough.

Preliminary Patent Search

Once you've figured out the basic design of your invention and documented it with sketches and written descriptions, I strongly recommend doing a preliminary patent search before moving forward. Many first-time inventors skip over this crucial step and end up wasting money and time developing a product that cannot be patented.

Following are a few ways to do a patent search yourself for free.

- **USPTO Patent Database.** Accessed through the Patent Application portal of the United States Patent and Trademark Office (USPTO) website, this free patent-search database provides descriptive text and images for granted and filed (pending) US patents.

- **Patent Scope.** Accessible via the World Intellectual Property Organization (WIPO) website, this free database of patents granted in various countries are searchable by country or globally and by multiple user-selected search fields.

- **Google Patents.** Google's database of patents worldwide is searchable by country, language, date, status (granted/filed), date range, and other user-defined search terms (keywords, USPTO or EPO format, etc.).

- **Free Patents Online (FPO).** This free global patent database is searchable by US patents (granted), US patent applications, WIPO patents, European patents (EP), and user-selected fields. This happens to be one of my favorites because it will categorize the search keyword and give it a rating of 1,000 or less, allowing you to quickly search for the patents that have those keywords in their filing.

- **Patent and Trademark Resource Center (PTRC).** If you don't have Internet access or don't feel confident doing a patent search yourself, you can go to a PTRC, provided you live near one, and do a free patent search with expert assistance. Most states have at least one PTRC, where patent/trademark librarians can show you how to use the search tools and help you find the information you need. A list of PTRC locations around the country is on the USPTO website.

Although I encourage inventors to do a preliminary patent search themselves, I always suggest enlisting the services of a patent search expert before putting time and money into designing their ideas. There are many affordable, reputable patent search agencies, but my favorite is Patent Search International (PSI). PSI's Ron Brown has been serving the inventor community with patent search support for decades. For $250, Ron will do a patent search and forward it to a registered IP attorney, who will provide a patentability opinion on whether to move forward with the invention. He has helped my clients save hundreds of thousands of dollars by not pursuing a patent for an idea for which a patent application had already been filed.

Preliminary Drawings, Illustrations, Models

Most indie inventors can save a bundle of money by sketching their ideas and "MacGyvering" mock-ups of their concept using materials they have on hand or can purchase at local hardware and crafts/hobby stores or online specialty stores, such as McMaster-Carr. Some inventors also have the skills and equipment to create photo-realistic images and concept prototypes, which are often needed for market research purposes. But many need some outside help creating these more realistic renderings of their ideas.

Here are a few low-cost ways to get presentation-worthy representations of your concept.

- **Local artists, artisans, tradespeople.** Local professionals are likely to give you a fair price and often a discount—especially if you're referred by someone they know. Reach out to your local inventors' club and social network to ask for recommendations and introductions.

- **Student interns and freelancers.** Students with drafting, illustrating, and model-making abilities often welcome the opportunity to get practical experience at a below-market rate. Many universities, community colleges, and trade schools have job boards where you can post freelance opportunities for students. Another option is to use an online platform that matches college students with freelance projects, often in the same areas, such as Slance and StudentFreelance.

- **Online freelance marketplaces.** On platforms such as Fiverr, HatchWise, LocalSolo, and 99designs, you can often get professional services at below-market rates. Just review each bidder's profile to make sure the person's credentials and work samples match your criteria.

PRODUCT DEVELOPMENT FUNDING

The product development phase of the invention process typically involves multiple rounds of designing, engineering, prototyping, testing, and fine-tuning before the invention is ready to roll out. Then, you'll need "looks like/works like" prototypes as well as manufacturing drawings and specifications. You'll probably also need to do a pilot production run, incurring not only the manufacturer's costs but also the cost of tooling, materials, and parts. Product testing always follows a pilot production run, which often results in revisions to manufacturing drawings, prototypes, and specs.

Once manufacturing drawings, prototypes, and specs are finalized, patent drawings and descriptions can be generated. Then a professional patent search must be conducted, after which the patent drawings and descriptions often need to be revised before filing the patent application.

Rarely can an inventor do all of that alone, and paying standard rates for these specialized services can be expensive. As a rule of thumb, the more complex the invention, the more expensive the product development.

That's why I encourage you to explore free and reduced cost sources of the technical and creative support you need. Following are some effective ways to help fund product development costs.

Grants for Prototyping

Some colleges/universities, state/local government agencies, and nonprofit organizations have grants to help cover the cost of developing prototypes and commercializing inventions. These grants typically target inventors or businesses in a specific location and/or industry sector. Most college/university prototype grant programs are solely for students, faculty, and/or alumni of those schools. Like all grant programs, prototype grants are in short supply and typically available for a limited period of time. Following are a few examples of prototype grants that, at this writing, are active and open to independent inventors.

- **Microfluid Circle Prototyping Grant.** Sponsored by Microfluid Circle, a "community of individuals and companies" facilitating the commercializing of microfluidic technology, this program awards two $50,000 in-kind, nonequity grants per year, to two inventors, for a year of prototyping design and fabrication services from uFluidix, a microfluidics manufacturer. The grant program is open to eligible inventors or startups with a novel product with a microfluidic component.

- **Nebraska Innovation Fund (NIF) Prototype Grant.** This initiative of the Nebraska Department of Economic Development (DED) offers grants of up to $150,000 for small businesses operating in Nebraska to develop a prototype for a commercial product. DED reimburses 66 percent or 80 percent (value-added agriculture projects) for a prototype project completed within 24 months. DED requires a matching contribution of 50 percent (2:1) of the amount requested or 25 percent (4:1) of the amount requested for value-added agriculture projects.

University Capstone Courses

The engineering departments of some universities offer a Capstone Course in which students provide engineering services in collaboration with, on behalf of, and at nominal cost to local entrepreneurs and inventors. In most cases, the capstone program seeks projects that enable students to perform various design and engineering processes through the course of the program. Rarely does a capstone project involve creating a set of engineering drawings or a prototype for an invention for which the design and engineering kinks have all been worked out.

- **Olin College of Engineering (Massachusetts)/Senior Capstone Program in Engineering (SCOPE).** Student teams work on projects sponsored by local companies and other institutions for the full academic year. The ideal project for SCOPE has one or more design and/or engineering problems to solve and enables student teams to perform multiple activities. SCOPE has worked on medical equipment, automated farm equipment, software development for mobile and social applications, and electronic communication systems.

- **Portland State University (Oregon)/Department of Mechanical Engineering Capstone Program.** Over the fall, winter, and spring semesters, seniors in the BSME Program work with local businesses to develop product design and engineering specifications, build prototypes, and perform benchmarking, parametric analysis, and other product development activities.

Maker Spaces for Inventors

Makerspaces—also called *FabLabs, hackerspaces,* or *TechShops*—offer access to design, engineering, and fabrication work spaces, machinery, and tools at below-market and often substantially reduced cost. Most provide free guidance or low-cost training on equipment and processes. Most offer monthly rates, and some offer weekly, daily, and even hourly rates.

A makerspace may be operated by a college or university, a public/private partnership, a state or local government agency, a nonprofit organization, or a for-profit entity. Most serve inventors and makers in a specific geographic area and/or sector(s), and some focus on a specific diversity group, such as women or people of color.

Makerspaces have become popular and are springing up throughout the country. They provide an economical and effective way to get the specialized design, development, engineering, fabrication, and testing needed throughout the inventing process.

By way of example, following are summaries of two of the myriad makerspaces in the United States today.

- **Art Design Portland (ADX)/Oregon.** I love the versatility and vibe of this makerspace, as reflected in this statement on the ADX home page: "It's a place of teamwork, mentorship, and staff who'll knock down walls to facilitate your vision. It's where challenges are celebrated, and the magic and mantra of getting shit done is a way of life." ADX offers five stocked workshops (wood, metal, print, design, jewelry), shared assembly space, dedicated workspaces, shared kitchen, Wi-Fi, classes, and private instruction. Two membership options offer flat monthly fees for bundled services, discounts, and 100 square feet of dedicated space: Startup, $450; Production, $700. Lease prices for smaller spaces are $30 to $100 per month.

- **Prototype PGH/Pennsylvania.** This nonprofit makerspace founded by women supports feminist innovators of all genders in the Pittsburgh greater metropolitan area. Members have access to equipment, workspace, and networking opportunities with fellow members, the all-volunteer staff, and partners such as the Center for Women's Entrepreneurship at Chatham University. The converted warehouse has fully equipped electronics, woodworking, metalworking, jewelry, and textile arts shops as well as CNC tools and other specialized equipment. Membership fees are sliding scale, ranging from $15 to $50 per month. Prototype PGH also offers a one-year business incubator program for $75 per year.

($) **Find the right makerspace near you.** Check out makerspaces within a
     reasonable driving distance to find the one that offers the workspace,
     equipment, support, pricing, and vibe that best fits your needs, budget, and
style. Ask colleagues for recommendations, search the Internet using your variables
(location, sector, women, etc.), and check out online directories such as Makerspaces
.make.co/, MakerDirectory, and MakeSchools (college/university makerspaces).

MAKERSPACE ENABLES A LEAN STARTUP AND REAPS INVALUABLE FRINGE BENEFITS

Scott Miyako, a mechanical engineer from the music industry, and Alex
Pletcher, an art director and designer from the TV/film production industry,
bootstrapped the launch of Portland Razor Company by pulling together
cash from selling cars and downsizing their lives. During their "scrappy startup
phase," they also leased space at ADX Makerspace in Portland, Oregon, to
take advantage of the low overhead that ADX offered. The cofounders paid a
monthly fee that covered tangibles, like a 100-square-foot office, use of common spaces in the wood shop, and utilities. The makerspace also provided
some valuable intangibles.

One of the key beneficial intangibles was the community element of ADX,
which Alex describes as "a self-guided MBA program." A small cohort of
startup founders renting space at ADX would come together to talk business,
stemming from a sincere interest in helping each other succeed. These meetups would start organically with someone posing a question about a product
or service they offered and would evolve into a full-blown whiteboard session
in the loading bay or wherever they happened to be. The questions could be
about anything: pricing structures and working with retailers, techniques for
working with new materials, how to use social media to get attention, the challenges of choosing people over profits, and so on.

Another intangible benefit was the observation that they could achieve a
horizontal expansion in the making industry. "At ADX, you can learn to build
it, build it yourself, or have ADX build it for you," Alex explained. "We liked the
idea of assembling our audience around a core idea and diversifying our products and services around that central idea. In essence, we are a straight razor

factory, but what we really offer is the ability for anyone to get a great shave. With our product you can shave yourself, we can teach you how to shave and care for a straight razor at our classes, or we can have a barber shave you— thanks to the barber shop we built at the front of our factory last year!"

Online Freelance Marketplaces

The best online marketplaces for product design and engineering projects are those that specialize in or have categories for freelancers in those fields. You might also want to use a platform that matches local talent with local clients. Although the project rates are usually higher than with student freelance/intern platforms, the rates are usually lower than going to a design or engineering firm. Popular freelance talent/project platforms with a design/engineering focus or category include Behance, Gigster, Guru, and Upwork.

Freelance job websites are also a good place to source affordable creative talent, such as packaging designers (boxes, containers), graphic artists (logos, product labels, marketing materials), web designers, and copywriters (web content, marketing copy, media releases). You can usually target freelancers in your area or in the United States.

Crowdsourcing Platforms

Sometimes referred to as *crowd-based innovation platforms* or *community invention platforms*, crowdsourcing platforms connect indie inventors with designers, drafters, engineers, protype/model makers, suppliers, and manufacturers. Rates are usually 10 to 35 percent lower than traditional sources of these services. Most invention crowdsourcing platforms also connect inventors with potential licensees; in some cases, the platform company itself may license select inventions crowdsourced on its platform.

By way of example, following are brief profiles of two crowdsourcing platforms for inventors.

- **CadCrowd.** This free crowdsourcing platform offers a wide range of design, engineering, manufacturing, patenting, marketing, and licensing services, provided by a global network of more than 20,000 curated freelancers. How it works:

(1) Investor posts a request for quotes; (2) bidders submit quotes; (3) client negotiates project with bidder of choice or cancels RFQ—or, the investor runs a design contest on CadCrowd. Freelancer fees average $50 to $120 per hour. CadCrowd's fees are deducted from freelancer receipts.

- **Quirky.** This free community-led invention platform pairs inventors with designers, renderers, engineers, and manufacturers. While developing their concepts on Quirky, inventors can keep their project private or make it public to get help and feedback from the community. Once satisfied with the invention, the inventor submits it to the Quirky Review team, which reports back within 45 days whether Quirky is interested in refining, testing, patenting, prototyping, and licensing the product. If the invention is licensed and produced by Quirky, inventors receive royalties and every "influencer" (member who assisted the inventor during the concept stage) receives a cut of the inventor's royalty share.

PATENT FUNDING

If you intend to sell your invention, you'll need to protect your intellectual property by filing a patent application with the USPTO—when the timing is right. It is usually best to file a patent application when, and only when, you've developed and validated your product and are preparing to bring your product to market.

The cost to patent an invention varies greatly and depends on:

- Type of patent (design, utility, or plant)
- Number of back-and-forth iterations during the USPTO patent examination process
- Fee rates of the patent search agency or patent attorney who does the professional patent search immediately prior to filing a patent application
- Fee rates of the patent attorney with whom you consult (if you file yourself) or who prepares and files the patent application.

Rarely is trying to patent an invention without legal counsel or services in the inventor's best interests.

For inventions in the utility patent category, some inventors opt to file a provisional patent application (PPA) once they've nailed down the concept, which gives them 12 months to develop the product. Filing a PPA is much less complicated and expensive than filing a regular patent application (RPA). For a small entity, the USPTO charges less than $200 for a PPA, and most inventors can prepare and file the application without the services of a patent attorney. If the inventor closes a licensing deal before the 12 months is up, the licensee typically assumes responsibility for the RPA process and expense. Otherwise, a nonprovisional regular patent application must be filed *before* the 12-month provisional period expires if the inventor wishes to hold the "invent" date and move forward with the patenting process.

Filing a PPA, which enables you to claim "patent pending," is also a good idea before launching a crowdfunding campaign to raise funds for your invention and before preselling your product. It's also a good idea to trademark your product name when you file a PPA or an RPA (if you forgo a PPA). Registering a trademark is not expensive, but it is an additional expense. You may also opt to hire an IP professional to do a trademark search to ensure the name you've chosen for your product hasn't already been registered to someone else.

In addition to filing for a patent in the United States (USPTO), you may also need or elect to file for international patents. That, of course, adds to your patenting costs.

Fortunately, there are ways to reduce the costs and to help fund the costs of patenting your invention.

Five Ways to Reduce Patent Costs

You can save a considerable amount of money by being fully prepared for the patenting process *before* enlisting the services of a patent attorney. Here's how:

1. Document every step of the inventing process in sequential order by date in a written or electronic inventor's notebook.

2. Develop a manufacturing-ready product before filing a non-provisional regular patent application. (If your invention falls into the utility patent category, you can file a provisional patent application, PPA, once you have a functional, looks-real proto-type and are ready to crowdfund or presell your invention.)

3. Write a concise, detailed description of your invention. The more precise and complete your description, the less time your patent attorney will spend preparing the application and going back and forth with the USPTO explaining and defending it.

4. Prepare or have prepared at least three sets of professional-quality patent drawings of your invention: one for your attorney, one for USPTO, and one for you.

5. Prepare a draft of the patent application yourself. From the USPTO website, download the transmittal form (template) and print the appropriate Nonprovisional Patent Application Guidelines (design, utility, plant). Refer to your inventor's note-book, description, drawings, and images; follow the directions explicitly; and take your time. If you have questions, contact the Patent and Trademark Resource Center (PTRC) nearest you for free assistance. Although drafting the application is challenging and time-consuming, it will reduce the amount of time your patent attorney spends (and the money you spend) preparing your patent application and interacting with the USPTO.

Professional Patent Search

Do-it-yourself patent searches are invaluable during the ideation and production development phases. Once you have a completed invention, though, it is imperative to hire an intellectual property expert to do a thorough patent search, which typically results in lower patenting costs. It also reduces the risk of having to redesign or abandon your invention if prior art pops up down the line.

Some patent attorneys prefer to conduct the patent search inhouse or to contract it to a patent search agent they work with. Other attorneys will be fine with you using a patent search agent of your choice. Patent searches conducted by patent agents are usually more affordable than those conducted by patent attorneys. It's also usually more economical to hire a patent agent directly than through your attorney, who will bill you for the patent search plus a fee for arranging it.

If you choose not to have a professional patent search done before filing a patent application and do not do one yourself, the USPTO will conduct a patent search as part of the patent application review process. In that case, the USPTO will charge you a separate fee for the patent search.

No-Cost Patent Advice and Assistance Options

Even if you intend to prepare and file the patent application yourself, it's a good idea to consult with a patent attorney before you start preparing the application and as needed during the patent examination process. Following are a few free and reduced-cost ways to get legal and other professional help with your patent application.

- **USPTO Patent Pro Bono Program.** Independent inventors and small businesses that meet USPTO's financial criteria are eligible for free legal assistance in preparing and filing a patent application. USPTO uses a nationwide network of independently operated regional programs to match inventors with volunteer patent professionals in their area.

- **USPTO Pro Se Assistance Program.** The *pro se* (do-it-yourself) patent program has two components: (1) assistance via online resources and in person at USPTO headquarters in Virginia, (2) an internal examination unit dedicated to examining pro se applicants. Both are provided at no cost (beyond standard USPTO fees).

- **Local Pro Bono Legal Aid Clinics.** Most states have nonprofit legal aid programs that can connect local inventors having limited financial sources with volunteer patent attorneys in their communities—such as Ohio Patent Pro Bono. Some university law schools operate similar programs—such as the Patent Clinic of the North Carolina School of Law (a registered USPTO patent clinic). The American Bar Association website features an annotated list of intellectual property pro bono resources for each of the 20 states with pro bono legal aid programs.

FUNDING TO BRING AN INVENTION TO MARKET

Once you have a looks-like/works-like prototype, CAD drawings, man-ufacturing/materials specs, trademarked product name, and patent pending, it's time to start marketing and selling your invention. As an independent inventor, you have two options for bringing your new product to market:

- License it to a corporation or direct-response TV company
- Bring it to market yourself

Each approach has its advantages and disadvantages—as well as costs. Going solo means you take full responsibility for marketing, selling, order fulfillment, manufacturing, packaging, distribution, and customer service as well as administrative stuff, such as product liability insurance and sales tax. If you have a financially sound business in operation at least two years *and* if your invention is an extension of that business, you might be able to secure traditional financing, such as bank loans or investment capital, to grow the business via the invention. If you start a business for the purpose of bringing your invention to market, you'll probably need alternative forms of funding geared toward ventures like yours, such as those described throughout this book. You'll also need to sell enough of your invention, through your website or an e-commerce site like Shopify or Amazon, to demonstrate its marketability to lenders and/or investors.

While some indie inventors are willing and able to run the whole show, many have no interest in starting and running a business. They just want to get their product into the market as quickly and easily as possible, with the least amount of cost to them, so they can start earning royalties. Some are eager to move on to their next invention. For inventors with that mindset, licensing is a funding option for bringing their product to market—shifting the costs and challenges of bringing it to market to the licensee—and getting paid for creating a great invention.

Licensing-Based Funding

Licensing your invention can be a powerful way to establish residual income while also reducing your up-front financial risk. For independent inventors, the three main options for pursuing a licensing deal are:

- Pitch your invention directly to corporations by courting the brand's product manager(s) or by participating in the brand's open innovation challenge.
- Pitch your invention to direct response TV companies.
- Pitch your invention to licensing companies.

Corporate Open Innovation Programs

Many large corporations in virtually every industry, from consumer products to technology, have open innovation initiatives, whereby the company seeks to license or buy inventions and innovative products that complement their brands. Typically, the corporate website will include a portal or a unique website will exist, where product needs are posted and inventors can submit their ideas. Some corporations employ or contract with product scouts, who seek new products from inventors on the company's behalf. If the invention is a fit, the corporation offers the inventor a licensing deal.

Other companies hold innovation challenges in search of a solution to a specific problems or an idea enabling them to pursue a unique opportunity. These open-innovation challenges (aka *competition*, *contest*) typically offer the "winners" a cash prize and/or a licensing deal.

Following are an example of a crowdsourcing platform for corporate innovation challenges as well as a corporate open innovation program.

- **Hero^x.** This crowdsourcing platform gives inventors direct access to open innovation challenges posted by corporations, research labs, government agencies, and philanthropic organizations. Eligible inventors or invention teams take on a challenge for a chance to win a cash prize and often a licensing deal. Most innovation challenges posted on Hero^x are for science- or technology-based innovations. For example, the GoFly Prize sponsored by Boeing in 2018 was a $2 million challenge to create a "safe, quiet, ultra-compact, near-VTOL (vertical takeoff and landing), single-person flying device capable of flying 20 miles."
- **Lifetime Brands.** Lifetime Brands is a leading developer and marketer of consumer household products, both its own and licensed products. The Innovation portal of the company's

website is informative and intuitive, making it easy to submit an idea. Although not required, patented ideas, market
research, CAD drawings, and prototypes will enhance and
expedite the review process. All ideas are evaluated by Warren
Tuttle, an authorized representative for Lifetime Brands and
president of United Inventors Association, who has extensive
experience working with inventors and bringing inventions
to market. Warren responds directly to each inventor, providing feedback on the idea. If Lifetime Brands is interested in
and ready to license the product, Warren guides the inventor
through every step of that process. Having known and worked
with Warren for years, I can attest to his expertise and to his
advocacy for independent inventors. Lifetime Brands receives 3
to 7 percent of net gross revenues.

Direct Response Television

Direct Response Television (DRTV) is television advertising that asks consumers to respond to the "infomercial," usually by calling a toll-free number to purchase the product. DRTV campaigns are produced and carried
out by DRTV companies, which license the product from the inventor.
Some DRTV companies run *multichannel* campaigns that include DRTV
first and extend to social media, mobile, radio, and retail. Most DRTV
companies cover all the costs in bringing the product to market—product refinement, test marketing, producing and airing commercials, order
processing, manufacturing, and distribution. Others require the inventor
to pay video production costs up front and sometimes manufacturing or
other costs. I strongly advise going with a DRTV company that assumes
all responsibilities, from inception through fulfillment, and that has a
portfolio of successfully sold products.

DRTV companies usually license a product for 18 to 24 months and
move it quickly through product refinement and test-marketing. If the
product is greenlighted, the selling cycle is short and fast-paced. Inventor
royalties run from 1 to 6 percent of net wholesale.

Not all inventions are well suited to DRTV. The ideal DRTV product
has a distinctive benefit that wows consumers, appeals to a broad market,
has a high markup, is highly demonstrable, and isn't available anywhere

else (initially). Each DRTV company specializes in one or more product groups, such as toys/games, kitchen/housewares, tools/hardware, etc.—such as the two featured here by way of example.

- **Allstar Marketing Group.** Allstar bills itself as a "consumer products company that uses direct response advertising to maximize the potential of innovative, quality products and sustainable brands." Allstar handles all aspects of the direct response campaigns—video production, media buying, product development, manufacturing, fulfillment, and customer service, at no cost to the inventor/licensor. Licenses consumer products in 12 categories.

- **Lenfest Media Group.** Lenfest is a consumer products company and direct response marketer that takes licensed products from concept through product development, market research, DRTV production and management, manufacturing, fulfillment, and retail distribution. Lenfest favors products that have been manufactured, packaged, patented, and sold in some capacity, but considers exceptional products at the concept stage. Royalty rates range from 2 to 5 percent of net sales.

AN INVENTIVE RETIREE RIDES THE INFORMERCIAL ROCKET TO SUCCESS

The idea for Saul Palder's invention came to him, as most inventions do, when he ran into a problem ripe for a solution: He couldn't find the cover to a food storage container. As the retired businessman contemplated ways to organize these common kitchen items, his mind went to the circular racks that hold poker chips. He envisioned containers and lids in a circular storage system that would spin around so everything would be easily accessible.

Saul went to work on a design. He had a prototype made and tested it, which sent him back to the drawing board. About that time, he was introduced to Hank Lippisch, a retired industrial designer. Saul hired Hank to prepare drawings for a prototype and for presentation to potential licensees and buyers. The two men met frequently at Saul's "corporate headquarters"—the

McDonald's on Route 128 in Newton, Massachusetts—to pore over blueprints, evaluate the viability of the design, and repeatedly ask, "What if?"

When the concept evolved to a workable solution, Saul turned to David Wolf, the IP attorney he'd consulted years earlier about the catalytic converter he invented. The Boston attorney did a patent search and found no prior art resembling Saul's Smart Spin. Saul and Hank finalized the design, and attorney Wolf filed the patent application.

Saul showed his Smart Spin to everyone he knew as well as complete strangers—and consistently got an enthusiastic thumbs-up. It was time to market his invention, which Saul didn't want to do but gave it his best shot. Although he made a few connections, he made no sales. But one of those connections led him to a local company, Merchant Media, a direct response TV and retail marketer.

Saul walked into Merchant Media with his patent, blueprints, and working prototype in hand. "I knew it was a great product within the first 10 seconds. Saul hit it!" said Michael Antino, president of Merchant Media.

Merchant Media licensed the rights to Saul's invention in fall 2003 and pulled the packaging, manufacturing, and other pieces together quickly. In fall 2004, Merchant Media launched Smart Spin, flooding the airways with infomercials. Before long, sales exceeded capacity, but Merchant Media was ready and ramped up production and marketing. With infomercials to 24/7 home shopping channels, catalogs, and finally retail, Smart Spin was everywhere. In less than six months, more than 6 million units were sold—and 13 years later, the sales keep coming.

Product Marketing and Licensing Companies

A top-notch product licensing company can detect a marketable invention and enhance its marketability, and then land the solid licensing agreement with a successful company. When that happens, the invention not only gets to market much faster than had the inventor peddled the invention directly to buyers and licensees alone, it also typically results in a higher return on investment for the inventor.

There are numerous product marketing and licensing companies, some better than others. To give you a benchmark of what to look for, here are profiles of two of better invention marketing and licensing firms to consider.

Edison Nation

Edison Nation licenses products to numerous consumer product man-ufacturing and retail partners (Bed Bath & Beyond, Home Shopping Network, Procter & Gamble, to name a few) and to As Seen on TV (ASOTV). Edison Nation also runs an open search for ideas in several categories that Edison Nation consider for developing in-house and then marketing to consumer product companies. No patent or patent pend-ing is needed, except for inventions accepted into Edison Nation's Insider Licensing Program.

All ideas are submitted online using Edison Nation's easy-to-use platform; the website clearly spells out everything you need to know. Registration to become a member and start checking out product innova-tion searches is free. Edison Nation charges $25 for each idea submitted. The invention can be submitted to either a specific Innovation Challenge (consumer products company), for ASOTV, for an open category, or for the Insider Licensing Program. It cannot be submitted to more than one of those four channels.

Edison Nation evaluates all idea submissions, and if an idea is a poten-tial fit for a company or ASOTV, Edison Nation pitches it to the com-pany or ASOTV. If the company or ASOTV bites, Edison Nation handles all the product development and licensing (company) or manufacturing/distribution (ASOTV). For products successfully licensed to a company, royalties are split 50/50 between the inventor and Edison Nation. For ASOTV, the inventor receives 7.5 percent of adjusted gross revenues. For some licensing deals, the partner receives a percentage of royalties as a success fee.

Lambert & Lambert, Inc.

This product marketing and licensing agency provides inventors and entrepreneurs with contingency-based representation for their inventions and product ideas, in a wide range of consumer products. Among the things I appreciate most about Lambert & Lambert are their transpar-ency and competency; they say what they do and do what they say. They are "licensing agents in search of great inventions, both with and without patents, to bring to market by way of a licensing agreement." A $199 fee is required to evaluate the idea, a necessary and involved process to weed out the "simply curious" and to determine whether the idea is licensable. If Lambert & Lambert takes on your invention, they get paid for their marketing and licensing services when, and only when, the invention is licensed and successfully brought to market.

Depending on how developed an invention is at time of submission, Lambert & Lambert services might include the following:

Patent assistance	Market research
Prototype development	Engineered drawings
Computer renderings	Manufacturing feasibility
Invention marketing materials	Networking with potential licensees
Trade show representation	Invention presentation
Licensing negotiation	Licensing agreement administration

The royalty percentage paid to Lambert & Lambert ranges from 25 to 30 percent of licensing revenues—again, depending on the invention's state of development at time of submission and acceptance by the agency to represent it.

$ **Beware of invention promotion scams.** Certain unscrupulous invention promotion companies lure inventors into paying hefty fees for their alleged promotional expertise and connections to big-name licensees on the false premise that this will hasten the path to lucrative licensing agreements. In reality, these scammers do little for their clients, whose inventions rarely, if ever, make it to market via the promotional company. The USPTO and Federal Trade Commission both provide information and resources to help you avoid and report invention promotion scams. You can also check with inventor associations and the Better Business Bureau.

Crowdfunding for Inventions

Once your product is ready to test-market, you can use rewards-based crowdfunding to raise capital to help fund the costs of bringing your product to market by preselling your product as the reward to backers. Some crowdfunding platforms also have online marketplaces where you can get some early sales transaction. Crowdfunding platforms that specialize in rewards-based campaigns for businesses—such as Indiegogo and Kickstarter—often work well for inventions.

A few niche crowdfunding platforms target innovative new products in certain sectors, usually technology innovations—such as:

- **B-a-MedFounder.** Equity- and rewards-based crowdfunding platform for medical device inventions and innovations.

- **Crowd Supply.** Donation- and equity-based crowdfunding platform and crowdsourcing platform providing technical and commercialization support for computer hardware inventions and innovations.

- **Mars Rising Network.** Crowdsourcing (free and low-cost resources) and rewards-based crowdfunding in partnership with Indiegogo and Kickstarter.

- **Techmoola.** Rewards-based crowdfunding platform for technology entrepreneurs and inventors.

(For more information on crowdfunding, check out the free, downloadable bonus chapter "Crowdfunding" at kedmaough.com.)

RESOURCES

With the multiple useful resources available to independent inventors and innovators, it's impossible to fit them all into the allotted space in this book. So here are the ones I rely on the most as an inventor and as an advisor to inventors.

Inventor's Digest. This print magazine and its digital companion, investorsdigest.com, are the go-to publications for practical information, entertaining content, and the latest concerns, challenges, cutting-edge developments, and causes for celebration pertaining to the inventing community.

inventRight. Cofounded by Stephen Key, inventor, entrepreneur, and author of the bestselling *One Simple Idea: Turn Your Dreams into a Licensing Goldmine While Letting Others Do the Work* and Andrew Krauss, inventor and former president of the San Francisco Inventor's

Alliance Group, inventRight offers workshops, webinars, consulting, and mentoring to inventors. The inventRight website also features informative articles and helpful resources.

IPWatchdog. Launched in 1999, IPWatchdog.com has been a trusted resource on intellectual property for tens of millions of unique visitors and is one of the leading sources for news, information, resources, analysis, and commentary in the patent and innovation industries. IPWatchdog also covers matters relating to trade secrets, copyrights, and trademarks.

United Inventors Association of America (UIA). UIA is a nonprofit membership organization dedicated to providing education resources and opportunities to the independent inventing community while encouraging ethical business practices among industry service providers. UIA inventor clubs around the country offer another source of resources and support. I am grateful to the UIA for its efforts on behalf of independent inventors across the country, and I am honored to be a board member of this stellar organization.

TARGET FUNDING VARIABLES FOR INVENTORS AND INVENTIONS

Use any combination of the following keywords to search the Internet for potential funding for your invention. For each search, specify one to three variables per each applicable keyword position—for example: inventor (keyword #1); prototype grant, capstone program, crowdsource (keyword #2); technology, medical devices (keyword #3); United States, Miami, Florida (keyword #4).

Keyword #1	inventor | invention | product developer | product development
Keyword #2	financing | grant | prototype grant | business loan | micro-loan | capstone program | crowdsource | crowdfunding | makerspace | patent legal aid | open innovation challenge | open innovation program | direct response TV | product licensing agency | product licensor

Keyword #3	name of industry sector | name of industry subsector | name of product type
Keyword #4	United States | name of city | name of state

CHAPTER

13

Funding for Research and Technology Ventures

Startups and small businesses engaged in the research and/or development and in the commercialization of scientific discoveries, new technologies, or technology-enabled innovations often have funding needs that are unique to those types of businesses. Although many of the funding solutions presented in this book can be utilized by most tech ventures, the funding options in this chapter specifically target research and technology companies.

One of my personal favorite funding opportunities for R&D and tech small businesses is the US federal government's Small Business Innovation Research (SBIR) and Small Business Technology Transfer (STTR) program. That said, only a small percentage of research/tech businesses qualify for an SBIR or STTR grant. Those that do make it into Phase I of an SBIR or STTR program often need bridge funding between Phase I and Phase II. Many also need funding before and after participating in an SBIR or STTR program.

Fortunately, SBIR/STTR grants/contracts aren't the only funding solution aimed at research and tech companies. Numerous other funding opportunities specifically target innovation- and technology-focused startups and/or small businesses.

FEDERAL SMALL BUSINESS INNOVATION RESEARCH AND TECHNOLOGY TRANSFER GRANTS

The Small Business Innovation Research (SBIR) program is a set-aside award system that provides nondilutive funding to domestic startups for the research, design, development, and testing of advanced technology and scientific innovations that have the potential for widespread commercialization. The Small Business Technology Transfer (STTR) program is a set-aside award system that provides nondilutive funding to domestic startups working in collaboration with domestic nonprofit research institutes to move scientific and technological advancements from the lab to the marketplace. Both programs are coordinated by the US Small Business Administration (SBA) Office of Technology.

The SBIR and STTR programs target early-stage companies engaged in the research and development of groundbreaking, high-risk, high-impact technologies that align with the research/research and development (R/R&D) initiatives of participating federal agencies. The programs are designed to facilitate the development of trailblazing innovations from the concept stage to the commercialization stage. Startups with low-impact ideas that don't align with federal R/R&D initiatives and startups with ideas that have already been designed, prototyped, and tested are not candidates for SBIR/STTR grants.

Other eligibility criteria are that the small business concern (SBC) has no more than 500 employees and is a for-profit entity, located in the United States, and at least 51 percent owned and controlled by one or more citizens (or permanent aliens) of the United States. SBIR requires, but STTR does not require, the principal investigator of the funded project to be primarily employed by the SBC. Further, STTR requires the SBC and its institutional partner to establish an intellectual property agreement prior to the onset of the program, the SBC perform at least 40 percent of the R&D, and a single partnering institution to perform at least 30 percent of the R&D.

Federal law requires certain US government agencies to set aside a percentage of their extramural budgets for SBIR and/or STTR awards. Currently, the set-aside is 3.2 percent for SBIR awards and 0.45 percent for STTR awards.

SBIR and STTR programs both have three phases: Phase I, concept development; Phase II, prototype development; Phase III, commercialization. The applicant must apply for each phase of the program in sequence, after having successfully met the benchmarks established for the preceding phase. Each federal agency sets its own funding cap, timeline, and benchmarks for each phase of an awardee project. SBIR/STTR funding may be in the form of grants and/or federal contracts.

SBIR Phase I awards typically do not exceed $150,000 total costs for six months, and SBIR Phase II awards typically do not exceed $1 million total costs for two years. STTR Phase I awards typically do not exceed $150,000 total costs for one year, and STTR Phase II awards typically do not exceed $1 million total costs for two years. As of November 20, 2018, federal agencies are authorized to issue a Phase I SBIR or STTR award of up to $252,131 and Phase II award of up to $1,680,879. Any SBIR or STTR award above those amounts requires a waiver.

SBIR and STTR do not fund Phase III of awardee projects. However, some federal agencies may provide follow-on funding in the form of grants or production contracts for products, processes, and services intended for use by the US government.

At this writing, 11 federal agencies participate in the SBIR program and 5 participate in the STTR program. Each participating agency issues one to three *solicitations* (open calls) for project/grant proposals per year. Each agency administers its own SBIR/STTR program and maintains its own SBIR/STTR website, which provide detailed submission guidelines for that agency's current and forthcoming solicitations.

 Don't Google! Go directly to the source to find SBIR/STTR grant opportunities. The two easiest, fastest ways to find current and upcoming SBIR/STTR solicitations (calls for proposals) are:

- Go to the SBIR Gateway website, where you can search current SBIR/STTR solicitation topics, link to individual participating federal agencies, and get the latest SBIR/STTR news.
- Go to grants.gov and do a basic search with the keyword *SBIR*.

ASSISTANCE AND FUNDING FOR PREPARING AN SBIR OR STTR APPLICATION

SBIR and STTR grants are extremely competitive, with applicant success rates of 15 to 20 percent for Phase I awards and 30 to 50 percent for Phase II awards. The application process is complicated, and the evaluation process is rigorous.

Due to the complexity of the SBIR/STTR process, most applicants enlist the services of advisors and grant writers with SBIR/STTR expertise. In fact, I wouldn't think of applying for an SBIR or STTR grant as a first-time applicant without specialized professional assistance. Fortunately, no-cost and low-cost SBIR/STTR preparation help is available, as is funding to help pay for SBIR/STTR training, consultants, grant writers, and other professional assistance.

Support from SBIR

A good first step is to utilize the training materials on the SBIR website, which include how-to tutorials and other resources; links to workshops, conferences, summits, and other events; and links to the SBIR sites of federal agencies participating in the program. Each agency website provides tutorials, tips, webinars, training events, and other resources specific to that agency's R/R&D initiatives and SBIR/STTR solicitations. All free!

A few of the federal agencies participating in the SBIR/STTR programs offer free "Phase 0" application assistance to a limited number of eligible first-time Phase I SBIR and STTR applicants each year. These free assistance programs typically target socially/economically disadvantaged small businesses (SDB), women-owned small businesses (WOSB), and small businesses located in underrepresented states and districts. Two such programs, both of which are administered by Dawnbreaker, a federal contractor, are:

- **Department of Energy (DOE) SBIR/STTR Phase 0 Assistance program.** Provides free Phase 0 assistance to eligible small businesses and qualified individuals who commit to form a company should they win a DOE SBIR/STTR award. Eligible parties receive one or more of specialized services (market research, proposal preparation, proposal review, IP consultation; financials; small business development training/ mentoring, etc.) following an initial assessment. Preference is given to SDB and WOSB businesses working in advanced technologies anywhere in the United States and businesses located in underrepresented states and districts.

- **National Institutes of Health (NIH) Applicant Assistance Program (AAP).** Offers free Phase 0 assistance to eligible new and previously unsuccessful Phase I SBIR/STTR applicants, who must apply for acceptance into the AAP. Support includes guidance and technical assistance in preparing the SBIR/STTR application; identifying appropriate market research; and guiding applicants through the process. NIH is particularly interested in small businesses owned/operated by individuals who are underrepresented in biomedical sciences, including minorities, individuals with disabilities, and women.

Two other SBIR resources for training and assistance in navigating the SBIR/STTR process are:

- **SBIR Road Tour.** This annual multistate tour, with stops in numerous cities, is hosted by local organizations that support "next generation" research and development entrepreneurs. SBIR/STTR agency program managers, SBIR staff, and guest speakers participate in panel discussions, give insights into the application and evaluation processes, and provided one-on-one consultations with attendees. Some tour stops are free to attendees; others require an entrance fee.

- **SBIR/STTR Events.** Numerous conferences, innovation summits, seminars, and other events are held throughout the year and the country, providing R&D entrepreneurs with access to SBIR/STTR trainers, experts, trainers, and representatives from participating federal agencies. Some events are national, others are regional. Some focus on the SBIR/STTR processes overall; others are industry- or agency-specific. You'll find an up-to-date events calendar on the SBIR Gateway website.

State and Regional SBIR/STTR Support

Most SBA Small Business Development Centers (SBDCs) have SBIR/STTR specialists on staff and/or on referral who can provide one-on-one advice and technical assistance at no or low cost to the client. Some SBDCs also hold SBIR/STTR workshops and host other events, such as SBIR Road Tour stops and agency-specific SBIR/STTR seminars. SBA Procurement Technical Assistance Centers (PTAC) may also provide SBIR/STTR support, often in partnership with a state SBDC network.

Some state governments, often in partnership with a local nonprofit organization or university/college, offer SBIR/STTR Phase 0/00 programs that provide SBIR/STTR training, technical assistance, grant writing, proposal review, and other professional services at little or no cost. Two such programs are:

- **Maine Technology Institute (MTI) SBIR/STTR Technical Assistance Program (TAP).** The TAP team offers eligible Maine-based companies free assessments to determine their suitability for the SBIR/STTR programs as well as free guidance and technical assistance in preparing, reviewing, and editing the proposal. In addition, MIT offers funds (via grants) to support applications with Phase I or Phase II activities throughout the application submission and evaluation processes.

- **VertueLab.** This Portland-based nonprofit organization offers no-cost and low-cost assistance to Oregon-based small businesses applying for an SBIR/STTR grant under the Federal and State Technology Partnership Program (FAST), funded by SBA. The 30 most promising receive one or more of the following services: feasibility assessment, connects to principal investigators and strategic partners, grant writing, technical review, business plan consulting, training and workshops, and assistance navigating the SBIR/STTR application process.

You may also need advice or professional services for the business components of your SBIR/STTR proposal—for example, accounting, business plan, legal, marketing, etc. The best sources for no-cost and low-cost business advice and technical assistance are your local Small Business

Development Center, SBA regional office, or SCORE office. (Please see Chapter 14, "Business Advice Funding.")

Another resource for professional help in preparing an SBIR/STTR application is private consultancies with SBIR/STTR specialization, such as BBC Entrepreneurial Training and Consulting and Greenwood Consulting Group. Just make sure any consultant or writer you hire to assist you is reputable and has SBIR/STTR experience.

You may also qualify for a Phase 0 grant to help pay for professional services needed or used to prepare an SBIR/STTR Phase I application or for a Phase 00 grant for costs associated with preparing an SBIR/STTR Phase II application. Many state economic development agencies, local universities, and local tech startup organizations offer Phase 0 and Phase 00 grants—such as those featured below.

- **Business Oregon SBIR/STTR Matching Grant Program—Phase 0.** Up to $50,000 for Oregon-based companies that receive an SBIR/STTR Phase I grant, for reimbursement of professional fees and other eligible out-of-pocket expenses directly related to preparing the Phase I application.

- **Phase 00.** Up to $100,000 to Oregon-based companies that intend to apply for an SBIR/STTR Phase II or Fast Track grant, to pay for professional fees and other out-of-pocket expenses directly related to preparing the Phase II or Fast Track application.

- **Wyoming SBIR/STTR Initiative (WSSI) Start with Phase 0/00 Program—Phase 0.** One competitive grant for $5,000 of services per month to a Wyoming-based small business or resident planning to submit an SBIR/STTR Phase I application. The $5,000 "contract" can be used to attend SBIR conferences and workshops, communication with and travel to federal agencies, consultant and mentor services related to preparing a Phase I proposal, writer, reviewer, and other expenses directly related to preparing the application. Each recipient is paired with an experienced mentor/principal investigator to assist with the application and to review the Phase I proposal.

- **Phase 00.** One $5,000 competitive in-kind contract per month, to a Wyoming-based small business or Wyoming resident who has received an SBIR or STTR Phase I grant and plans to apply for an SBIR/STTR Phase II grant. Can be used to attend conferences and workshops, communication with and travel to federal agencies, consultant and mentor services related to preparing a Phase II proposal, writer, reviewer, and other expenses directly related to preparing the application.

LEVERAGING DOD FUNDS TO PUT INNOVATIVE SOLUTIONS INTO THE HANDS OF WARFIGHTERS

Beacon Interactive Systems began as a bootstrapped startup operating out of a rent-controlled apartment on Beacon Street in Brookline, Massachusetts. Using customer financing as the funding path forward, the company experienced significant growth by delivering its collaborative enterprise software solutions to customers in both the private and public sector. Private-sector customers include MetLife, IBM, and Olympus as well as global firms like the pan-European venture capital entity E-Start.

During the 2002 economic downturn in the software industry, the leadership team successfully navigated the company into the federal marketplace via funding from the US Navy's Small Business Innovation Research (SBIR) Program. As a direct result of this federal funding, Beacon is now delivering Mission Critical shipboard systems that streamline maintenance, safety, and operational energy management to every ship, submarine, and aircraft carrier in the US Navy.

"The SBIR program not only provided us with the financial resources to explore the technology we wanted to develop and really thought would enable maintainers and sailors to keep the ships ready, it also provided a valuable resource—an engaged customer," said Beacon CEO ML Mackey.

As Beacon president Mike MacEwen explained, "What we get back from the customers is that they like and appreciate what we have done for them, what we've done for their organizations, what we've done for their people. That's a really satisfying day for us here at Beacon."

FEDERAL INNOVATION CHALLENGES

In July 2010, the US General Services Administration released an innovation challenge platform, Challenge.gov, that enables the US federal government to crowdsource innovative solutions to challenging problems. Federal agencies periodically post select innovation challenges on Challenge.gov, and entrepreneurs, innovators, independent inventors, and everyday citizens from across the United States compete for cash prizes. At this writing, more than 60 federal agencies have run more than 1,000 challenges offering well over $250 million in cash prizes for the best ideas.

The Challenge.gov platform provides comprehensive information on each challenge, including challenge overview, prizes, eligibility requirements, challenge schedule, challenge requirements, judging criteria, sponsoring/collaborating federal agencies, and support materials (videos, webinars, white papers, presentations, etc.). To give you a glimpse into the variety of innovation challenges run by various US federal agencies, following is a quick rundown of a few winners:

- **Easy EHR Issue Reporting Challenge.** Winners of this Department of Health and Human Services challenge created software tools to help clinicians report usability and safety issues with electronic health records (EHR) faster, more efficiently, and in alignment with their regular clinical workflow. The 2018 EHR awards consisted of a $45,000 first place grant, a $25,000 second place grant, and a $10,000 third place grant.

- **Virtual Reality (VR) Heads-Up Display (HUD) Navigation Challenge.** Winners of this National Institute of Standards and Technology (NIST) challenge each created VR HUD prototypes allowing navigation with unimpeded visual aids. The results will support America's First Responders and help the NIST Public Communications Research Division advance research for user interface technology. The 2018 NIST awards consisted of two $25,000 first place grants, one $15,000 third place grant, one $10,000 fourth place grant, one $7,500 fifth place grant, and one $5,000 sixth place grant.

- **Wildland Fire Sensors Challenge.** Winners of this challenge sponsored by the Environmental Protection Agency in collaboration
  with five other federal agencies created sensor technology for
  the development of affordable, transportable, easy-to-use, and
  reliable instruments that can be deployed near a wildfire to
  inform firefighters and community health officials to assess,
  report, and forecast levels of four air pollutants. The 2018
  Wildland Fire Sensors Challenge awards consisted of a $35,000
  first prize grant and a $35,000 second prize grant.

STATE AND LOCAL FUNDING FOR
TECH STARTUPS AND SMALL BUSINESSES

States and regions that have strong technology-based economic development (TBED) initiatives often offer funding support for technology-based
startups and small businesses. The funding may be in the form of grants,
innovation challenges, business competitions, loans, or investment capital. TBED-based funding may be administered by a state or local government entity (usually department of commerce or economic development)
or by a nonprofit economic development organization (EDO). Two representative state funding programs for technology companies follow.

State of Iowa Financing Programs for Technology Companies

The Iowa state government offers three programs for Iowa-based small
technology companies in the advanced manufacturing, bioscience, and
information technology industries.

- **Iowa Proof of Commercial Relevance (POCR).** Offers low-interest
  term loans of up to $25,000 to eligible companies having a vali-
  dated concept or intellectual property and demonstrated proof
  of concept (functional prototype) of an innovative technology
  solution. Funds can be used to seek market validation of a product or service and a business model prior to commercial launch.
  Requires a 1:2 (private:public) funding match.

- **Iowa Demonstration Fund.** Offers financing of up to $125,000,
  primarily in either a low-interest loan or a royalty arrangement,

to eligible companies having high-growth potential and market-ready innovative technologies or products having a clear potential for commercial viability. Funds can be used for marketing and business development activities to help the business reach a position to attract follow-on private sector funding. Requires a 1:2 (private:public) funding match.

- **Iowa Innovation Acceleration Fund.** Offers debt or royalty-based financing to eligible businesses through two programs, each of which corresponds to the specific stage of growth of investment-grade, high-growth companies having a competitive and protectable product, mature technology, or process. Both programs require a 1:1 (private:public) funding match. (1) The PROPEL program awards up to $300,000 to accelerate market development in companies that have a key management team in place, a validated business model, and an established customer base generating substantive revenue. (2) The INNOVATION EXPANSION program awards up to $500,000 to fund product refinement, expansion of product lines, and marketing activities in companies that have a complete management infrastructure, demonstrated historical profitability, and established customer base.

State of Pennsylvania Ben Franklin Technology Partners (BFTP)

Launched in 1983, BFTP is one of the longest-running and most robust technology-based economic development programs in the United States. BFTP provides both early-stage and established tech companies with funding, business guidance, technical assistance, and access to a network of resources. Funded and administered by the Commonwealth of Pennsylvania, Ben Franklin Technology Partners:

- Makes direct investments in promising, technology-oriented businesses throughout the commonwealth to fund critical commercialization activities and growth needs.

- Offers no-cost and low-cost business and technical assistance, including business plan review, technical assessments,

intellectual property counsel, marketing advice, operations
strategies, and funding strategies.

- Creates and fosters partnerships between technology entrepreneurs and investors, business incubators, research labs (federal, university, corporate), state/regional/local business assistance resources, and economic development organizations.

BUSINESS COMPETITIONS FOR TECH STARTUPS

Numerous business pitch, business plan, and innovation competitions targeting technology startups take place throughout the country. Some are national or international in scope; others are open only to local startups. Some focus on a broad range of technology sectors; others focus on a specific sector. A few target tech companies majority-owned by women, minorities, or veterans. Some pitch competitions take place during a conference; other tech startup competitions are discrete events or even virtual competitions. Competitions for technology innovations and startups may be sponsored by state or local government agencies, universities, investor groups, trade organizations, corporations with open innovation initiatives, or other organizations. Most business competitions for tech startups offer cash and/or in-kind prizes, and the cash is usually a grant but can be equity-based. Winners and finalists also receive media attention and access to industry leaders, investors, and often advisors. Two of the dozens of tech startup competitions currently in force are feature below.

(For more information on business pitch, business plan, and other business competitions, check out the free, downloadable bonus chapter "Competition-Based Funding" at kedmaough.com.)

Arizona Innovation Challenge

This initiative of the Arizona Commerce Authority (ACA) awards up to $3 million annually, split into two competitions. Each challenge, held in spring and in fall, awards up to 10 winners up to $150,000 each in nondilutive capital. In addition, awardees receive a full scholarship to Venture Ready, ACA's 12-month business mentorship program, during which each company is paired with an entrepreneur in residence and guided through the commercialization of a scalable product or service.

Startup Battlefield

This pitch competition takes place at the annual TechCrunch Disrupt conference in San Francisco, produced by TechCrunch, the premier online publisher of technology news and creator of Crunchbase, the database of tech startups and their founders and funders. Early-stage tech startups from around the world vie for the Disrupt Cup (trophy), a $100,000 equity-free prize (grant), and the attention of investors and media. Participation is free and open to all pre-Series A startups. Past winners include successful tech companies such as Dropbox, Mint, Yammer, and Zenefits.

INCUBATOR- AND ACCELERATOR-BASED FUNDING FOR TECH STARTUPS

There is no shortage of business incubators and accelerators that focus on technology startups in the United States. They're in every major city and usually in smaller cities populated with numerous tech companies and a university or two nearby. Incubators and accelerators come in both for-profit and nonprofit varieties. Some are a public/private partnership between an investment group, university, local or state government agency, and/or nonprofit organization. Others are affiliated with local tech startup ecosystems, such as Technology Square in Atlanta, Georgia—an entire city block housing several startups, corporate innovators, venture capitalists, academic researchers, and 10 technology incubators/accelerators.

All incubators/accelerators focus on a specific industry or on one or more specific sectors. The focus typically aligns with the interest and expertise of the staff, which may comprise entrepreneurs, investors, industry experts, and/or academicians. A *lot* of incubators/accelerators focus on one or more technology verticals—such as Dreamit, a venture fund and accelerator with three accelerator programs: healthtech, urbantech, and securetech. Some incubators/accelerators focus on tech startups founded and led by women, minorities, veterans, or other underrepresented entrepreneurs. For example, the digitalundivided BIG Incubator focuses on tech startups founded and led by Black and Latinx women.

For more information on start-up funding offered by business incubators and accelerators, please see Chapter 19, "Incubator and Accelerator-Based Funding."

Center for Entrepreneurial Innovation (CEI)

The Center for Entrepreneurial Innovation (CEI) in Phoenix, Arizona, is a division of Maricopa Community College District and receives additional funding from the City of Phoenix and the US Economic Development Agency (EDA). CEI focuses on Arizona-based early-stage startups in bioscience, medical technology, software, and cleantech. The program, which lasts 18 to 36 months, includes pro bono mentoring and access to grants and equity funding. CEI also offers clients affordable workshops, furnished workspace, marketing services, and use of facilities.

Techstars

Considered one of the best and largest technology startup accelerators, Techstars selects over 300 startups per year to participate in its multiple accelerator programs. Techstars runs accelerators in numerous sectors (alchemist blockchain, fintech, energy, future home, Internet of things, farm to fork, healthcare, and more), which are conducted in several cities around and outside the United States. Current US Techstars locations are Atlanta, Austin, Boston, Boulder, Chicago, New York City, and Seattle.

Techstars selects 10 companies for each cohort. Each Techstars Accelerator portfolio company receives:

- $100,000 convertible note and $20,000 cash stipend (for living expenses during program) in exchange for 6 percent common stock.

- Ninety days of free personal mentoring and office space to accelerate the business, culminating in a Demo Day before investors.

- Free hosting, accounting, and legal support, plus numerous credits and perks.

- Access to Techstars' global network of mentors, founders, industry leaders, and investors during the accelerator program and for life.

CROWDFUNDING FOR TECH STARTUPS AND SMALL BUSINESSES

Technology companies have had success raising capital on the leading crowdfunding platforms that cater to businesses, such as Fundable, Indiegogo, Kickstarter, and Wefunder. Crowdfunding platforms that target independent inventors also target technology startups, such as B-a-MedFounder, Crowd Supply, and Techmoola. Other crowdfunding platforms that target or are effective for research and technology startups are Experiment, Innocentive, Republic, RocketHub, SeedInvest, and SeedUps.

(For more information on crowdfunding, check out the free, downloadable bonus chapter "Crowdfunding" at kedmaough.com.)

Experiment

Endorsed by Bill Gates, Experiment is a rewards-based crowdfunding platform for funding and sharing scientific discoveries, with 20 different project categories—from biology to computer science, ecology, materials sciences, neuroscience, and more. The project and the scientist (academic, corporate, or independent) are vetted to ensure both meet Experiment's criteria. Experiment is an all-or-nothing crowdfunding platform; only if the funding goal is met are the funds collected from backers and released to the scientist—less Experiment's 8 percent platform fee and the 3 to 5 percent third-party payment processing fees. The funding success rate is about 46 percent, and the average amount of funds raised per campaign is a bit over $4,000. The fund-raiser rewards backers by sharing progress reports during the experiment and the scientific results upon completion of the experiment. Backers are typically a combination of the fund-raiser's network of supporters and Experiment members.

Republic

Republic is an equity-based crowdfunding platform that enables the American public and professional investors to invest in US tech startups in all sectors. It is an all-or-nothing crowdfunding model. A startup can raise up to $1.07 million per 12 months on Republic. If the funding goal is not reached, the stock offering is canceled and all funds (held in escrow during campaign) are returned to backers. If and when the funding goal is reached, then all funds are collected, the stock offering is transacted, Republic takes its cut and pays third-party expenses, and the remaining funds are released to the startup. Republic charges a platform fee of 6 percent of the total funds paid in cash and 2 percent of securities issued during the campaign. Third-party costs include credit card processing, document preparation for the offering, and any attorney fees.

ANGEL INVESTMENT GROUPS TARGETING TECH STARTUPS

Technology and technology-enabled startups are target investments for many of the 5,000 or so accredited angel investors in the United States. If you're located within driving distance of a city with a robust or emerging technology industry, you should be able to find angel investment groups or syndicates nearby that focus on tech startups in your sector and area. You can also find and connect with potential angel investors on an online angel platform. (For more information on angel investors, check out the free, downloadable bonus chapter "Equity Funding" at kedmaough.com.)

Search for angel investment groups and/or individual angel investors that target tech startups in your lane—that is, targeting companies in your sector, stage, location, diversity demographic (of founders), and so on. For example, if my startup was in the medical device lane, I'd search for angel investors in the medtech sector. A few possibilities for me to investigate would be Bio/Med Investor Network, Life Science Angels, Mass Medical Angels (MA2), and WINGS. As for founder demographics, some angel investment groups target tech startups with underrepresented founders, such as Black Angel Tech Fund and Chloe Capital.

By way of example, let's take a quick look at two tech-focused angel investment groups with two different investment focuses.

Atlanta Tech Angels (ATA)

ATA, one of the nation's top angel investing networks, works with venture capital affiliates in Atlanta and across Georgia to evaluate and fund top-tier early-stage technology companies in Atlanta and surrounding areas. ATA members provide seed and early-stage capital to entrepreneurs seeking $200,000 to $3 million, an investment range not generally served by VC funds. ATA members also provide their portfolio companies with mentorship, industry expertise, and valuable contacts. Collectively, Atlanta Technology Angels and its affiliate, Gwinnett Angels, screen hardware, software, digital media, life sciences, cleantech, and industrial technologies as well as financial services and consumer products and services.

Propel(x)

This San Francisco–headquartered angel investing platform focuses on funding early-stage companies that are built around a groundbreaking scientific discovery or technology with intellectual property—what Propel(x) refers to as "deep technology startups." In its first year of business (2018), 40 companies raised over $9 million in funding from accredited angels, institutional investors, and Hubble Investments (a broker-dealer, FINRA/SIPC member, and Propel(x) affiliate). At this time, only accredited investors can invest via the Propel(x) platform, and Propel(x) curates all companies raising funds on the platform. Minimum investment per angel is $3,000. Propel(x) requests the startup to reserve $200,000 of its capital raise for its Propel(x) fund-raising. Propel(x) charges a 5 percent success fee for investment amounts of $200,000 and an 8 percent success fee for investment amounts of less than $200,000. Propel(x) covers all fund-raising–related costs, such as syndication formation, broker review, escrow account, and investor verification.

VENTURE CAPITAL GROUPS TARGETING TECH STARTUPS

One of the frequently quoted statistics is that four states, or sometimes it's six or eight states, control the majority of research and technology investment capital in the United States. There is, of course, truth to that. Where volumes of technology companies proliferate, so, too, do investors and investment capital often congregate to fund them. But that's changing, as technology clusters and ecosystems emerge and expand in other parts of the country. And some VCs in Silicon Valley, Boston, Houston, and other technology hot spots do sometimes invest in hot tech startups in other parts of the country.

That said, if a VC group is all over tech startups in your lane but focuses on companies in Chicago and you're located in Kansas, don't waste your time or theirs trying to get your foot in the door. Target your search on venture capital groups that are in the market that match all your variables—location, sector, stage, size, revenues, makeup of founding team, and so on. The more closely your variables align with their investment focus, the better your odds of getting the opportunity to pitch your business.

(For more information on venture capital funding, check out the free, downloadable bonus chapter "Equity Funding" at kedmaough.com.)

Bolt Capital

"Venture capital at the intersection of hardware and software" is how the aptly named venture capital group Bolt Capital bills itself. Bolt is led by general partners who are experienced founders and engineers and have created billions of dollars of market cap at companies like Airbnb. Bolt Capital focuses on pre-seed, pre-product companies, often writing founders their first check and initially investing up to $1 million. Individual Bolt investors make their investment decisions independently, typically take the *lead investor* position (first VC investment in company), and are amenable to coinvesting with others.

Bolt also offers Bolt Bold, an incubation/investment deal in which Bolt provides the capital and resources to help build the foundation of the company. Bolt Build provides equity investments of $200,000 to $500,000 as well as office space and a prototyping lab at the idea stage.

Stout Street Capital

"Colorado's fastest-growing venture capital firm," Stout Street Capital is an early-stage seed fund that invests on technology companies innovating in sectors such as artificial intelligence, advanced materials, data analytics, fintech, robotics, software, and more. The firm focuses on underserved markets, particularly in the middle of the country with an emphasis on the Rocky Mountain area. Stout Street targets post-revenue, seed-to-series-A investments in companies valued at less than $10 million. Portfolio companies include Agility Robotics, Bitsbox, and Pilotly.

ONE TECHNOLOGY, THREE FOUNDERS, AND A CROWD OF ANGELS

What happens when a busy emergency room physician comes up with a great idea that solves a common problem, but he doesn't have the knowledge or time to work out all the design and engineering kinks and to build a business around his technology? The doctor in question went to the Micro-Inventors Program of Oregon (MIPO) and talked with a business counselor—me. After Sean and I discussed his invention, situation, and options, he took my advice to find an engineer or industrial product designer to help him refine and test his technology—a clog-preventing bathtub and shower drain stopper.

New technology requires research, development, and tooling to refine the design and build a prototype. Sean asked his college buddy David, a mechanical engineer, to help him with the design. David agreed and came onboard as cofounder of their two-man side-hustle business.

David's work proved that the grip and rip technology of Sean's bathtub drain story was indeed revolutionary. It prevented bathtub and shower drains from getting clogged!

Meanwhile, Sean and David realized that they also needed to bring in someone who had the business experience they lacked. They found Bill, who had decades of startup experience and success. As the company's new CEO, Bill helped tune up the business plan, mentored Sean and David on key administration and financial matters, and brought in investors.

While Sean and David fine-tuned and patented the Dynamic Drain, the three founders raised $750,000 in angel investment capital in the form of a convertible promissory note. Their angels were mostly personal and professional connections in the area, many of whom were Bill's peers from his previous startup successes. The founding team also sold a small amount of stock in their emerging enterprise. The capital kept things moving along, covering the costs of production-grade tooling, packaging, marketing, and working capital.

Then, Sean, David, and Bill did what innovators often do. They licensed the Dynamic Drain to PF WaterWorks, which began utilizing the technology under the trade name DrainEASY. That was several years ago. PF WaterWorks continues to incorporate DrainEASY in numerous products sold nationwide, and Sean, David, and Bill continue to receive the royalties.

TARGET FUNDING VARIABLES FOR RESEARCH AND TECHNOLOGY VENTURES

Use any combination of the following keywords to search the Internet for potential funding for your technology startup or small business. For each search, specify one to three variables per each applicable keyword position— for example: technology, startup (keyword #1); equity financing, venture capital (keyword #2); med tech, artificial intelligence (keyword #3); United States, Cleveland, Ohio (keyword #4); minority owned, veteran owned (keyword #5).

Keyword #1   technology | tech | high tech | research | R&D | startup | small business | business | company | high growth company

Keyword #2   financing | grant | loan | crowdfunding | innovation challenge | incubator | accelerator | business plan competition | business pitch competition | royalty financing | equity financing | investment capital | angel investor | venture capital | technical assistance | SBIR STTR | gov

Keyword #3   name of industry sector | name of industry subsector | name of product type

Keyword #4   United States | name of city | name of state

Keyword #5   (applicable diversity variable) hub zone | low income | woman owned | minority owned | veteran owned | disabled | LGBTQ | immigrant | refugee

PART FIVE

Funding for Startups and Small Businesses

CHAPTER 14

Business Advice Funding

Raising sufficient capital to launch or expand your business is crucial. But it won't buy success if you don't have the business know-how to make it happen. Although most entrepreneurs wear many hats and have many strong suits, no one knows it all and can do it all well. I often say that if you want to fail at business, do everything yourself, don't get advice, and don't create a community to support you. It's what I call *brilliance failure*. It's when you reach a certain level of knowledge or expertise and you know what you don't know, but instead of asking for help, you try to figure it out on your own or put it off—which often impedes or delays progress. I know this to be true because I once suffered from brilliance failure, but now I always ask for expert advice, even when I think I know the answer.

Sometimes, the founder or founding team *does* have the expertise to cover all the critical bases, but they don't have time to do it effectively or quickly enough. Likewise, entrepreneurs lacking certain types of expertise often lack the resources to acquire that knowledge or to hire staff that does. Nor can many small businesses afford to hire private advisors and consultants.

What many entrepreneurs don't realize is that you can get the same high quality of expert advising and assistance at no cost or low cost to you. For example, as a director of a Small Business Development Center, an extension of the US Small Business Administration (SBA), I can provide my clients with *free* business advising and coaching, for which I would charge at least $200 an hour as a private consultant. I can also refer my clients to other SBDC counselors in my state with different areas of expertise. In Oregon, we have 20 SBDCs and upwards of 120 advisors in various disciplines. That means business owners in Oregon—and all other states—can get help in multiple areas from some of the best experts in the area at no cost to them.

If, in reviewing your startup or expansion plan, I found that you needed $8,000 in business advising across multiple disciplines, and SBDC can provide those resources at no cost to you, that is essentially an $8,000 grant. Let's say that I and the other SBDC counselors in my area were unable to provide or find no-cost resources for some of your needs, but I could connect you with qualified consultants willing to provide those services at a significant discount. Instead of charging their standard $200 per hour, they've agreed to charge you $100 per hour for five hours of services. Altogether, you would receive $8,000 worth of expert help at a cost to you of $500. What's more, that 40 hours of advice and assistance enabled you to achieve what might have taken months or years for you to achieve alone. If that's not a funding option, what is?

You see, target funding isn't just about getting cash. It's also about getting as many resources as possible at no cost or low cost in order to reduce the amount of cash you need to come up with to move your business forward.

Now, I realize that isn't easy. Finding the expert advice, services, and other resources you need at no or nominal cost can take time and effort. You also have to know where to look and what to look for, and many new business owners don't know what they need, what is available to them, and how to find and get it—much less for little or no cost. That's why I think a navigator, such as an SBDC counselor or a business coach, is essential to any business. A navigator is similar to a project manager, guiding you to all the advisors and other resources you need to support your business—not only when you first start out but also when it's necessary to pivot or realign the business. A strong business navigator will have a vast network of purposeful connections and will continually build that network. A good navigator will also guide you in building your own network.

This chapter is sort of like a navigator for finding real-life navigators near you who can provide and/or connect you with no-cost and low-cost business coaching, advising, consulting, training, and assistance.

$ **If a business advisor tells you he or she can give or get all the help you need, find another advisor.** It is impossible for any one person—no matter how brilliant and experienced and well connected—to have expertise or alliances in every facet of business development. It is far better to work with a good navigator and to surround yourself with a team of experts.

US SMALL BUSINESS ADMINISTRATION (SBA)

The SBA partners with the following nonprofit networks that counsel, mentor, and train aspiring and existing small business owners throughout the United States.

SCORE

With more than 10,000 advisors and 300 chapters nationwide, SCORE is one of the largest small business education and mentoring network in the United States. SCORE educators and mentors are retired and working business owners, executives, and managers with experience across more than 60 industries. SCORE's mentoring and training initiatives encompass every stage of the business life cycle: prestart, startup, in operation, and transitioning.

SCORE's offerings include:

- No-cost one-on-one business counseling to entrepreneurs and small business owners on a wide range of business topics
- No-cost and low-cost webinars and workshops on various aspects of small business startup and ownership
- No-cost access to an extensive, searchable online library and to downloadable tools such as templates, checklists, and e-guides

One of the challenges of using SCORE is that because all SCORE mentors are volunteers, the strong advisor you need or have been working with may not be available or may stop volunteering with SCORE. My favorite part of using SCORE is the SCORE Mentor Match Program—a searchable online tool that enables you to search for the type of mentor you need. This can be helpful if you haven't found or choose not to work with a navigator. Just remember that a navigator will not only help you find but often will also introduce you to experts whose expertise they can vouch for. Visit the SCORE website to find a chapter near you to select and connect with a mentor; to sign up for a local workshop, webinar, or on-demand course; and to browse SCORE's robust online library.

> Entrepreneurs with access to a mentor are five times more likely to start a business than those without a mentor. Almost 90 percent of businesses launched by SCORE clients are still in business one year later, compared with the national average of 75 percent of startups that survive the first year.

Small Business Development Centers (SBDC)

The nationwide network of SBDCs provides no-cost business advising and assistance along with no-cost and low-cost business training to new and existing small businesses that employ or will employ workers over and above the business owners. The SBDC operates 1,000 centers throughout the United States and its territories. Several states also have outreach centers in rural and outlying areas. Local SBDCs are hosted by colleges and state economic development agencies. Each local SBDC is staffed with business counselors whose expertise spans multiple disciplines and who know the business climate, regulations, ecosystems, and service providers of the areas they serve.

Applicants for an SBDC business advisory position go through a stringent interview and vetting process. In fact, most SBDC business advisors have an MBA or the equivalent and years of small business experience and are recruited by SBDC because they have expertise in a particular area. I joined the SBDC because I wanted to be part of a group of exceptional business experts who are giving back to their local small business community.

SBDC programs are designed to guide every type of small business through every stage of and in every area of business—from planning to licensing, funding, marketing, staffing, financial management, operations management, and more. All SBDC locations offer individualized, face-to-face business advising and assistance. Each statewide SBDC program also offers a variety of business education and training modules. The types of services, training, and resources vary somewhat from state to state, primarily because they are based on local needs and economic development strategies. Some SBDCs offer specialized programs, such as exporting, rural businesses, cybersecurity, franchising, or technology transfer. Several SBDCs offer scale-up assistance to potentially high-growth small businesses in certain industry sectors that are generating at least $1 million in annual revenue.

To find SBDC locations and to learn about the SBDC services in your state, visit the website of America's SBDC, the nonprofit association of the nationwide network of Small Business Development Centers. For information on SBA Veteran's Business Outreach Centers and Women's Business Centers, please see Chapter 4, "Funding for Veteran-Owned Businesses," and Chapter 7, "Funding for Women-Owned Businesses."

Almost 70 percent of pre-venture entrepreneurs start a business after receiving SBDC counseling. For SBDC clients that have established businesses, the average employment growth is nearly 10 times and the average sales growth is nearly 4 times the national average for all businesses.

OTHER GOVERNMENT AGENCIES PROVIDING SMALL BUSINESS ADVICE

Most federal programs that support small businesses are under the wing of the SBA. Two other federal agencies that support small businesses are the Office of Small Business Utilization (see Chapter 17, "Government Procurement–Based Funding") and the US Commercial Service (see below).

Most state governments work in partnership with local Small Business Development Centers (SBDC), with the SBDCs providing all or most of the business counseling and training. Sometimes, a state or local economic development corporation or commerce department offers its own no-cost or low-cost small business advising, training, and support services.

Following are examples of business advising services provided by a federal government agency, a state government agency, and a local government agency.

US International Trade Administration:
Exporting Advice and Assistance

The US Commercial Service (CS), part of the US International Trade Administration (ITA), operates 108 offices throughout the nation and in US embassies and consulates in 78 countries. The CS global network of trade professionals offer, for a fee, custom international trade counseling, market intelligence, business matchmaking, and commercial diplomacy tailored to the client's needs. Fees for customized services are based on the company's size, with small businesses paying the lowest prices. A fee schedule is posted on the ITA website (export.gov).

The website provides no-cost access to:

- Educational content on all aspects of exporting—articles, videos, webinars
- Export tools and guides
- Seminars conducted at CS offices
- Insights on the best international markets for US products and services
- Current information on international trade trends, problems, and solutions

This is a valuable program for anyone seeking guidance and connections for selling goods or service across international channels. In fact, I recently went through this very program so that I could fully understand the steps involved in exporting.

Department of Commerce

The Washington State Department of Commerce offers a wide range of services for startups and small businesses—including three programs that include free business advice.

Export Assistance. International trade experts provide consulting and assistance with key aspects of exporting—such as creating an export plan, clarifying international trade law issues, finding an interpreter, risk mitigation, market research, trade show support, and business matchmaking.

Growing Rural Economies. This program helps entrepreneurs and small business owners in rural communities start and grow their enterprises by providing access to capital, networking, mentorship, technical assistance, and education/training.

StartUp Washington Economic Gardening. This program is designed to help entrepreneurs "get over the inevitable hump" of launching a new business. Specialized professionals certified by the National Center for Economic Gardening, hosted by the Edward Lowe Foundation, guide and assist the company's management in analysis of core strategy, market dynamics, generating qualified sales leads, innovation, financial management, and other key areas.

New York City Department of Small Business Services
The City of New York offers numerous services for startups and small businesses, including the following programs that provide no-cost business advice and training.

NYC Small Business Solutions (SBS). This series of educational courses and seminars covers a wide range of topics—including business planning, funding, financial management, intellectual property, government contracting, social media, marketing, e-commerce, and more. Most are live events held at Business Solutions locations throughout the City's five boroughs or at libraries, banks, and community centers. Some are webinars.

NYC Construction Mentorship. NYC SBS runs two four-month intensive mentoring and training cohorts each year for owners of City-certified M/WBE construction or construction-related businesses that have been in operation at least two years and have annual revenues of at least $150,000.

WE Legal. WE NYC (Women Entrepreneurs New York City) hosts legal clinics in which women entrepreneurs can get one-on-one legal advice on business formation, contracts, intellectual property, and other business legal matters from the City's top law firms.

WE Connect Mentors. WE NYC members have access to weekly group mentoring sessions with a WE Mentor of their choice. They also have access to an event series in which small groups of women business owners participate in discussion/brainstorming sessions led by a WE Mentor.

CHAMBERS OF COMMERCE

Most local chambers of commerce refer their small business members to providers of no-cost and low-cost business counseling, training, and mentoring in their area—such as a Small Business Development Center, SCORE location, economic development corporation, or business council. Some chambers of commerce offer business advice directly to their members.

For example, the Aurora (Illinois) Chamber of Commerce has a Business Advisory Council comprising business leaders who provide mentoring to owners of early-stage companies and counseling to owners of established small businesses. These one-on-one professional services are available at no cost to chamber members. As another example, the Greater Vancouver (Washington) Chamber of Commerce, in partnership with the City of Vancouver, runs a Small Business Assistance Program that provides no-cost business counseling and technical assistance to eligible mid- to low-income small business owners.

Some chambers are demographic-based. For example, there are Asian American, Hispanic, LGBT, Native American, and women chambers of commerce—which may be national with local chapters or only in a certain area.

Another thing to keep in mind is that chambers of commerce are membership organizations that charge dues, which can range from a few hundred dollars to a couple of thousand dollars a year, depending on the size and type of business. I suggest checking with your SBDC counselor or other navigator to determine whether and which chamber (or chambers) might be beneficial to you.

LOCAL MEETUPS AND NETWORKING GROUPS

Attending local meetups can be a good way to get business advice and to make connections that can lead to other resources. To find no-cost and low-cost meetups and other networking events for entrepreneurs, small business owners, or a particular industry in your area, you can search an online event platform such as Meetups or Eventbrite.

Likewise, local networking groups for entrepreneurs, small business owners, or certain industry sectors host gatherings where peers exchange information and resources. Some peer-to-peer networking groups also host panel discussions and guest speakers who have specialized knowledge, advice, and resources they're usually willing to share. Through a networking group, you might meet and develop a rapport with an industry expert who could become your advisor or mentor.

Following are two of the myriad local entrepreneur support communities that offer no-cost business advising and coaching.

1 Million Cups

1 Million Cups is a no-cost program of the Kauffman Foundation that is designed to educate, engage, and inspire entrepreneurs around the country. Based on the notion that entrepreneurs discover solutions by conversing with other entrepreneurs over cups of coffee, 1 Million Cups enables entrepreneurs to discuss their business ideas and issues with other entrepreneurs in their local communities. Each presenter has six minutes to talk about who they are, what they're doing, and why they're doing it. Each presentation is followed by a 20- to 30-minute question-and-answer session that culminates in the ultimate question: "What can we as a community do to help you?"

1 Million Cups presentation events are organized by more than 800 volunteer organizers in 180 communities in 40+ states and one US territory. Anyone can attend a 1MC event, which is a good way to get familiar with the program before presenting your company. Businesses in operation less than five years can apply online to present at 1MC. All industries are welcome. Presentation applications are reviewed and approved by local organizers. Community organizers may also provide individualized coaching.

To join a 1MC community and to apply to be a presenter, you must first register (free) at the 1 Million Cup website. Once registered, you can also view videos of past 1MC presentations from around the country, which are searchable by industry and location.

Business Networking International

BNI is my favorite networking association. It boasts more than 233,000 members in 8,399 local chapters worldwide. As a member, you meet weekly to discuss business and to support each other through referrals. There is virtually no competition, because each business invited into the group complements the others and duplication is rarely in play. For example, a local chapter may have an accountant, lawyer, massage therapist, business advisor, tech founder, web designer, bank executive, and so on.

When I joined BNI several years ago, I was part of a chapter made up of about 30 members, and in one year our group generated more than one million dollars in referrals. It was amazing, and to this day many of my solid contacts came from that BNI chapter, including my lead photographer and business attorney.

FOUNDATION-SPONSORED SMALL BUSINESS COUNSELING PROGRAMS

Several foundations in the United States offer programs to educate, mentor, and assist entrepreneurs and small business owners. Many of these programs are provided at no cost or low cost.

Mansmann Foundation Peer Mentoring Pods

Mansmann Foundation, a noncharitable organization, offers low-cost ($50 per month) Peer-to-Peer Business Mentoring PODS and one-on-one counseling to founders and owners of small businesses located in low-income communities in and around Pittsburgh, Pennsylvania. The PODS consist of 10 to 15 business owners who meet once a month for two hours with a professional facilitator. The PODS focus on collaborative problem solving and facilitating the growth of their businesses, with topics ranging from business planning to product development, sales and marketing strategies, pricing for profit, financial reports, cash-flow issues, hiring practices, and operations efficiency.

Goldman Sachs 10,000 Small Businesses

This philanthropic small business development program of the Goldman Sachs Foundation consists of the following integrated components:

- A business education curriculum comprised of nine modules and four clinics, designed and codelivered by Babson College, the national leader in entrepreneurship education
- A network of support—including one-on-one business advising, technical assistance, resources, and networking opportunities
- Access to capital through local, regional, and national mission-based lenders

The program is delivered through more than 100 partnerships between local community colleges, business schools, community development financial institutions (CDFIs), and nonprofit organizations in 30 markets throughout the United States. Applicants accepted into a 10,000 Small Businesses cohort receive scholarships and the entire program at no cost.

BUSINESS GUIDANCE TRANSFORMS A SKILLED BUILDER INTO A SUCCESSFUL BUSINESS OWNER

Launched in 2006, DiStefano Brothers Construction is a residential design build remodeling company based in South Kingstown, Rhode Island. Owner Peter DiStefano, a highly skilled and experienced tradesman, had limited experience managing finances and positioning his company for future growth. So, when earnings became stagnant, Peter applied for and was accepted into a 10,000 Small Businesses cohort in Rhode Island.

After Peter completed the program, his company changed dramatically. Revenues increased 180 percent, and he opened another location, purchased a fleet of trucks, and hired 13 new employees—achievements Peter credits to the marketing and financial management skills he acquired through 10,000 Small Businesses.

The company has since grown to 35 employees and now has a five-person design team. Peter's goal is to grow DiStefano Brothers Construction into a $30 million company and to bring on additional employees. Because, he says, "What I enjoy most about being a small business owner is hiring people."

LEGAL CLINICS FOR SMALL BUSINESSES

Numerous bar associations and law schools throughout the United States provide no-cost legal clinics and/or other legal support to small businesses in economically depressed communities and/or with limited financial resources. For example, the Washington, D.C., Small Business Legal Assistance program offers free monthly walk-in clinics that provide current and aspiring business owners with the opportunity to consult one-on-one with a volunteer attorney about legal documents and legal issues common to startups and small businesses.

Another example is the Lewis & Clark Law School's Small Business Legal Clinic (SBLC) in Oregon, held three times each month, which provides business transactional legal advice to low-income and emerging small businesses at no cost. Clients meet one-on-one with business attorneys who specialize in various areas of corporate law. The SBLC matches attorneys with clients needing services within the attorney's area of expertise.

To search online for pro bono legal services in your area, use the following keywords:

small business + legal clinic or legal services +
pro bono + name of your city or state

ONLINE BUSINESS MENTORING PLATFORMS

This relatively new option for no-cost and low-cost business advice connects entrepreneurs and small business owners with advisors or mentors in their community, their industry sector, or an area of business in which the business owner lacks expertise. Some business advising/mentoring platforms are rather exclusive, accessible only to heavily vetted entrepreneurs with a business of a particular stage, sector, revenue level, growth rate, or other criteria.

With some business advising/mentoring platforms, the advising or mentoring sessions are conducted solely online, usually via a chat format, such as Slack. With others, the entrepreneur or business owner communicates with the mentor or advisor first by e-mail and then by phone, e-mail, Skype, and/or face-to-face meetings.

I've briefly profiled two of the many online business mentoring platforms, below, as examples, because they have good reputations and are no-cost. Other business advice/mentoring programs you might want to check out are: 10X Factory, Clarity, eMentorConnect, Find A Mentor, Mentor City, Mentor Selector, and Sky's the Limit.

Mercy Corps Micro Mentor Program

Provided by Mercy Corps, a nonprofit organization, MicroMentor is a no-cost, easy-to-use social platform that connects entrepreneurs with volunteer mentors who are ready, willing, and able to help solve problems and build businesses. Both entrepreneurs and mentors create profiles on MicroMentor. Each entrepreneur can search for and reach out to mentors of interest to them; likewise, mentors can search for and reach out to entrepreneurs they think they can and want to help. When a match is made, the mentor and mentee work out the details of their mentoring arrangement—how they will communicate, when, and about what. The MicroMentor site also features an Ask and Answer page (free access) that is searchable by expertise, industry, and question or keyword or your choice.

Pacific Community Ventures Small Business Advising

Pacific Community Ventures, a nonprofit community development institution, offers a Small Business Advising program that "leverages technology and volunteerism" to match you with the best pro bono advisor for you, in your town or anywhere in the country. For example, if you're located in Cleveland but the most qualified advisor for your needs is in Boston, Small Business Advising can arrange that hookup.

Here's how it works: You create an account on the Small Business Advising website and a short online profile about you, your business, and your challenges or opportunities. Provided you meet the program requirements, Small Business Advising then finds a potential advisor for you to work with and introduces the two of you by e-mail. If you and your advisor agree to work together, the two of you schedule a day and time to connect either in person or by phone, e-mail, FaceTime, Google Hangouts, Skype, or whatever works best for you and your advisor.

Most participants in the Small Business Advising program have a business located in the United States with an operating history of at least a year, annual revenues of at least \$100,000, and at least one part-time or full-time employee. Consideration and often exceptions are made for businesses that don't meet all of that criteria but have "compelling social missions" or create jobs for people in economically distressed areas.

TARGET FUNDING VARIABLES FOR BUSINESS ADVICE FUNDING

Use any combination of the following keywords to search the Internet for potential no-cost and low-cost business advising and assistance for your business. For each search, specify one to three variables per each applicable keyword position—for example: small business (keyword #1); technical assistance, business education (keyword #2); Detroit, Michigan, economic development, gov (keyword #3); hub zone, low income (keyword #4).

Keyword #1 business | small business | startup | microenterprise | entrepreneur

Keyword #2 business advice | business counseling | business advising | technical assistance | business mentor | business mentoring | legal advice | legal clinic | business education | networking

Keyword #3 United States | name of city | name of state | federal | gov | economic development | community development | chamber of commerce

Keyword #4 (applicable diversity variable) hub zone | low income | woman owned | minority owned | veteran owned | disabled | LGBTQ | immigrant | refugee

Grants for Startups
and Small Businesses

A grant is an endowment of money and/or resources that is granted (gifted) for a specific purpose and at no cost to the recipient. You don't pay it back, or pay interest on it, or give up equity in exchange for it, or provide goods or services in reciprocation of it. A grant also comes with bragging rights—the opportunity for the grantor and you to tout how the funds are helping your business achieve a noteworthy goal. That can generate interest and boost confidence in your business among potential partners, investors, lenders, and even other grant-making organizations.

A business grant can be a sweet piece of a business funding pie. Yet, few small business owners take advantage of this free source of capital—primarily because they don't know about it or because they've bought into the notion that grants are hard to find and hard to get. In fact, you've probably read some of the articles, blog posts, books, and websites claiming that the vast majority of grants are for charitable organizations and few to none are available to commercial ventures. To that I say, not quite and not even!

True, a larger percentage of government and foundation grants are for not-for-profit projects than for-profit companies. But many government agencies and nonprofit foundations do make grants to small businesses, and they're not the only grant games in town. Many colleges and universities, research and technology institutions, nonprofit organizations, trade associations, private companies, and private individuals also offer grants to startups and/or small businesses.

Grant opportunities for privately held, for-profit enterprises are out there. In fact, grant opportunities aimed at small businesses are actually on the rise. The challenge is to find grants that are meant for entrepreneurs like you and businesses like yours—which is where target funding comes into play.

TARGET FUNDING: WHERE YOUR BUSINESS VARIABLES MEET THE GRANTORS' MISSION

All grant programs are mission-driven, and that mission (focus) always relates to achieving or furthering a specific common good. That common good, or positive social impact, may be as complex and far-reaching as finding a cure for multiple sclerosis or as simple and provincial as sustaining and developing Main Street businesses in a certain community. Target funding helps you find grant programs with missions that align with your business funding variables.

Business variables that are commonly linked with the missions of grant programs that are open to small businesses include:

- Location of business—for example: a specific district or community, city or town, county, state, region, country
- Size or stage of business—for example: small business, midsize business, microenterprise, startup, early stage, high growth
- Adversity or diversity demographic of business owner—for example: minority, woman, veteran, disabled, immigrant/ refugee, low-income
- Industry sector or subsector—for example: sustainable energy or solar, health or medical devices, retail or e-commerce
- Funding use or project—for example: storefront improvements, add new jobs, export portable solar cooking stoves, launch an adaptive clothing line for children

For example, let's say I'm counseling the owner of a bakery located in the Germantown district of Philadelphia, Pennsylvania. He purchased the building, a former café, and opened a bakery in that retail space two years earlier. To help retain existing customers and attract new customers, he decided to give the storefront a facelift, redecorate the café space, and purchase equipment that would enable him to expand his product line. He's secured a $20,000 InStore forgivable loan from the City of Philadelphia Department of Commerce, and now he's seeking grant funding to help cover the remaining renovation and expansion costs.

To help him find a grant that aligns with his business, I might do an Internet search using the following variables (keywords):

grant + retail business + Philadelphia + storefront improvements

When I did exactly that, I found two grants for which he might qualify on the first page of search results:

- **Storefront Improvement Grant.** This program of the City of Philadelphia, Department of Commerce reimburses up to 50 percent of eligible improvements to a maximum of $10,000 for a single commercial property or $15,000 for a multiple-address or corner commercial property in eligible corridors of Philadelphia (including, as I discovered, most of Germantown).

- **Loan Match Grant.** This program of The Merchants Fund (TMF), a private foundation that makes small grants to small businesses in the City of Philadelphia, is a stabilization grant of up to $10,000. To qualify, the business must be located in Philadelphia, be in operation no more than three years, and be the owner's primary source of income. In addition, the applicant must be working in partnership with a sponsoring agency, such as a community development corporation, and contribute funding to the project by way of a matching loan, personal funds, or contributions from state or local government agencies.

As another hypothetical example, let's say I'm counseling the owner of a startup in Portland, Oregon, that produces medicinal and wellness cannabis products. The owner, who happens to be African American, seeks funding to develop product packaging, create a website, and market his product line to distributors and retailers.

An Internet search for that client might consist of the following variables (keywords):

grant + cannabis + business + minority owned + Portland Oregon

When I tested that out, I immediately found the Cannabis Business Development Equity Program, an initiative of Prosper Portland, the city's economic development agency. The service provider for the program is NuLeaf Project, a local nonprofit organization whose mission is "building inter-generational wealth for people of color through the legal cannabis industry." The Cannabis Business Development Equity Program, which was initiated in 2017 and is expected to run for at least a few years, offers monetary grants as well as grants of in-kind services to cannabis entrepreneurs of color in Portland, Oregon:

NuFuel   Annual grants of $5,000–$30,000.

NuNetwork Pairing with a cannabis-industry global thought leader for one-on-one mentoring and business coaching.

NuSchool   Business accelerator program with customized education and technical skill building.

Grants for startups and small businesses come in many different shapes and sizes, and they can come from several different types of organizations. Let's go over the most common providers of business grants.

A STABILIZATION GRANT RESTORES THE SOUND OF MUSIC TO AN HISTORIC NEIGHBORHOOD

Elizabeth Vander Veer Shaak, a violinist and bowmaker, established Mount Airy Violins & Bows in 2003. Located in the historic Mount Airy community of Philadelphia, Mount Airy Violins & Bows offers custom-crafted bows and string instruments and an array of services, from restoration and repair to renting and rehairing. The music shop also rents instruments and has a small space for concerts.

Mount Airy Violins & Bows was in need of an upgraded HVAC. The window units were inadequate and very loud when turned on. Whenever an instrument was tested or a concert was happening, the window units had to be turned off. Properly working and reliable HVAC systems are important to a stringed instrument business. If the store's units were to break down, excess humidity could set in and potentially warp and damage the delicate instruments.

Elizabeth applied for a grant from The Merchants Fund, a private foundation dedicated to providing financial assistance to merchants in Philadelphia. Her goal was to use the grant to upgrade all the primary rooms of her shop and work on the remaining rooms over time.

TMF awarded Mount Airy Violins & Bows a $10,000 stabilization grant in the spring of 2016. The funds were used for the first round of HVAC upgrades. The project not only saved the business money but also provides an enhanced environment for concerts and better preserves the instruments.

GOVERNMENT AGENCIES

The US Small Business Administration (SBA) oversees three federal programs that award grants to small businesses in certain industries that are achieving outstanding results in specified innovation-driven endeavors.

- Regional Innovation Cluster Initiative (see Chapter 10, "Industry Cluster Funding")
- Small Business Innovation Research (SBIR) program (see Chapter 13, "Funding for Research and Technology Ventures")
- Small Business Technology Transfer (STTR) program (see Chapter 13, "Funding for Research and Technology Ventures")

In addition, numerous federal agencies participate in the US government's Innovation Challenge program, which offers "prizes" (grants) for innovative ideas and innovations submitted by the public (individuals) or private companies. (See Chapter 13, "Funding for Research and Technology Ventures").

Some state and local governments offer grant programs for small businesses and/or startups. Sometimes referred to as *business incentive grants*, these programs are aligned with the state, county, or city's economic growth initiatives. See Chapter 9, "Economic Development Funding," for the scoop on small business grants, loans, and other funding provided by local and state government agencies and by community development organizations.

Following are a few examples of the types of small business grants offered by local and state government agencies.

Cleveland (Ohio) Job Creation Incentive Grant Program

This program is offered to new businesses locating (or relocating) to the City that create at least five new full-time jobs within the first year as well as to existing businesses located in the City with substantial job growth. Restaurant and retail business are ineligible for the program. Grantees receive a monetary award of 0.5 percent of new payroll for up to three years. New businesses may also be eligible for a $5,000 moving assistance grant. For more information, visit the Rethink Cleveland website of the City of Cleveland Economic Development.

Montana Trade Show Assistance Program

This grant reimburses 50 percent ($3,000 award cap) of allowable and approved costs to exhibit at a domestic or international trade show outside Montana, at which the business has not previously exhibited. Accessible to private-sector, Montana-based companies that market a product made in Montana or that adds value to a Montana-made product. Eligible expenses are booth rental, booth equipment/furniture/carpeting rental, booth utility costs, signage/flyers specific to the show, shipping/storage/drayage, and show labor. For additional information, visit the Made in Montana page of the Montana Department of Commerce website.

NYC Love Your Local

Longstanding nonfranchise small businesses from across the five boroughs of New York City can apply to receive up to $90,000 in grant awards. Selected businesses use grant funds to cover the costs of improvement projects recommended by industry experts, from whom the business owner receives 20 hours of in-depth, one-on-one business counseling. Awardees also take part in the NYC Love Your Local interactive map and social media campaign. For additional information, visit the NYC Department of Small Business Services (SBS) website.

FOUNDATIONS

A foundation is a nongovernmental, nonprofit organization or charitable trust that makes grants for cultural, educational, religious, scientific, societal, or other philanthropic purposes. Some corporate and private foundations make grants to for-profit enterprises. Following are two examples of foundation grants that are open to for-profit businesses.

Bill & Melinda Gates Foundation

The Gates Foundation works with businesses, governments, academic institutions, faith-based groups, individuals, and charitable organizations on a wide range of national and global economic and societal issues. "In developing countries, it [the Foundation] focuses on improving people's health and giving them the chance to lift themselves out of hunger and extreme poverty. In the United States, it seeks to ensure that all people— especially those with the fewest resources—have access to the opportunities they need to succeed in school and life." Visit the Gates Foundation website to learn about current grants open to for-profit entities and how the foundation's grant process works.

Leona M. and Harry B. Helmsley Charitable Trust

The Helmsley Charitable Trust aims to "improve lives by supporting exceptional efforts in the U.S. and around the world in health and select place-based initiatives." The Trust provides grantees with financial resources, involvement with and monitoring of the project, and other resources. Many of the Trust's grant programs are reserved for nonprofit entities, and the Trust does not accept unsolicited proposals for most of its initiatives. That said, the Trust does issue requests for proposals (RFPs) for some of its initiatives, some of which are open to for-profit entities. All active RFPs are posted on the Helmsley Trust website, and each RFP specifies whether that initiative is open to for-profit applicants.

For example, at this writing the Trust has one RFP open to both for-profit and not-for-profit entities. The Future Technologies Initiative (FTI) of the Helmsley's Type 1 Diabetes (T1D) program seeks to "incubate proof-of-concept, early-stage research and development" of "novel insulin and glucagon delivery technologies" and "novel sensing technologies." FTI offers grants of up to $750,000 per project and will consider supporting one or more projects with a maximum term of 24 months. We're talking deep biomedical science and technology here. Not surprisingly, then, the qualification requirements, applicant vetting process, grant distribution, benchmarking, and management processes are rigorous.

PRIVATE GRANTS

An individual, group of individuals, financial institution, privately held company, or other entity that is neither a government agency nor a not-for-profit organization may offer grants to startups and/or small businesses. Many such private grants target startups and/or small businesses in one or more cities or states. Other private grants target startups and/or small businesses in a specified industry sector, or in both a certain industry and a certain location.

Connecticut Next: Entrepreneur Learner's Permit and Growth Grants

Connecticut Next (CTNext), a network of "passionate people" who support "busy entrepreneurs," is a subsidiary of Connecticut Innovations, a venture capital organization providing equity investments, strategic guidance, and partnership connections to Connecticut startups. The Entrepreneur's Learner's Permit program offers reimbursement grants of up to $1,500 for startups costs incurred by first-time entrepreneurs in biotechnology, green technology, and information technology industries. The Growth Company program offers grants of up to $25,000 to Connecticut-based early-stage companies with high growth potential and in high-growth industry sectors.

Federal Home Loan Bank of Indianapolis: Elevate Small Business Grant

Federal Home Loan Bank of Indianapolis (FHLBI) is an independent regional cooperative bank that is privately capitalized and owned by its member banks, credit unions, community development financial institutions (CDFIs), and insurers throughout Indiana and Michigan. Small business customers of FHLBI member banks can apply for an Elevate Small Business grant of up to $25,000. The grant applicant must be sponsored by the local FHLBI branch. Elevate grants can be used for capital expenditures, workforce training, or other eligible needs to assist with the growth and development of the business.

($) **Cultivate connections with changemakers and leaders in your lane.** An introduction or referral from an influencer within the grant maker's network can weigh in your favor. It could also help you get invited to apply for a plum grant program that is a great match for your venture but does not accept unsolicited proposals.

GRANTS FROM NONPROFIT ORGANIZATIONS

Nonprofit organizations such as trade associations, community development corporations, and groups or networks supporting entrepreneurs, small business owners, or inventors sometimes offer grant programs to for-profit ventures. A few examples follow.

CFDA/NYCDC Fashion Manufacturing Initiative

The Fashion Manufacturing Initiative (FMI), introduced in 2016, is a $6 million private-public partnership fund of the Council of Fashion Designers of America (CFDA) and the New York City Economic Development Corporation (NYCEDC). FMI offers grants of up to $300,000 to fashion manufacturing companies for the purpose of purchasing equipment, making capital and technology upgrades, workforce training, or relocation costs to within the City's five boroughs. Recipients of relocation grants are required to contribute a 25 percent match of the award; recipients of grants for other uses must contribute a 33 percent match. FMI grant recipients also have access to a database of fashion industry manufacturers and to a series of programs for the New York City manufacturing community, hosted by NYCEDC and CDFA in collaboration with industry leaders and experts.

National Association for the Self-Employed Growth Grants®

The NASE Foundation, the philanthropic arm of the National Association for the Self-Employed (NASE), a nonprofit membership association of self-employed business owners, awards one Growth Grant of up to $4,000 each month. To be eligible for the grant, the solo entrepreneur must be an NASE member in good standing ($120 a year for basic membership). The online application is much less involved than the grant application packages required by many grant-making agencies and organizations. The NASE selects grantees at its discretion based on business need, proposed use, probability of the grant satisfying the funding need, and the potential impact of the grant on the overall growth and success of the business. For more information, visit the NASE website.

Growth Grants a Welcome Hand up for Microentrepreneurs

Since its inception in 2006, the NASE Growth Grants program has awarded more than $1 million to owners of very small businesses throughout the United States. A check for a few thousand dollars can make a big difference to a one-person operation trying to grow and thrive. For example, Elisha Tiffee, owner of a Cinnaholic franchise in Dallas, Texas, a vegan bakery specializing in pastries such as cinnamon buns, cakes, cookies, and brownies, used her $4,000 NASE Growth Grant for expansion signage and an event catering display. David Speidel of Columbia Missouri, owner of SPRADCO (Speidel Research and Development Company), an energy and environmental consulting and engineering firm, used his $4,000 NASE Growth Grant to purchase new testing and sampling equipment. Darlene Molnar, an interior designer with clients in Washington, D.C., Virginia, and Maryland, used her $4,000 NASE Growth Grant to hire a professional photographer to roll out an aggressive marketing campaign.

COLLEGES AND UNIVERSITIES

Grant programs for entrepreneurs, small business owners, startup teams, and independent inventors are sometimes offered by various departments (business, science, technology) of academic institutions. In some cases, the applicants must be undergraduate, graduate, or postgraduate students of the college or university. Other college/university grant programs target startups and/or small businesses engaged in a certain area of research, innovation, or technology—such as the grants associated with the SBIR/STTR programs. (See Chapter 13, "Funding for Research and Technology Ventures.") Following are a few examples of the many grant programs offered to small businesses in various sectors by academic institutions throughout the United States.

Brown University, Jonathan M. Nelson Center for Entrepreneurship Grants

Brown's Nelson Center for Entrepreneurship offers a three-tiered business grant program—which I like because each grant is aimed at a critical early stage of business development.

Explore Grants of up to $500 are offered to fund the early discovery work of individual students or student teams pursuing any type of venture. Explore grant recipients work directly with Nelson Center staff to strategize how best to identify an unmet need and how best to determine which key assumptions and hypotheses to test. Explore teams often receive additional guidance from Brown alumni and industry experts.

Expand Grants are available for individual students or student teams that have identified an unmet need and are ready to start developing or testing a value proposition or solution to that need. Many Expand recipients use the grant funds to build prototypes or a "minimal viable product" for use in testing the problem they've identified. Expand grantees work closely with Nelson Center staff to develop a plan; they also have access and often make use of industry mentors and alumni experts.

Brown Venture Founders Grants, a partnership of Nelson Center for Entrepreneurship and Slater Technology Fund, offers new Brown graduates up to $50,000 to launch and grow their startups in Rhode Island. The Venture Founders program also provides grantee founders with dedicated mentorship, co-working space, and other resources for growing their startups.

Texas Women's University Women's Enterprise Training and Micro Grant Program

Launched in 2018, this grant program of TWU's Center for Women in Business (CWB) offers $5,000 grants to existing or emerging women-owned businesses in Texas with five or fewer employees. As a requisite to receiving the grant funds, grantees must complete a small business course hosted by TWU in Denton, Texas. Grant funds may be used for a variety of expenditures, including equipment, machinery, technology, inventory, raw material, fixtures, property improvements, and marketing.

University of Oregon, RAINmaker Grants

The Paul Anthony Troiano RAINmaker Fund offers seed grants (per year) of up to $5,000 for five student-led and -owned for-profit startups supported by the Regional Accelerator and Innovation Network (RAIN), Eugene node, at the University of Oregon. All current UO students, including undergraduates who are juniors and above and graduate students, in all disciplines may apply. UO students who graduated in the term immediately prior to the application deadline may also apply. Students in the School of Music and Dance are especially encouraged to apply.

 Consider alternative business grants—such as business competitions, business incubators/accelerators, and matched savings grants—which are more plentiful and easier to access than traditional grants. Please see Chapter 18, "Matched Savings Funding" and Chapter 19, "Incubator- and Accelerator-Based Funding." To learn about grants awarded to winners of business pitch, business plan, and other business competitions, check out the free, downloadable bonus chapter "Competition-Based Funding" at kedmaough.com.

TARGET FUNDING VARIABLES FOR GRANT FUNDING

Use any combination of the following keywords to search the Internet for potential grants for your business. For each search, specify one to three variables per each applicable keyword position—for example: small business, microenterprise, self employment (keyword #1); grant (keyword #2); United

States, New Mexico, economic development, gov (keyword #3); veteran owned, disabled (keyword #4).

Keyword #1	business | small business | startup | microenterprise | entrepreneur | self employment
Keyword #2	grant | business grant | growth grant
Keyword #3	United States | name of city | name of state | economic development | community development | gov | trust | foundation | org | edu
Keyword #4	(applicable diversity variable) hub zone | low income | woman owned | minority owned | veteran owned | disabled | LGBTQ | immigrant | refugee

CHAPTER

16

Funding for a Franchise

It has been said that opening a franchise is going into business for yourself without going it alone—and, I might add, without starting from scratch. The franchisor puts in the work and capital to develop and prove the concept, bring it to market, build a successful enterprise around it, and create a franchise system whereby others can own and operate a replica of the business. I call it a Business in a Box, as you literally get a box and unwrap it, and a fully formed business pops up and customers come rolling in. As a franchisee, you pay the franchisor for the right (license) to sell its products and/or services under the franchisor's brand and business model for a specified period of time. You also take on the work and costs of opening, operating, and growing your franchised business.

When buying a new franchise from a franchisor, you pay an up-front franchise fee—which vary, depending on the brand, from a few thousand to millions of dollars, with the majority falling in the $50,000 to $200,000 range. Some franchisors also charge a territory fee, which is usually optional and for an extended territory. The franchisor may include training in the franchise fee or charge a separate training fee, and some franchisors offer more advanced training at additional cost. If the franchise is a brick-and-mortar business, startup costs will also include signage, decor, and either rent and leasehold improvements or real estate construction. In addition, you'll need capital to cover expenses such as equipment, supplies, inventory (if applicable), professional fees (legal, licensing, etc.), insurances, advertising/marketing, utilities, and taxes. If the business requires staff, you'll also have hiring and payroll expenses.

When buying an existing franchise (*resale*), you pay the agreed-upon purchase price to the selling franchisee. The franchisor must authorize the resale, and a new franchise agreement will be drawn up between you and the franchisor, for which the fees and terms may differ from the franchise seller's. Many franchisors charge a resale transfer fee, paid by either you or the selling franchisee. Some franchisors will require you to go through their orientation and/or training program, for which you will be charged. You may also incur additional costs, such as for new equipment, lease-hold/building improvements, and inventory or other operating expenses.

Most franchisors collect recurring royalty and/or advertising/marketing fees, usually on a weekly or monthly basis. Franchise royalty fees average 5 to 6 percent of gross sales (less sales tax) but can go as low as 1 percent or as high as 50 percent. Some also charge an annual renewal fee, which is typically considerably less than the initial franchise fee.

Most franchisors require a new franchisee to pay 40 percent of the initial franchise fee with their own cash and/or other nonborrowed resources. Some new franchisees can pay the entire franchise fee out of their own pockets; most need to secure financing to help cover the initial franchise fee and/or other startup costs. Likewise, many franchise resale buyers need to finance a portion of the purchase price and/or other business expenses.

FREE ADVISING FOR PROSPECTIVE FRANCHISE OWNERS

There is no shortage of franchise consultants in the United States, many of which charge for their expertise and some of which provide guidance at no cost to the franchisee. Those that offer free advising or consulting to potential franchisees are typically franchise brokers who receive commissions on the franchise fees paid to the franchisor by new franchisees that the broker has referred to the franchisor.

A competent and credible franchise consultant will advise and guide you through the process of opening a franchise and will connect you with franchise opportunities and financing sources that are suitable for you. The challenge is to vet the franchise consultant before engaging his or her services. The International Franchise Association or your local Small Business Development Center may be able to provide you with a few recommendations. The Association of Small Business Development Centers has an agreement with FranNet, a leading franchise consulting company with more than 100 franchise consultants across the country. Other franchise trade organizations or a local SCORE office are also potential sources for a referral.

FINANCIAL INCENTIVES FOR NEW FRANCHISE OWNERS

Franchise companies sometimes offer a discount or a rebate on one or more of their franchise fees as an incentive for signing on new franchisees. These incentive programs are usually offered for a limited period of time, usually for a year, which may be extended for another year if the program is working and the franchisor is focused on adding new franchise units. For example, Penn Station East Coast Subs offered a rebate of the first year of royalty payment to new stores opened in 2017 and extended the program throughout 2018. Other franchise brands offer financial incentives to new franchises in certain territories—again, usually for a limited period of time. For example, Sonic Drive-In offers a discount on its licensing fee to new units in select locations, and Long John Silver's 2018 incentive program offers no initial franchise fee, free hardware for its drive-thru-of-the-future system, and a reduced royalty schedule for three years for new franchise owners.

Some franchise companies offer financial incentives to new (first unit) franchisees owned by entrepreneurs of a certain diversity group. For example, Global Franchise Group, which has six quick service restaurant (QSR) franchise brands, including Roundtable Pizza and Marble Slab Creamery, offers 25 percent off the first-store franchise fee to veteran-owned stores and 15 percent off the development fee of two or more stores owned by a woman or a minority. Weed Man offers veteran franchisees 25 percent off the initial franchise fee, and Edible Arrangements gives veterans $10,000 off the first-store franchise fee.

Less common is a franchisee discount program with an indefinite or at least a longer timeline—like the FASTSTART program offered by FASTSIGNS. With FASTSTART, new franchisees get a 50 percent discount off the first year's royalties as an incentive for them to invest that money into marketing their new FASTSIGNS business.

Financial incentives are essentially granting—franchise funding you don't have to pay back or pay interest on. Getting a discount or rebate on franchise fees is great, provided the franchise brand is also affordable and up your alley. Finding potential franchising opportunities that hit all of those marks will take some research on your part—a process that can be facilitated by enlisting the free assistance of a reputable franchise advisor, such as an SBDC counselor or a FranNet consultant.

> VetFran, a program of the International Franchise Association (IFA), gives aspiring veteran franchise owners access to more than 600 US franchise brands that offer financial incentives to veteran franchise owners. For more information, please see Chapter 4, "Funding for Veteran-Owned Businesses."

FINANCING OPTIONS FOR FRANCHISEES

Some franchisors provide their own debt financing to franchisees, often on a case-by-case basis and typically in addition to referring franchisees to third-party lenders. Anytime Fitness, MaidPro, Signal 88 Security, Snap-on Tools, and Weed Man are but a few of the many franchise brands that offer direct financing to select franchisees. Some finance the entire debt burden, while others finance a portion (fraction) of the debt. The franchisor may provide flexible loan terms—for example, a loan based on simple interest, no principal, and a balloon payment in 5 or 10 years, or with the first payment due in 6 months or 12 months down the line. As an alternative to making loans to franchisees, some franchisors will guarantee a loan or a specified portion of the loan. Other franchisors help fund costs in other ways—such as building a new store for and leasing the location to a new franchisee, or allowing the franchisee to pay the initial franchise fee in installments.

In many cases, however, the franchisee will need to secure debt financing from a source other than the franchisor—whether for up-front franchise fees, equipment, real property acquisition/construction, leasehold improvement, or operating expenses. Because of the unique aspects of the franchisor-franchisee partnership and the finance solutions required to support that business model, franchisors often encourage franchisees to seek financing from lenders that specialize in franchise financing and with whom that franchisor has a relationship. In fact, many franchisors will introduce qualified franchisees (new or existing) to its affiliated lenders.

The accessibility of business loans for the purchase, opening, improvement, or operating expenses of a franchise business is similar to that of an independent small business and is more accessible than for nonfranchise startups. To qualify for a franchise business loan, borrowers need to have good credit and sufficient liquid assets and valuable collateral. Lenders also consider the success, stability, and growth potential of the franchisor. In addition, most lenders expect the franchisee to kick in at least 25 percent of the initial franchise fee and startup costs—as do most franchisors.

$ **Check the franchisor's Franchise Disclosure Agreement (FDD) for financing options it offers.** Item #10 of the FDD (a legal document all franchisors must supply to potential franchisees) will indicate whether the franchisor offers financing directly to its franchisees and/or works through affiliated third-party lenders.

Lending Marketplaces Specializing in Franchise Financing

A lending marketplace is an online lending platform, typically owned by a fintech company, that connects borrowers with suitable lenders in its database and brokers loans through that network of lenders. You may be able to secure a business loan with a general business lending marketplace like OnDeck and Prosper. However, given the intricacies and complexities of the franchisor-franchisee partnership and of financing a franchise, you may be better off using an online lending marketplace that caters to franchisees—solely, primarily, or as an area of specialization.

Among the most popular lending marketplaces specializing in franchise financing are ApplePie Capital, Benetrends Financial, BoeFly, FranFund, and Guidant Financial. Let's take a quick look at two of those marketplaces, ApplePie Capital and Benetrends.

ApplePie. The first online lender dedicated solely to franchise financing, ApplePie offers a wide range of SBA, startup, business, and equipment loan options—including remodel/refresh and refinance/recapitalization loans—through a network of diverse lenders. In addition, the company has secured more than $500 million from investors to make its own

ApplePie Core loans. Lends exclusively to new and existing franchisees in 50 states. Features include: growth-oriented capital, competitive and variable interest rates, interest-only grace period on new units, 5- to 10-year payment terms, flexible collateral options, and no prepayment penalty options.

Benetrends. A preferred partner of the International Franchise Association (IFA), Benetrends provides both franchise and small business financing solutions through its lending network. Its signature product, The Rainmaker Plan, is a 401(k)/IRA rollover funding program that enables penalty-free and tax-free use of retirement funds to start a business. Benetrends also brokers SBA loans, equipment and large asset loans, and other business loans as well as equipment leasing with buyout options. A financial solutions supplier to the franchise industry for more than 30 years, Benetrends boasts a 97 percent SBA loan approval rate, amounting to some $12 million per month in client approvals.

A POWER COUPLE TAPS INTO SPECIALIZED FRANCHISE FUNDING TO ROW INTO THEIR FUTURE

Gyee and Bob O'Malley, a Massachusetts couple who had professional careers in healthcare and IT consulting as well as five rental properties, wanted to add to and diversify their income stream. Gyee was looking for something she was passionate about that could run as a semi-absentee owner and build a large business around. Their ultimate goal was to eventually leave their corporate jobs.

When searching online produced nothing that fit their bill, the O'Malleys connected with FranNet and used FranNet's matching process to identify franchise opportunities that better met their goals and needs. After narrowing it down to and carefully evaluating about five franchise brands, they decided on RowHouse, a network of boutique fitness studios for indoor rowing enthusiasts.

FranNet connected the O'Malleys with Benetrends Financial, which provided free customized prequalification for an SBA loan as well as guidance in utilizing Benetrend's Rainmaker program, which allows tax- and penalty-free use of retirement funds to start a business. The couple used the Rainmaker financing, which enabled them to move forward with their three-store franchise deal and begin construction debt-free, reserving their ability to secure an SBA loan later to expand their business.

Direct Lenders Specializing in Franchise Financing

If you prefer to borrow directly from a more traditional lender, then I suggest targeting your search to financial institutions that specialize in franchise financing—such as Bank of America, Bridge Group Financing, PNC Financial Services Group, and United Community Bank. Most banks and other financing companies that focus on franchise financing offer SBA loans as well as other loan products that complement the franchise business model, including startup financing and equipment loans. By way of example, here are brief profiles of two direct franchise lenders.

- **Bridge Group Financial Group.** A wholly owned subsidiary of BankUnited, N.A., Bridge Group Financial Group (BFG) provides financing solution solely to US franchisees of regional and national brands. BFG's Franchise Lending division offers a suite of fixed-rate loans, including loans for acquiring and developing new units as well as for acquiring, reimaging, and relocating existing franchises. BFG also offers equipment loan and leasing options for various types of equipment and assets across several industries.

- **United Community Bank.** UCBI is a regional bank providing personal, corporate, retail, and small business banking and financial advisory services to 140 communities in Georgia, North Carolina, South Carolina, and Tennessee. With its small business franchise financing program, UCBI works with the franchisor to develop a concept-specific lending plan geared to the individual franchisee's needs. UCBI has preferred lender status with many regional and national franchise brands and finances new, existing, and multistore franchisees. Loan sizes range from $150,000 to $10 million, with repayment terms of up to 10 years (equipment) and 25 years (real estate) and equity injection requirements as low as 10 percent (real estate) and 15 percent (leasehold improvements). United Community Bank offers SBA loans as well as other business loans to its franchise customers.

To improve your chances of finding a suitable direct lender, ask for a recommendation from a franchise consultant, the franchisor you want to partner with, or a franchise trade organization such as the International Franchise Association.

SBA LOANS FOR SMALL FRANCHISE BUSINESSES

The Small Business Administration (SBA) has a soft spot for both new and existing franchises! In fact, about 10 percent of all SBA loans—primarily SBA 7(a) and SBA CDC/504 loans—go to franchisees. An SBA-guaranteed loan is a great financing option for franchisees that can't get a conventional bank loan, as long as they meet the qualification criteria *and* the franchisor is one of the 2,500 or so vetted franchisors on the SBA's Franchise Directory. If your franchise brand is not on the directory, the franchisor can apply for inclusion by submitting its Franchise Disclosure Document (FDD) to the SBA; if it measures up, the franchisor will be added to the directory.

An SBA loan has advantages over many other loan options—such as more favorable interest and terms, lower down payments, no prepayment penalty, and loans of $5,000 to $5 million. It also has some disadvantages—such as the lengthy and complicated application process, stringent use provisions (i.e., franchise royalty excluded), strict adherence to the 5 Cs of creditworthiness, and 10 to 30 percent collateralization. (For more information on SBA loans, check out the free, downloadable bonus chapter "Debt Funding" at kedmaough.com.)

FIRST COMES LOVE, THEN COMES ENTREPRENEURSHIP

Charlotte, North Carolina, residents Kia and Clarence Lyons decided long before they said "I do" that, once they'd saved up enough money (as they had to pay for their $30,000 wedding), they would start their own business. The couple also planned to start a family, so Kia researched businesses that would enable them to "break into entrepreneurship" without being all-consuming. The Lyons chose to open a Popbar franchise, a quick service restaurant (QSR) that serves up healthy popsicles.

Armed with a great location, 20 percent of startup costs, good credit scores, and plenty of collateral (real estate), they applied for a loan at the local branch of a large bank and were rejected. They tried a smaller community bank and got another no, but the loan officer referred them to Carolina Small Business Development Fund (CSBDF). CSBDF is a nonprofit community development financial institution (CDFI) that provides loans to Main Street businesses and targets minority entrepreneurs like the Lyons.

Kia and Clarence received a CSBDF loan for 80 percent of the approximately $375,000 they needed for startup costs, including build-out and equipment. They opened their Popbar franchise in January 2017 and have been serving pops of gelato, yogurt, and sorbet on a stick happily ever after.

RESOURCES

Franchise Direct. Founded in 1998, Franchise Direct is among the pioneering Internet lead-generation platforms for franchise brands and is one of the world's leading online portals for franchise opportunities, knowledge, and resources—including franchise financing sources. The online franchise opportunity directory can be searched using a variety of filters: industry, location, investment amount (franchise fee), low-cost brands, brands offering special financing, SBA-approved brands, and more.

Franchise Times. The *Franchise Times* print magazine combined with its online content portal is the definitive source of news and information for the franchise industry. The website is loaded with resources, including a directory of franchise finance sources and a directory of franchise opportunities. The online content is free; the magazine is by paid subscription.

International Franchise Association (IFA). Founded in 1960, IFA is the most prominent franchise trade association in the United States, with over 1,300 franchisor members, 13,550 franchisee members, and 675 supplier members. In addition to its extensive advocacy and best-practices work, IFA provides news, information, educational opportunities, and resources to franchisors and franchisees. Through its online directories, events, website, and relationships with franchisor members, IFA keeps franchisees abreast of franchise opportunities in the United States and in 70 key franchise markets around the world. The IFA website also includes a directory of suppliers, including providers of franchise financing, many of which have alliances with IFA and IFA franchisor members.

TARGET FUNDING VARIABLES FOR FRANCHISE FUNDING

Use any combination of the following keywords to search the Internet for potential franchise funding for your business. For each search, specify one to three variables per each applicable keyword position—for example: franchise, business (keyword #1); financing, loan (keyword #2); United States, Pennsylvania, economic development (keyword #3); immigrant, minority owned (keyword #4).

Keyword #1   franchise | franchisee | business | small business | startup

Keyword #2   financing | franchise financing | loan | equipment leasing | franchisee discount

Keyword #3   United States | name of city | name of state | economic development | community development

Keyword #4   (applicable diversity variable) hub zone | low income | woman owned | minority owned | veteran owned | disabled | LGBTQ

Government Procurement–Based Funding

The United States federal government is the largest purchaser of goods and services in the country, and more than $100 billion in federal procurement contracts annually goes to small businesses. State and local government agencies, too, buy a substantial amount and variety of products and services from a wide range of companies, including small businesses.

Government contracting and subcontracting can help launch or accelerate a small business. The guarantee of ongoing revenue provided by a government contract, which can extend three or even five years, can help stabilize cash flow. The stature of being a government contractor can help attract commercial clients and secure financing to operate or expand the business.

But bidding against big corporations for government contracts is a formidable task. To level the playing field, the federal government, as well as virtually all state governments and many local governments, have established programs that "set aside" certain procurement contracts for small businesses. Those set-asides are sometimes mandated but are more often "preferred" goals.

Those set-aside goals might open the gates to the government contracting playing field, but they don't exactly level the playing field. Selling to the government is much different than selling to the commercial sector, and competing for government contracts poses significant challenges for small businesses. The government procurement process, especially at the federal level, involves navigating a maze of complex rules, regulations, paperwork, and procedures. Every federal agency has different set-aside goals and contracting procedures. Likewise, every state and sometimes individual counties and/or cities within a state have their own procurement requirements and processes.

In recognition of this reality, multiple programs have been established to provide procurement education, advice, and assistance at no cost or low cost to small businesses. Getting free or substantially discounted business assistance that enables you to create a new revenue stream—saving money on the resources needed to make money—is a great funding opportunity!

FEDERAL PROCUREMENT PROGRAMS FOR SMALL BUSINESSES

The US Small Business Administration (SBA) oversees federal small business procurement programs and works with 24 federal agencies toward the goal of awarding 23 percent of prime government contracts to eligible small businesses. Of that 23 percent, 5 percent is reserved for small disadvantaged businesses, 5 percent for women-owned small businesses, 3 percent for service-disabled veteran-owned small businesses, and 3 percent for small businesses in historically underutilized business (HUB) zones.

The SBA and its partnering agencies and organizations offer procurement assistance programs to help small businesses:

- Determine whether the company offers products and/or services the government buys and has the resources to provide those goods and/or services
- Get the proper certification(s) to participate in federal government contracting programs
- Receive business training and mentoring to learn how federal contracting and subcontracting work
- Qualify for exclusive set-aside and sole-source contracts
- Partner with established contractors as a subcontractor
- Identify and bid on federal contracting opportunities

All companies that wish to participate in SBA procurement assistance programs must be certified by the SBA as a small business enterprise.

In addition, the SBA oversees the following small business contracting programs.

- **8(a) Small Disadvantaged Business Development (BD) Program.** Offers procurement assistance and contract opportunities to small businesses that are at least 51 percent owned and managed by an economically or socially disadvantaged individual. Requires SBA small business certification and 8(a) BD certification.

- **Historically Underutilized Business Zone (HUBZone) Program.** Offers procurement assistance and contract opportunities to small businesses located in economically depressed areas designated as HUBZones. Requires SBA small business certification and HUBZone certification.

- **Service-Disabled Veteran-Owned Small Business Program.** Offers procurement assistance and contract opportunities to small businesses that are at least 51 percent owned and managed by a US veteran with a service-related disability. Requires SBA small business certification.

- **Women-Owned Small Business (WOSB) Program.** Offers procurement assistance and contract opportunities to small businesses that are at least 51 percent owned and managed by a woman. Requires SBA small business certification and WOSB certification.

To take advantage of the SBA's federal procurement opportunities for small businesses, one must first learn how to contract with the federal government, which is a complicated process, and secure the appropriate certification(s). Many for-profit companies offer government contracting training, certification, and consulting—for a price, often a hefty price. Why pay a premium price for federal contracting assistance from a private company when several federal agencies and some nonprofit organizations provide top-notch federal contracting education, certification, guidance, and technical assistance—at no or nominal cost to small businesses? Following are some great sources of free and affordable federal procurement assistance.

- **Minority Business Development Agency (MBDA).** The MBDA, an agency of the US Department of Commerce, operates 28 MBDA centers around the country, each of which is focused on promoting the growth of minority business enterprises (MBEs) in that respective region. This includes providing free assistance to clients in acquiring 8(a) and other relevant procurement certifications, understanding government contracting processes, and identifying and accessing federal (as well as state, local, and commercial) contracting opportunities.

- **SCORE.** Supported by the SBA, SCORE is a nationwide non-profit organization offering no-cost and low-cost business counseling provided by a network of more than 11,000 volunteer mentors. SCORE mentors with expertise in government procurement are available at SCORE offices throughout the country to provide advice and assistance to startups and small businesses interested in government contractor or subcontracting.

- **SBA Commercial Market Representatives.** Located in six offices around the country, commercial market representatives (CMRs) help small business owners find and bid on subcontracting opportunities through prime contractors with federal agencies. A CMR directory is on the SBA website.

- **SBA Learning Center.** The SBA website's Learning Center has a free online course that helps small businesses understand the basics of federal government contracting. The SBA website also features a Contracting Guide that covers the basics of small business contracting with the federal government.

- **SBA Mentor-Protégé Program.** This program matches a certified 8(a) small business (*protégé*) with a corporate business executive (*mentor*) for the purpose of enhancing an 8(a) firm's capabilities to successfully compete for federal government contracts. The mentor, or Business Opportunity Specialist (BOS), provides multiple forms of support, including business development, technical training, financing, subcontracts, and assistance in securing and fulfilling prime contracts.

- **SBA Procurement Center Representatives.** Through offices in six key areas around the country, a network of procurement center representatives (PCRs), each specializing in contracts awarded by one or more specific federal agencies, provide procurement counseling to small businesses and assist small businesses with the contracting process and payment issues. A PCR directory is on the SBA website.

- **SBA Procurement Technical Assistance Centers.** This network of almost 100 Procurement Technical Assistance Centers (PTACs) with 300 offices nationwide is the go-to source for small businesses who do or want to contract with federal, state, and/or local government agencies. (Both the Association of PTACs website and the SBA website feature a director of PTAC locations.) Each PTAC offers one-on-one government-contracting assistance at no cost or nominal cost. A PTAC counselor in your area can help you to:
  - Determine whether your business is ready for government contracting
  - Get the appropriate certifications
  - Register your business in various government procurement databases
  - Market your business to government agencies
  - Find and bid on contracts
  - Measure your performance and comply with contract audits

- **SBA Small Business Development Centers.** Your local SBDC business counselor can provide you with free government contracting advice and connect you with local sources of government contracting training and assistance.

- **SBA Women's Business Centers.** Each of the 100+ Women's Business Centers (WBCs) across the United States works with local SBA offices and community partners to provide women entrepreneurs with free counseling and assistance with all aspects of business development, including government contracting.

SBA SUPPORT AND A SMART STRATEGY LEAD TO GOVERNMENT CONTRACTS AND GROWTH

ELYON International, headquartered in Vancouver, Washington, provides management consulting, information technology, geospatial, and professional support services to a diversity of government and commercial clients nationwide. Founded in 1997 by army veteran Carmen Nazario, ELYON is an SBA-certified 8(a) and HUBZone small business enterprise as well as both an Oregon and Washington State-certified woman-owned, minority-owned, and veteran-owned small business.

In its early years, ELYON contracted solely to civilian companies and organizations. To help her better understand the government contracting landscape, Carmen sought advice and assistance from SBA Small Business Specialists in Portland, Oregon, and Vancouver, Washington, and attended government contracting workshops. She was also awarded an SBA 8(a) Academy scholarship sponsored by SBA and Howard University School of Business. This invaluable and no-cost guidance and training helped Carmen to develop a road map for targeting the "low-hanging fruit"—that is, contracting opportunities for which ELYON qualified under one or more of its government procurement set-aside certifications.

ELYON'S first government contract was as a subcontractor to a large US Department of Defense contractor. "Government contracting is complex, and there's a big learning curve," explained Carmen, ELYON CEO and president. "Starting small, as a subcontractor, was a big help because we could ask the prime contractor questions, and they sometimes provided help with paperwork, especially security paperwork when we had to onboard employees."

The government contracting training and experience also helped Carmen to better market herself and her business, resulting in ELYON's growth in federal and civilian sectors. ELYON's success under Carmen's leadership has been recognized with the US Small Business Administration's (SBA) Portland District 2009 Minority Business Person of the Year award, Hispanic Chamber of Commerce 2014 Bravo Award, Northwest Mountain Minority Supplier Development Council's 2014 Supplier of the Year Award, SBA Portland District 2017 Graduate of the Year, and SBA Region 10 2017 Graduate of the Year.

STATE AND LOCAL GOVERNMENT PROCUREMENT PROGRAMS

Your local Procurement Technical Assistance Center (PTAC) can help you register with your state, county, or municipal procurement agency, research potential contracting opportunities with that agency, and respond to contracting opportunities that align with your business. To find a PTAC in your area, use the searchable PTAC directory on the Association of Procurement Technical Assistance Centers website.

You can also visit the procurement office or website of your state or local government to find out whether it has a small business procurement program and, if so, the rules and other details of that program. In most cases, there are no or nominal fees to apply and to register for a state or local small business contracting program. Some state and local procurement offices offer free orientation and training for small business contractors or will refer you to the local PTAC, SBA, SBDC, or SCORE office for government procurement training and counseling.

Following are examples of state, county, and municipal small business procurement programs.

Texas Economic Department

The state government of Texas requires all Texas state agencies to "make a good faith effort" to award contracts for construction services and commodity purchases to qualified small business enterprises that are certified as historically underutilized businesses (HUBs). The Texas Comptroller's office administers the State's HUB certification and registration process. To obtain HUB certification, the business must be:

- A for-profit entity, located and operating in Texas, that meets the size standards prescribed by Texas Administrative Code
- At least 51 percent owned and operated by a resident of Texas who is an Asian-Pacific American, Black American, Hispanic American, Native American, American woman, or service-disabled veteran

In addition, the Texas Department of Transportation (TxDOT), as an agency funded by the U.S. Department of Transportation, has a

Disadvantaged Business Enterprise (DBE) program that awards contracts to eligible SBA-certified minority-owned and women-owned small businesses.

The Texas Economic Department refers small businesses to local SCORE mentors, SBA Small Business Development Centers, and Procurement Technical Assistance Centers for government procurement training and counseling.

Cuyahoga County (Ohio) Office of Procurement and Diversity

The Cuyahoga County government seeks to award contracts to certified small business enterprises (SBEs), minority business enterprises (MBEs), and women business enterprises (WBEs). To qualify, an SBE must be located and doing business in Cuyahoga County, and an MBE or WBE must be located and doing business in the Cleveland Contracting Market, which includes Cuyahoga, Geauga, Lake, Lorain, Medina, and Summit Counties.

The County has its own SBE/MBE/WBE certification application, but also has a "quick certify" application for SBEs, MBEs, and WBEs certified by the State of Ohio or the City of Cleveland. Prior to certification and registration, the County's Small Business Enterprise Program provides opportunities for small firms to develop business skills, to learn contracting regulations and processes, and to effectively bid on contracting and subcontracting opportunities.

Metro (Portland, Oregon)

Metro is the governing agency for the 24 cities and three counties that make up the greater Portland metropolitan area, "the urban heart of Oregon." Metro solicits bids and proposals from business that are certified by the State of Oregon's Certification Office for Business Inclusion and Diversity (COBID)—that is, minority-owned, women-owned, service-disabled veteran-owned, and emerging small businesses. Through the Oregon Procurement Information Network (ORPIN), Metro requests bids from COBID-certified contractors for public improvement projects between $5,000 and $50,000 and requests proposals from COBID-certified contractors for professional, technical, and scientific services projects between $10,000 and $50,000.

The COBID website links to the Oregon Procurement Information Network (ORPIN) website, which directs visitors to the website of Business Oregon, an Oregon State government agency, for procurement assistance resources. The Business Oregon's Resources page lists organizations that provide procurement assistance to small businesses, including AVITA Associates (my consulting business!), the Government Contract Assistance Program (Oregon's Procurement Technical Assistance Center, PTAC), Oregon Department of Transportation (ODOT), three SCORE chapters, and local SBA and SBDC offices.

TARGET FUNDING VARIABLES FOR GOVERNMENT PROCUREMENT-BASED FUNDING

Use any combination of the following keywords to search the Internet for potential government contracting-related funding for your business. For each search, specify one to three variables per each applicable keyword position—for example: small business enterprise, government procurement (keyword #1); technical assistance, financing (keyword #2); New Mexico, gov, economic development (keyword #3); women business enterprise (keyword #4).

Keyword #1   small business enterprise | minority business enterprise | women business enterprise

Keyword #2   government procurement | government contracting | SBE certification | MBE certification | WBE certification | SBA 8(a) certification | financing | loan | technical assistance | business training | business resources | United States | name of city | name of state | federal | gov | economic development

Keyword #3   (applicable diversity variable) hub zone | disadvantaged | inclusion | diversity | woman owned | minority owned | veteran owned | disabled | LGBTQ

PART SIX

Funding for the Unbankable

Matched Savings Funding

A matched savings grant, commonly known as an *individual develop-ment account* (IDA), is a special savings account established for the pur-pose of helping low-income, low-wealth individuals save money toward an asset-building expenditure, such as starting or expanding a business. For every dollar the accountholder deposits in the IDA account, the IDA sponsor makes a matching contribution (*grant*) of one dollar or more. To participate in an IDA, the accountholder agrees to save a set amount of money within a defined timeline. The IDA accountholder also receives financial education and credit counseling as a requisite to participating in the IDA program.

Once the training requirements and savings goal are met, the spon-sor's matched funds are deposited into the entrepreneur's account. The entrepreneur/business owner then has the option to either use the com-bined funds (savings plus matched grant) to pay for the targeted business expense(s) or to deposit the money into a business capitalization account for later use.

Let's say you open an IDA program in which you will save $100 a month for 18 months and the IDA sponsor will kick in $5 for each dollar you save (5:1 match). At the end of 18 months, you would have $10,800 in your IDA ($1,800 you saved + $9,800 matched saving grant)—in addition to interest earned—to help fund your business.

Out of all the funding options available, the IDA program is my favor-ite to share with my clients because it is so versatile. It can be used to build a business, to go to or finish college to acquire knowledge and creden-tials needed for a business, or even to make disability accommodations in your workplace that may not be supported by a state agency or Medicare/ Medicaid. In addition, once you've met the requirements and reached your savings goal, you not only get the matched grant, you also can withdraw the funds you saved to use for your business; you aren't required to keep any of those funds in savings. Another benefit is that you can go through the program more than once, as long as the goals are different. Where else can you get a 5 to 1 match, or 4 to 1, or 3 to 1, or even a 2 to 1 return on the money you save? Certainly not your bank. Meanwhile, you learn how to properly save money.

IDA programs, which have been used as an asset-building strategy since 1990, are partnerships between a sponsoring organization (state or local government agency and/or a nonprofit organization) and a financial institution (bank, credit union, community development financial institution). A sponsoring organization may operate the IDA program independently or as a regional or statewide collaborative. The sponsoring agency/organization provides the matched funding and typically provides the training and technical assistance as well; the financial institution holds and reports on the savings account.

State laws authorizing the establishment and funding of IDA programs have been enacted in each of the 50 states. At least one IDA program exists in every state, and most states have multiple IDA programs. Funding for an IDA program always comes, in part, from state coffers. Funding may also come from the financial institution partnering with the organization or agency sponsoring the IDA program and/or from foundations and other charitable organizations. The largest funder of IDA programs is the federal Assets for Independence (AFI) program; however, the US government suspended funding for AFI in 2017, a suspension that continues at this writing.

You must be a resident of the state in which you apply for an IDA, and you must complete the financial education courses specified by the organization sponsoring the IDA program. Not all IDA programs allow the matched savings funds to be used for business expenses; many IDA programs are reserved for buying a home and/or a higher education goal.

Eligibility criteria and other terms and conditions—such as maximum household income level, allowable business expenses, minimum and maximum accountholder deposits, amount of matched dollar contributions, savings time period, and allowable withdrawals—vary from program to program. Some IDA programs target a certain diversity group, such as minorities, Native Americans, or women.

SOURCES OF IDA MATCHED SAVINGS FUNDING

Following are a few representative IDA programs that can be used to help fund a microenterprise or small business.

($) **If you receive disability benefits, check with your case worker to determine whether participation in an IDA might affect your benefits.** Many government agencies that fund IDA programs require that the accountholder's deposits to an IDA be made from earned income. Because benefits such as SSD, SSI, and SSDI are not considered earned income, you would need another source of income to contribute to an IDA. You will also need to ensure that you don't exceed the asset limit set by the SSI program; otherwise, you could lose benefits.

Austin (Texas) Individual Development Account Program

This IDA program is sponsored by the City of Austin's Neighborhood Housing and Community Development (NHCD) agency and accounts are held and administered by Velocity Credit Union.

Eligibility	Resident of the city of Austin or qualifying surrounding area. Complete 16 hours of financial education, 8 hours of which must be completed prior to enrollment in the IDA program by way of graduating from the 8-hour Realizing the American Dream class.
Goal	$25 minimum, $200 maximum per month, up to $2,000 total.
Match	3:1. Deposited monthly into a reserve fund held by the City of Austin.
Withdraw	Funds released directly to the vendor for an approved business asset purchase.

Community Action Partnership (CAP) of North Dakota

Eligibility	Residents of North Dakota that meet the household income requirements at time of acceptance into the IDA program. Completion of 10 hours of financial literacy training and 8 hours of asset-specific training.
Goal	$25 minimum per month, for at least six consecutive months. Up to $2,000 within 24 months.
Match	2:1.
Withdraw	Funds must be saved for and spent on a business asset within 24 months.

Mercy Corps Northwest

Mercy Corps Northwest (MCNW) is the nonprofit arm of Mercy Enterprise Corporation, an Oregon-based community development financial institution (CDFI) working to improve the economic self-sufficiency and community integration of low-income citizens throughout the region. MCNW serves as the US economic development office of Mercy Corps Global, a Portland-based international nonprofit relief and development agency. Almost 40 percent of MCNW's business programs' clients come from Hispanic, African American, Asian, American Indian, and other minority communities. The majority of MCNW clients live at or slightly above the federal poverty line and below 80 percent of median family income (MFI); rarely do clients have household incomes exceeding 200 percent of the prevailing federal poverty rate.

Eligibility	Resident of Oregon or Washington state, for use in launching a microenterprise or small business that will build the household's assets and contribute to the community's and state's economic strength. Completion two months prior to achieving savings goal of at least one of five authorized classes, four conducted by MCNW and one by Portland State University's Business Development department. Other business workshops may qualify, determined on a case-by-case basis.

Goal	6–24 months. Monthly deposits required. Targeted savings amount and timeline based on the participant's budget and the length of time needed to implement the participant's business plan. Graduating participants are also preapproved for a $1,000 low-interest, credit-building loan. Oregon participants may participate in a second IDA under certain circumstances.
Match	5:1.
Withdraw	Matched savings grant funds disbursed upon completion of training and attainment of savings goal. Funds must be utilized for approved business expenses within four months.
Use	Primarily hard asset purchases, such as equipment and machinery. Business and/or professional training expenses allowed. Up to 25 percent of funds for sustainable marketing, such as website design, signage, and professional branding. Vehicle purchases only if the vehicles is the business's primary asset—for example, food cart or truck, taxi, delivery business, farm truck.

A MATCHED SAVINGS GRANT HELPS TURN A FANCIFUL DREAM INTO A THRIVING BUSINESS

In 2011, Celese N. Williams was a single mom of a three-year-old, employed at a desk job making barely over minimum wage, and struggling to make ends meet. A lifelong amateur artist, Celese wanted to turn her face-painting hobby into a business. Although she had little knowledge of how to run a business and no one to ask for advice, she took a leap of faith. Using her employer's computer after work, Celese built a basic website and opened a business account with what little money she had. The banker told Celese about the matched savings grant program offered by Mercy Corps Northwest, a local branch of the global nonprofit agency dedicated to helping economically disadvantaged people transform their lives.

She worked and saved for three years, during which she also attended Mercy Corp Northwest's Business Foundations classes. For every dollar Celese put into her individual development account (IDA), Mercy Corps contributed five dollars. In 2013, she received her matched savings grant and bought her first-ever computer. Celese says that having her own laptop was "a turning point for her business" and that the business seminars were also "a huge asset," giving her the knowledge and tools to grow her business.

The success of her business enabled Celese to get off public assistance completely, quit her "desk job" and focus solely on her business, and support her daughter. She was even able to attend college, and in 2017 received an associate degree in art, becoming a first-generation college grad in her family.

In business now for seven years, Mystique's Fancy Faces not only provides gainful employment for Celese but also enables her to employ five contract employees to assist her with events—which are much in demand. She's worked with "dream clients" throughout the Portland, Oregon area, including Nike, Columbia Sportswear, the Oregon Zoo, Hewlett-Packard, Intel, and many others. She was contracted to face paint for a national ad campaign for T-Mobile, and in 2018, she landed the biggest opportunity of her career—face painting for an upcoming Disney film.

HOW TO FIND AN IDA PROGRAM NEAR YOU

An easy way to locate an IDA program is to use the Find an IDA Program map on the website of Prosperity Now (formerly CFED), a research and advocacy nonprofit organization with a mission to help "open the door to financial opportunity" to low-income and low-wealth individuals throughout the United States. This interactive map of the United States pinpoints more than 1,000 IDA program providers across the nation. Clicking on an IDA location icon activates a pop-up window that contains a website link and/or contact and program information (including allowable use of funds) for that IDA provider.

Another way to find IDA programs in your area is to contact the agency or organization that oversees the statewide IDA (*asset building* or *matched savings*) program (*initiative*) in your state—such as the Midas Collaborative in Massachusetts, the Ohio CDC Association's Assets Ohio program, and the Oregon IDA Initiative. I love the Oregon IDA Initiative's website—which enables you to search for IDA providers by county and type (business, education, home purchase, home repair). When I searched the site for business IDAs in Washington County (the Portland Metro area), a dozen IDA programs popped up—including one that focuses on entrepreneurs with disabilities and four that focus on minority-owned small businesses. I also discovered that about a quarter (22 percent in 2017) of all IDA participants in my home state of Oregon use their IDA funds to start or expand a microenterprise.

TARGET FUNDING VARIABLES FOR MATCHED SAVINGS GRANTS

Use any combination of the following keywords to search the Internet for potential matched savings funding for your business. For each search, specify one to three variables per each applicable keyword position—for example: business (keyword #1), matched savings, IDA (keyword #2); Ft. Lauderdale, Florida, Broward County (keyword #3); disadvantaged, low income (keyword #4).

Keyword #1	business | small business | microenterprise
Keyword #2	matched savings | individual development account | IDA | grant | program | asset building
Keyword #3	name of city | name of state | name of county | economic development | community development | gov | org | CDFI
Keyword #4	(applicable diversity variable) disadvantaged | low income | woman owned | minority owned | veteran owned | disabled | LGBTQ | immigrant | refugee | urban | rural

CHAPTER
19

Incubator- and
Accelerator-Based Funding

Incubators and accelerators are organizations designed to help entrepreneurs fine-tune and advance their early-stage businesses. The organization may be a for-profit company (e.g., venture capital firm or large corporation), nonprofit organization (e.g., community development corporation or corporate foundation), government agency (e.g., state or local commerce or economic development department), or public institution (e.g., university or research lab).

Most business incubators and accelerators are intensive, goal-driven, problem-solving, action-based (*experiential*) programs in which entrepreneurs work closely with a team of experts. The support provided may include mentoring, free or low-cost workspace, technical assistance, pro bono or low-cost business services, free or discounted business resources, and access to grants, loans, or investment capital.

Incubators and accelerators often have a vested interest in the success of startups in their programs—by way of either the funding the organization itself receives or their equity stakes in cohort companies. Consequently, incubators/accelerators tend to surround their cohorts with highly specialized and exceptional quality mentors. Mentors are typically successful entrepreneurs, corporate executives, thought leaders, industry experts, and/or investors with expertise in the incubator's or accelerator's target area—which may be defined by industry sector, geographic location, and/or founder demographic (e.g., women, minorities, LGBTQ, veterans).

Not all incubators and accelerators are created equal; some are extremely beneficial, while others are moderately helpful. It depends on the quality of the curriculum and mentors as well as on selecting the right program for your venture. The better ones provide invaluable support in getting new companies off the ground and on the fast track to success. Many of my clients have launched successful companies as a result of the mentorship and other resources provided by incubators and accelerators.

INCUBATORS VERSUS ACCELERATORS

The terms *incubator* and *accelerator* are sometimes used interchangeably. Although there are some overlaps in what incubators and accelerators provide, when and why they provide that support differs. Incubators nurture (*incubate*) startups at the ideation and beginning stage, with the goal of building out the minimum valuable product, business model, and founding team. Accelerators fast-track (*accelerate*) startups that have some market traction at the early or growth stages, with the goal of rapidly, substantially, and exponentially growing (*scaling*) the business.

Incubators generally run 12 to 24 months, provide services tailored to the needs and agenda of the founder/founding team, and rarely offer funding. In contrast, accelerators are usually highly structured, with the agenda set by the accelerator, typically run three to six months, and often offer equity-based funding. Virtually all incubators and accelerators provide connections and often introductions to potential funding sources, primarily equity investors. All incubators and accelerators provide mentoring, coaching, and hands-on learning opportunities as well as an array of resources, usually at low cost and some at no cost to participants.

INCUBATORS

The majority of incubators are nonprofit organizations or public/private partnerships (such as a university and a corporation), but some are for-profit entities. Most focus on ventures in a certain state or city and in a specific industry, but some are open to founders from anywhere in the United States and in a broad range of industries. Incubators operated by local or state nonprofit organizations, often in partnership with local/

state government commerce, community development, or economic development agencies, may focus on economically or socially disadvantaged entrepreneurs. Although many incubators target startups with high growth and high revenue potential, some are designed for entrepreneurs with promising but more modest business ideas.

Halcyon Incubator

The nonprofit Halcyon Incubator was founded and is funded by S&R Foundation. Halcyon is an immersive incubator held twice a year, during which a diverse cohort of social entrepreneurs from around the United States receive extensive support to transform their ideas into scalable, sustainable for-profit social enterprises. Each venture selected for a Halcyon cohort receives a $10,000 living stipend and free participation in the 18-month program, which has two phases:

1. **Residency (5 months).** Fellows live and work at Halcyon House (Georgetown, DC) with "unfettered" access to expert guidance as well as core programming that includes skill development workshops and a Demo Day in front of partners and investors.

2. **Post-Residency (13 months).** Fellows continue to work at Halcyon Incubator and to receive free access to all resources to further build their networks, secure funding, and grow their ventures with guidance from Halcyon's network of mentors, advisors, and supporters.

The Hatchery Chicago

Opened in December 2018, the Hatchery Chicago is a nonprofit incubator for food and beverage entrepreneurs in the Chicago greater metropolitan area—providing no-cost and low-cost entrepreneurship training, mentoring, resources, and workspace as well as access to corporate partners and funding sources. The Hatchery's 67,000–square foot facility features 56 private production-ready kitchens, a large shared kitchen, walk-in dry/cold/freezer storage, coworking space, meeting rooms, events space, loading docks, and food truck allocation. Up to 100 incubating startups and tenants have secured access to the facility 24 hours a day, 7 days a week. The incubator's nonprofit partners are microlender Accion Chicago, an anchor tenant at The Hatchery, and Industrial Council of Nearwest Chicago (ICNC), a nonprofit community development corporation that has provided no-cost and low-cost services to local manufacturing, food processing, and technology startups and small businesses since 1967.

Ventures

Ventures is a nonprofit certified community development financial institution (CDFI) for aspiring entrepreneurs with "limited resources and unlimited potential" in the Seattle, Washington, greater metropolitan area. Ventures serves local entrepreneurs for whom traditional business development services are out of reach—particularly women, people of color, immigrants, and individuals with low income. This support includes general business and specialized training, legal clinic, one-on-one consulting, mobile coaching, a commercial kitchen, a retail store in the popular Pike Place Market, booth space at the Seattle Gift Show, an online business directory, capital (low-interest loans, matched savings grants, peer-to-peer crowdfunding), and ongoing support from the Ventures network of advisors. Participants pay $50, $100, or $200 (according to income) for the initial training program. Fees for additional workshops and classes are on a sliding scale; those who can't afford the minimum sliding scale are encouraged to pay an appropriate amount.

THREE DIVERSE ENTREPRENEURS, ONE INCLUSIVE SMALL BUSINESS INCUBATOR

Earica Brown, Abdul "Doolie" Mohamud, and Francine Moo-Young come from different backgrounds but have a few key things in common. They share their home base of Seattle, their creativity, their entrepreneurial spirit, and their participation in Ventures, a nonprofit organization that provided them with a suite of incubation services to start and grow their own businesses.

In 2016, Earica launched Viavoya, a photography and videography company that works exclusively with corporate clients. Viavoya's team of experienced digital and aerial photographers and videographers document corporate incentive travel, destinations, and events and create corporate portraiture, marketing visuals, and social media imagery.

In 2013, Doolie, a refugee from Somalia who immigrated to the United States in the early 1990s, is the maker and marketer of Doolie sauce, a blend of chili peppers, coconut, lemon, and African seasoning based on his grandmother's recipe. The chunky "salsa-esque" dip/marinade/sauce is sold in numerous markets and grocery stores.

Born in Jamaica, Francine graduated from the Fashion Institute of Design and Manufacturing (FIDM) in Los Angeles and worked for iconic LA fashion brands for 10 years before moving to Seattle. Francine opened Moo Young Studio and Workshop in 2010, where she handcrafts wearable leather art, ranging from clothing to handbags to shoes to umbrellas, and conducts leather fashion design workshops.

Earica, Doolie, and Francine each had the vision, talent, and determination to pursue their entrepreneurial dreams. Ventures provided the free and affordable specialized training, mentoring, and technical assistance they needed to make their dreams a reality. The result: three very different but equally successful businesses.

ACCELERATORS

In contrast to incubators, the majority of accelerators are for-profit entities, although some are or partner with nonprofit organizations. Some accelerators focus on ventures in a certain city (or cities) or certain state (or states); others are open to startups throughout the United States or the world.

MassChallenge

Launched in 2010 and headquartered in Boston, MassChallenge is among the world's premier accelerators for high-potential startups across all industries, from across the globe, at zero cost and with zero equity taken. Every year, MassChallenge runs one program in each industry-agnostic accelerator (Boston, Israel, Mexico, Switzerland, Texas, United Kingdom) and in each vertical accelerator.

Designed for early-stage startups, MassChallenge industry-agnostic accelerators are four-month programs providing hands-on support from mentors and experts, free coworking space, tailored workshops, a network of corporate partners, and the opportunity to win a portion of more than $2 million in cash prizes (grants and scholarships).

Designed for later-stage startups, MassChallenge's vertical accelerators are six-month programs in which each startup is partnered with a corporation, institution, or organization that supports the startups with product validation, codevelopment opportunities, strategic investments, customer connections, and advisor introduction. They also get free coworking space in Boston and the opportunity to win cash prizes.

Startup52

Founded in 2016, Startup52 is the first exclusively diversity-focused accelerator in New York City. Startup52 runs two 12-week accelerators per year, each with a cohort of up to 15 startups with at least one founder from an underrepresented community (people of color, women, veterans with disabilities, immigrants, LGBTQ, etc.). Startup52 targets technology and technology-enabled ventures in diverse sectors—including AI, IoT, edtech, biotech, cleantech, fintech, mobile, SaaS, big data, security, hardware, robotics, gaming, consumer products/services, education, fashion, media/entertainment, and travel.

In exchange for a 5 percent equity stake in each startup, Start52 provides one-on-one mentoring from experts, investors, and successful entrepreneurs; networking opportunities; free coworking and meeting space; professional services (legal, accounting, human resources, branding, design, etc.); industry-specific discussions and sessions; and frequent exposure to seed investors, angel investors, and venture capitalists (during and after program; free and discounted).

Techstars Music Accelerator

Run by Techstars, one of the world's top technology accelerators, in partnership with leading companies in the global music industry, Techstars Music Accelerator is held annually in Los Angeles. Startups in each cohort receive $20,000 cash stipend (for living expenses while in LA) and a $100,000 convertible note upon acceptance into the accelerator, in exchange for 6 percent common stock in the company, with an equity-back guarantee. The 90-day program includes hands-on mentorship from music artist and music executives on the Techstar team; experiential exposure within the music industry; connections to Techstars' network of founders, alumni, and mentors; perks worth over $1 million; free office space in LA for the duration of program; Demo Day and other investor connections; and lifetime access to Techstars.

ACCELERATING AN ARTFUL, IMPACTFUL BRAND

Soapbox Theory was launched in 2001 on the premise that positive, diverse, and quality representations of Black culture matter. At the time, founder Kayin Talton Davis was a mechanical engineering student. She was often the only woman and only person of color in her classes, and the bias and exclusion of several classmates weighed heavily on Kayin. As a distraction and spirit-lifter, Kayin returned to drawing, and illustrations of unapologetic Black joy and pride decorated the margins of her class notes. That's when she launched Soapbox Theory—a line of greeting cards celebrating Black culture.

To help fund her venture, Kayin entered and won the 2017 Pitch Black business competition, a platform to connect mainstream startup ecosystems with talented black founders. That led to her joining the first cohort of XXcelerate, a 12-month business-building program in Portland, Oregon, designed by women entrepreneurs, for women entrepreneurs. The experience enabled Kayin to clarify the role she wanted to play within her company as it grew, define her goals for the brand, and refine and focus her marketing efforts. Having honest dialogues with other small business owners about the challenges they faced and how they worked through them was also helpful.

Today, Soapbox Theory, in partnership with Screw Loose Studio, produces handcrafted greeting cards, apparel, plates, lunchboxes, and other printed items bearing Kayin's colorful artwork. The brand's fiercely loyal customers often purchase multiple products, and Soapbox Theory has made the gift lists of Huffington Post, *Essence*, BuzzFeed, and numerous independent blogs and was featured in an interior design article in *HGTV Magazine*.

INCUBATOR/ACCELERATOR

Although far fewer in number than either incubators or accelerators, several organizations offer both incubation and acceleration tracks. These incubators/accelerators can guide and support select ventures from ideation through to successful launch and fully functional growth company. In some cases, a startup will participate only in the incubator or only in the accelerator.

Founder Institute

Formed in 2009 and headquartered in Silicon Valley, Founder Institute (FI) is one of the world's leading preseed startup accelerators, with chapters in more than 180 cities across 60 countries. FI provides high-potential technology and technology-enabled startups with a support network and a structured process to support their ventures at three stages:

1. **Idea Stage.** Helps aspiring, solo, or full-time employed founders validate ideas to build a team and launch a business.

2. **Prototype Stage.** Helps founders and founding teams with an initial product to secure advisors, generate revenue, and begin to raise capital.

3. **Early Company Stage.** Helps established companies at the prefunding stage to generate traction, scale their business, and raise growth capital.

The program runs 3.5 months. Each week, participating founders attend a three-hour (or more) evening session, where they receive training, evaluation, feedback, and assignments from 20 to 40 mentors per cohort. Founders spend the rest of the week working on their businesses and completing assignments, which are real-life tasks (not theoretical). Graduates receive a lifetime of support from the Founder Institute's network of CEO mentors, investment support, and invitations to FI events. Founders or founder teams pay a $50 nonrefundable application fee and a course fee ($800–$1,000) that is fully refundable before the third session of the program.

Each founder graduate contributes 4 percent equity warrants into a 15-year pool. When a liquidity event occurs, the pool's financial returns are distributed equally across the cohort—with graduates, mentors, directors, and the Founder's Institute each receiving 25 percent.

Propeller

Founded in 2009, Propeller is a nonprofit organization that provides both incubation and acceleration support to help a diverse community of entrepreneurs in New Orleans, Louisiana, launch and grow small businesses and nonprofit organizations that address social and environmental disparities. The Propeller Incubator offers low-cost coworking space, event space, workshops, seminars, and other events, including pitch competitions. The Propeller Accelerator offers four tracks: food, water, health, and education to support local social entrepreneurs at whatever stage they're in—developing an idea, launching an early-stage startup, or expanding an established business. Each startup in the accelerator program is paired with a mentor in its field, given free access to experts in all areas of business, and connected with funding sources.

Pay attention to the fine print. Make sure you know, understand, and fully agree with all the costs, terms, and conditions of participating in an incubator or accelerator program. Better yet, consult with your business attorney before signing any agreements or other legal documents. This is especially critical if participation is contingent upon the incubator or accelerator, or its collective, receiving an equity stake in your company or a share of your future revenues. You should also ensure that you can leave the program before completion without unfair financial and/or legal repercussions and that participation will not infringe upon your ability to bring on investors and/or board members.

RESOURCES

Accelerator Info. Online list of accelerator programs at US universities that have dedicated centers for entrepreneurship. Searchable by state and industry, with a hot link to each program.

The MBA Is Dead. Online database of hundreds of incubators and accelerators around the world. Searchable by region (US, Canada) or subcategory (e.g., blockchain, fintech, women, university).

Seed-DB. Database of close to 200 accelerators around the world. Option to list alphabetically (*a–z* or *z–a*), location (alphabetically or reverse alpha by city name or "worldwide"), number of companies accelerated (ascending or descending order), dollar amount of exits (per accelerator), total dollar amount of capital raised (per accelerator), average dollar amount of capital raised (per accelerator).

Seed Accelerator Rankings Project (SARP). Website reporting the results of the annual survey and ranking of seed accelerators in the United States. Lists the 26 top-rank accelerators for each year since 2016.

TARGET FUNDING VARIABLES FOR BUSINESS INCUBATORS AND ACCELERATORS

Use any combination of the following keywords to search the Internet for potential incubators and/or accelerators for your business. For each search, specify one to three variables per each applicable keyword position—for example: business incubator, pre-seed (keyword #1); USA, Minneapolis (keyword #2); food and beverage, consumer products (keyword #3); LGBTQ, founder (keyword #4).

Keyword #1	business incubator | business accelerator | startup | pre-seed | seed | idea stage | growth stage
Keyword #2	United States | name of city | name of state
Keyword #3	name of industry sector | name of industry subsector
Keyword #4	underrepresented | disadvantaged | diversity | inclusion | women | minority | veteran | disabled | LGBTQ | immigrant | refugee | founder | founding team

PART SEVEN

Ready, Set, Fund!

Creating Your Target Funding Map

A target funding map is your action plan for taking aim at the funding opportunities you have identified as the best fit for your funding goals. It charts the course for meeting every funding goal you have set over the timeline you have established. Depending on your funding goals, which are driven by your business objectives, you might create a target funding map for 30 days, 60 days 90 days, 120 days, or longer. For that matter, your target funding map could cover your funding goals over a period of 6 months, 9 months, or 12 months. However, I generally recommend not going past a year because funding opportunities often change or end, and one you'd targeted might not be available.

For example, the owner of a successful teahouse plans to open a similarly modeled wine bar in 120 days (four months). She's developed the business plan; leased the location; acquired business licenses, permits, and insurance; named the wine bar; lined up a contractor for storefront and leasehold improvements; and enlisted a pro bono architect (her spouse) to create the design/construction plans—all funded with her own resources. She also has created a target funding map built around her funding goals over a 180-day timeline (six month). Each funding goal is associated with a specific business objective—an essential must-acquire or must-do— she must fund in order to successfully launch her wine bar as planned. Her target funding goals might include securing funding for storefront improvements, leasehold improvements, equipment, furnishings, inventory, website, logo, signage, marketing and advertising, hiring and training employees, and so on.

The point is, target funding is about planning your funding and funding your plan. The plan is your target funding map, which you create by pinpointing the funding opportunities that align with both your time-sensitive funding goals and your funding-related business variables. These are the same variables associated with the funding options discussed in the preceding chapters of this book.

Creating a target funding map, then, is actually a four-step process:

1. **Define your funding goals**, including the timeline for achieving them.

2. **Define your target funding variables**—the keywords you'll need to track down potential funding sources (funding providers).

3. **Identify potential funding opportunities**, which involves finding and researching potential funding sources to uncover potential funding opportunities (specific grants, loans, investment capital, etc.) to target.

4. **Create your target funding map**—a step-by-step plan for pursuing the potential funding opportunities you've identified for each of your funding goals.

A target funding map is essential to target funding, a process that thousands of startup founders, small business owners, and independent inventors have used to help fund their businesses. My favorite part of advising or training entrepreneurs on target funding is the moment when the process clicks for clients and they "get" that target funding is a tool for finding funding that targets them.

ARE YOU READY TO START TARGET FUNDING?

In order to map out and implement a target funding plan, you need to assess how prepared you are, or are not, to pursue each funding option you are considering or will/should consider. Certain types of funding require you to have certain things in place, meet certain standards, and provide certain information in a certain format. Putting those things in place and pulling those materials together can require resources and take time—sometimes weeks or months.

Business funding is both a numbers game and a timing game. The time frame between application and funded can range from a couple weeks to several months, depending on the funding type and source. Some funding opportunities have application deadlines; others are first come, first served. You don't want a missing game piece to throw you off course or out of the running for a funding opportunity you need to meet your funding goals and, with them, your business objectives.

Following are some simple measures you can take to gear up for target funding.

Review Your Financial Standing

Before you can develop your target funding strategy and build your target funding map, you need to review your financial situation. Actually, before and while you fund your business, I encourage you to check your credit scores, both personal and business (if you have a business score), using a free site such as Credit Karma. You should also assess your financial statements, if you have them, and if you don't, prepare them or hire an accountant to prepare them for you. (Remember, you might be able to get pro bono or low-cost accounting assistance through your local Small Business Development Center or SCORE office.)

Knowing where you stand financially is important to target funding, enabling you to:

- Determine whether and how your financial standing might impact your target funding process. For example, a high credit score might qualify for a low-interest SBA or bank loan. A modest credit score and low income might qualify for a CDFI or government economic development loan.

- Address any errors in your credits scores and begin to address any deficits in your financial standing, with the goal of improving your credit score and other financial measures and, with them, your funding options.

- Answer a potential funder's questions about your financial standing immediately, accurately, and fully.

- Provide potential funding sources with copies of your financial statements, if and as required.

When I went bankrupt many years ago and entrepreneurship seemed like a distant dream, my credit score plummeted to the high 400s. I worked diligently to increase it. Today, my credit score is above 800, and I still use Credit Karma to monitor my credit score, which motivates me to sustain a healthy credit score and improve it.

It is *always* advantageous to know your financial status and to be proactive, rather than reactive, in repairing and rebuilding your financial strength.

Identify and Quantify Your Skin in the Game

All potential funders want an accounting of—and you need to know for your own planning and management purposes—the funding contributions you've made to your business, specially:

- The amount of cash you've put into the business. The funder may also ask where that cash came from—for example, savings, inheritance, gift from family or friend, sale of personal assets, personal loan.
- Assets purchased for the business and their value.
- Available liquid assets and their value.

I suggest creating a spreadsheet to record your contributions to date as well as future cash contributions, business asset acquisitions, business assets used to secure business loans, etc. Please note that this tracking sheet is not a substitute for business accounting programs and documentation. Its purpose is to help gauge and keep track of the assets you put into and put up for your business.

Here is an example of an owner contributions tracking sheet for a fictitious small business that makes and markets household furnishings and decor from upcycled materials.

Owner Contributions

Investment	Value/Available*
Carpentry equipment and tools	$ 12,000
Truck	$ 15,000
Computer and printer	$ 5,000
401(k)	$150,000*
Total	**$182,000**

Identify and Quantify Any Outside Funding You Have Received

Lenders, investors, and many grant makers will want to know about any external funding you've received for your business—specifically, when received, where it came from, type of funding, how much, and for what purpose. If you've received debt funding, potential funding sources will also want to know whether and how the loan was secured. This information may also be required or useful to any business advisors and consultants you work with. Keeping track of this information will also aid you in your target funding processes, and a spreadsheet is an easy way to record that data.

Funding Received

Date	Source	Amount
04/18	Business competition	$5,000 cash
		$5,000 in-kind (computer, printer)
08/18	Inheritance	$10,000
Total		**$20,000**

I often tell my clients to think of target funding as a pizza pie with at least six slices. Each slice represents a different funding option and amount, which collectively make up the entire pie. If you had $100,000 to invest, you wouldn't want your financial planner to invest all of it in one stock option. They would tell you that is foolish and that diversification minimizes the risk of losing any funds. Same goes with target funding. Diversification is key.

Identify Any Needed Prerequisites for Target Funding

In order to qualify and apply for a particular funding opportunity, the funder may require you to have certain business protocols in place and to present certain materials. Several times over the years I've seen entrepreneurs find a great funding opportunity with a small window in which to apply only to realize they don't have some specific requirement in place, like a business plan or a pitch deck.

For example, you'll need to have a strong elevator pitch ready to reel off at a moment's notice in conversation, a cover letter, as part of a presentation, or to participate in a business competition. Most sources of debt funding and equity funding will want to see your business plan and financial statements, and many also want to see a feasibility study and/or SWOT analysis (strengths, weaknesses, opportunities, threats).

You'll need a pitch deck and to set up an investment offering in order to raise investment capital. You'll need a proposal to apply for grants and government procurement contracts and the proper business certifications to bid on government and corporate contracts as well. Typically, it takes between 40 and 100 hours—as well as either training and technical assistance or a professional grant writer—to prepare a federal Small Business Innovation Research (SBIR) or Small Business Technology Transfer (STTR) grant proposal.

For crowdfunding, you'll need rewards, a short video about your business and/or product, and intellectual property protection if your venture is product-based. You'll also need a video along with a sales sheet for licensing and direct TV funding. A website or at least a splash page with contact links is either required (preselling on a crowdfunding platform) or advantageous for some funding options.

Depending on the stage of business and the type of funding you're targeting, you may also need to have your business structure, business license, business insurances, business banking account, and/or core management team in place.

Being prepared will enable you to take advantage of the funding opportunities you target. That's the beauty of target funding, because the process tasks you to research potential funding opportunities, during which you will discover what all the qualification and application requirements are—including deadlines. That way, you can add funding needed to attain any missing prerequisites—*and* factor the time required to secure that funding and those resources—to your target funding map.

DEFINE YOUR FUNDING GOALS

Identifying and defining your funding goals is the first step in creating a target funding map—and a step too often skipped by entrepreneurs operating in "just do it" mode. It is impossible to effectively fund your business if you don't know exactly what you need the funding for, how much you need, when you need it, and why you need the expenditures in question.

Need is an operative word when it comes to setting target funding goals. Every entrepreneur I've ever known has aspirations to add bells and whistles and some niceties and even frills to their businesses. But usually, those "extras" are wants and wishes, not needs. I say, if you can afford them without having to fund them and without eroding profits, go for it. But, in my quite strong opinion, the only things that should be funded with money or resources from an external source are the things you truly need to have or do to start, build, stabilize, sustain, or expand your business.

I will never forget the first time I walked into one of the offices I ended up leasing before I purchased my own space. The entrepreneur was so proud to show me around. The furniture was stunning, and clearly a lot of money was put into remodeling the space. He told me he needed all that high-end furniture because clients were being seen there. When I asked how he paid for it all, he said with his credit card. He was out of business within six months. He needed attractive furniture to create a welcoming, professional environment for clients. He didn't need furniture that cost $30,000!

Setting your funding goals is Priority One in creating an effective target funding map and implementing it. Following is a simple three-step process for defining your funding goals.

Identify Your Funding Needs

Make a list of each expenditure you need to make and fund in order to move your business forward or keep it on track. If the only thing that comes to mind is a pressing funding need, such as working capital to fill customer orders, put that at the top of the list. But don't stop there. Consider the goals you've set for the business in the weeks and months ahead. What resources will you need 30 or 90 or 180 or 365 days from now to achieve those business goals? Will you likely or potentially need funding for any of those resources?

Remember, target funding focuses on getting the funding you need when you need it. That requires planning and preparing for upcoming funding needs, which then become funding goals to which an actionable plan and a timeline will be established in the target funding map.

When listing a funding goal, be specific. For example, if you need to purchase equipment, itemize each piece of equipment needed, when you need it, and the cost. You might also include a note referencing the business objective the expenditure enables—for example, "to diversify product line to increase revenues and to improve production efficiency to increase profit margins." Some funding providers, such as investors, want to know not only how the money will be spent but also how it will advance the business or bottom line. That kind of information is useful when you prioritize or need to reprioritize your funding goals.

Be realistic with your funding goals, too. Make sure a goal is attainable, based on your financial standing, stage of business, revenues and revenue projections, and other funding considerations. Make sure to factor in any prerequisites you might need in order to apply and/or qualify for certain funding options. For example, a funding goal to purchase a building within 30 days is probably not realistic because commercial real estate loans typically take longer than that.

Record your funding goals on a spreadsheet or in a notebook so you can refer to and modify your funding goals as your target funding progresses.

Funding Needs/Goals

Lease retail space; 3 months + security deposit	
Leasehold improvements	
Storefront improvements	
Register, dollies, forklift	
Delivery van	

Website	
Social media training	
Hire store clerk; 3 months	

Quantify Your Funding Needs

In theory, assigning a cost to each funding goal might seem like a snap. In practice, accurately costing out each resource takes some work. By *work*, I mean research and comparison shopping—to which some entrepreneurs are adverse, preferring to "guestimate" costs.

Again, being realistic is important. Target funding is smart funding, and smart funding means knowing what you need so you don't come up short or overspend. If you borrow $25,000 to purchase a delivery van for which you paid $30,000 (20 percent kicked in by you), when—had you done some comparison shopping—you could have purchased a nearly identical van for $25,000, you've borrowed $4,000 more and contributed $1,000 more than needed. On the other hand, if you underestimated the cost at $20,000 and borrowed $16,000 and set aside $4,000 for your contribution, but the best price you could get was $30,000, you'd be in a pickle. You'd need to either find another way to fund the $10,000 difference or go through the rigamarole of finding another vehicle the lender will approve.

So do a little research to accurately estimate costs, and record them in your funding goal worksheet. Here's an example:

Funding Needs/Goals

Expenditure	Estimated Costs
Lease retail space; 3 months + security deposit	$ 5,000
Leasehold improvements	$ 3,000
Storefront improvement	$10,000
Register, dollies, forklift	$ 4,500
Delivery van	$15,000
Website	$ 2,500
Social media training	$ 1,000
Hire store clerk, 3 months	$ 7,250
Total	**$48,250**

Prioritize Your Funding Goals

Now it's time to determine the timeline and priority of each funding goal.

1. Consider the following factors:
    - Can any of the resources be acquired at no cost or lower cost? For example, in the upcycle business example, could the social media training be obtained through a local community college or Small Business Development Center? Could the owner barter a product or carpentry services in exchange for web design services?
    - Can you do any of the targeted contractual work yourself? For example, in this case, could the owner and a volunteer team of fellow tradespeople do any of the storefront improvements?
    - When is funding needed for each funding goal? Make sure to consider the availability of any prerequisites (i.e., grant proposal), the resource (product/materials/person), and any funding opportunity you've already identified (city's annual, first-come/first-serve storefront façade grant program).
    - Could any of the funding goals be postponed or eliminated? If postponed, what is the new timeline for funding that goal?

2. Identify any idea or concerns that need further research and consideration—such as no-cost or reduced-cost alternatives to any of the funding goals before you can firm up a timeline and establish the priority for that/those funding goal(s).

3. Establish the timeline for securing funds for each funding goal. You can designate when you need the funds by number of days, weeks, or months; just use the same convention for naming all funding-goal timelines.

4. Update your funding goals worksheet. Add the timeline you've set for each funding goal. Make note of any homework you need to do to resolve the issue. Sort (or list) the funding goals in groups according to the timelines, with the shortest timelines

at the top. Following is an example of what the upcycle maker's prioritized funding goals might look like:

Funding Needs/Goals

Expenditure	Estimated Cost	Timeline	Options to Explore
Lease retail space, 3 months + security deposit	$ 5,000	60 days	Showroom at shop
Leasehold improvements	$ 3,000	60 days	
Social media training	$ 1,000	60 days	Free/reduced training
Website	$ 2,500	60 days	
Storefront improvement	$10,000	60 days	
Register, dollies, forklift	$ 4,500	90 days	
Delivery van	$15,000	90 day	
Hire store clerk, 3 months	$ 7,250	90 days	
Total	**$48,250**		

5. Research and come to a decision about any no-cost and reduced cost options for meeting a funding goal.

6. Prioritize your target funding goals—based on which are the most critical to achieving the business objective associated with the funding goal. Number them sequentially in order of priority. Sort the funding goals in order of priority.

Once you've decided your funding priorities, update your worksheet to reflect any changes. Here's what the upcycle furniture shop's funding priorities might look like:

Prioritized Funding Goals

Priority	Expenditure	Estimated Cost	Timeline	Plan
1	Lease retail space, 3 months	$ 5,000	60 days	Insufficient space and foot traffic at shop
2	Leasehold improvements	$ 3,000	60 days	
5	Website	$ 2,500	60 days	
6	Social media training	$0000	60 days	SBDC: Free!
3	Storefront improvement	$10,000	60 days	
4	Register, dollies, forklift	$ 4,500	90 days	
7	Hire store clerk, 3 months	$ 7,250	90 days	
8	Delivery van	$15,000	180 days	Hold-off; evaluation 120 days
	Total	**$47,250**		

DEFINE YOUR TARGET FUNDING VARIABLES

Now comes the fun part—when you identify all the potential variables that you can use to target funding sources and resources that align with you and your business. I suggest you create a list of funder *eligibility variables* and your corresponding *qualifier variables*. Your qualifier variables are the keywords you will use to search for matching eligibility variables (keywords) of potential funding sources for your business.

Eligibility Variables	Qualifier Variables
Business Size/Scalability	
Small business	Small business
High-growth, scalable startup	
Small business	

Eligibility Variables	Qualifier Variables
Business Stage	
Research and development	Operating
Prelaunch	
Startup	
Operating	
Business Location	
State	Oregon
County	Lane
City	Eugene
Rural	Downtown urban renewal
Urban renewal zone	
Economic development zone	
Industry cluster	
Industry	
For example:	
Agriculture	Retail
Construction	Creative/arts
Creative/arts	
Health/well-being	
Research/technology	
Retail	
Specialized Focus	
Social cause	Home furnishings and decor
Niche	Sustainability
Demographic of Owner(s)	
Gender	Woman
Ethnicity	Age 50+
Veteran	
Disability	
Other (LGBTQ, immigrant, age 50+)	

IDENTIFY POTENTIAL FUNDING OPPORTUNITIES

With your prioritized funding goals and target funding variables in front of you, you're ready to track down and vet potential funding solutions for your venture. I think of this search-and-research mission as a journey of discovery. Even after more than 20 years of searching for and researching funding solutions for startups, small businesses, and inventions, I sometimes find a new funding source or an amazing resource I didn't know about.

I also think of every target funding campaign as a unique organism, with its own personality and idiosyncrasies, around which the target funding process is adapted. That said, the Target Funding methodology I've created (and personalize with each targeted funding campaign) guide and facilitate the process. In terms of identifying potential funding opportunities, that involves the following:

- Researching any potential funding sources (providers of funding) and funding opportunities (specific funding program, i.e., SBIR grant) you're already aware of.

- Conducting variables-driven Internet searches for potential funding sources for your funding goals.

- Researching each funding source that you discover online to determine whether that source offers any funding opportunities that align with your funding goal(s) and funding variables.

- Reaching out to your network and to community influencers for recommendations of potential funding solutions for your funding goals.

- Researching funding sources and solutions recommended by others to identify any funding opportunities that align with your funding goal(s) and funding variables.

- Recording your findings in a spreadsheet.

Are you ready to get this search party started? Just follow this 10-step guide to identifying potential funding opportunities for your target funding goals.

1. Create a spreadsheet (or database) for recording and managing essential information about potential funding solutions you find and research. This funding solution workbook might include the following column headers.
   - Source
   - Opportunity
   - Eligibility
   - Specs
   - Website
   - Contact

2. Add your funding goals to your funding solutions workbook, in order of timeline.

3. Identify the funding options (funding types, i.e., accelerator, SBA loan, venture capital) you are considering. To help brainstorm possibilities, review the funding options discussed in the chapters of this book that relate to your business.

4. Create a keyword search guide, listing your target funding variables and funding option preferences. For example:
   - Business location: Eugene, Oregon
   - Business size/stage: Small business
   - Owner demographic: Woman, immigrant, Jewish
   - Funding options: matched savings grant, storefront (facade) improvement grant, interest-free business loan, expansion loan, equipment loan, business vehicle loan
   - Industry: Retail
   - Sector/specialization: Home furnishings, home decor, upcycled, sustainability

5. List your funding specifications and eligibility factors. For example:
   - Amount needed: $47,250 estimated total expansion costs ($10,000 for storefront improvements, $4,500 for equipment, $10,500 for startup expenses, $7,250 for job creation, and $15,000 for a vehicle)
   - Collateral: 401(k)
   - Credit scores: 730 (personal), 87 (business)

- Years in business: 5 years
- Number of employees: 3, including owner
- Annual revenues: $220,000
- Five-year revenue projection: $500,000
- 100 percent privately owned; no investors

6. Research potential funding sources and funding solutions you've already identified.

   6.1 Open your funding solution workbook.

   6.2 Go online and search for the funding source.

   6.3 Go to the website of the funding source and navigate to the funding services/programs page or portal.

   6.4 Review the funding solutions offered. Check for the following details and any other information that is relevant to you:

   - Type(s) of funding offered
   - Eligibility requirements for each funding solution offered: e.g., location, size, stage, business structure, years in operation, revenues, industry/sector/specialty/ social impact, owner demographic, patent/patent pending, etc.
   - Funding specifications: i.e., amount, terms, conditions, allowable use(s) of funds, collateral, percentage of cost funded, etc.
   - Application requirements: i.e., application form and/ or proposal, business plan, financial statements, SWOT analysis, video, prototype, patent/patent pending, etc.
   - Funding cycle: documents required; time length (estimated determination and funding dates)

   6.5 Record your findings in the funding solutions workbook (spreadsheet).

7. Search for and research potential funding sources, using your keyword search guide.

   7.1 Do multiple search queries, using different combinations of keywords (variables) for each search. I usually limit each search query to five or six words. For example:

- **Keyword search #1.** Eugene Oregon + gov + small business + storefront improvement
- **Keyword search #2.** Eugene Oregon +art + business
- **Keyword search #3.** woman owned + small business + grant + Oregon + Eugene
- **Keyword search #4.** woman owned + small business + loan + Oregon + Eugene
- **Keyword search #5.** encore entrepreneur + small business + financing

7.2 Go to the website of each potential funding source the search query generates and navigate to the funding services/programs page or portal.

7.3 Review the funding solutions offered. Check for the following details and any other information that is relevant to you:
- Type(s) of funding offered
- Eligibility requirements for each funding solution offered: i.e., location, size, stage, business structure, years in operation, revenues, industry/sector/specialty/ social impact, owner demographic, patent/patent pending, etc.
- Funding specifications: i.e., amount, terms, conditions, allowable use(s) of funds, collateral, percentage of cost funded, etc.
- Application requirements: i.e., application form and/ or proposal, business plan, financial statements, SWOT analysis, video, prototype, patent/patent pending, etc.
- Funding cycle: documents required; time length (estimated determination and funding dates)

7.4 Record your findings in the funding solutions workbook (spreadsheet).

8. Reach out to your social network(s) for funding recommendations and resources.

Who do you know who might be able to suggest a funding solution for your business—or connect you with someone or an organization that can? Who are your fellow entrepreneurs, mentors, champions, and kindred spirits? The people who root for, care about, and are interested in you and your business usually want to help. All you have to do is ask. So ask those people first, with a personalized query. You can use a more general query to post, message, tweet, and/or text your entire network or select categories within your network (i.e., colleagues and friends; excluding customers and competitors). Ask your connections to pass word along to their connections.

At this point, you're looking for suggestions and names, but not necessarily introductions. It's usually best to hold off on direct contact until you've researched the funding source, created your target funding map, and are ready to launch your target funding campaign. But if an introduction is made or offered, take advantageous of that opportunity to introduce yourself and your business and to learn about them.

9. Reach out to government agencies, nonprofit organizations, and influencers that support entrepreneurs and businesses in your community and industry. Introduce yourself to the economic development team in your region, as a member of the business community focused on contributing to the local economy. Identify the top 10 organizations in your community, industry, demographic, or customer market. Reach out and make a connection. Cite your connection to the group or the cause it supports. Deliver your elevator pitch. Share that you're seeking funding for your business and what you intend to do with it. Then, ask if they could recommend a good source of business funding.

10. Research funding sources and solutions recommended to you.
    10.1 Open your funding solution workbook.
    10.2 Go online and search for the funding source.
    10.3 Go to the website of the funding source and navigate to the funding services/programs page or portal.
    10.4 Review the funding solutions offered. Check for the following details and any other information that is relevant to you:

- Type(s) of funding offered
- Eligibility requirements for each funding solution offered: i.e., location, size, stage, business structure, years in operation, revenues, industry/sector/specialty/ social impact, owner demographic, patent/patent pending, etc.
- Funding specifications: i.e., amount, terms, conditions, allowable use(s) of funds, collateral, percentage of cost funded, etc.
- Application requirements: i.e., application form and/ or proposal, business plan, financial statements, SWOT analysis, video, prototype, patent/patent pending, etc.
- Funding cycle: documents required; time length (estimated determination and funding dates)

10.5 Record your findings in the funding solutions workbook (spreadsheet), as in the example table.

Source	Opportunity	Eligibility	Funding Cycle
City of Eugene Loan Program	Art Loan: $10,000–$100,000 term loan. Below-market fixed interest. Flex terms. 50 percent matching funds. Secured with business assets or personal guarantee.	New or existing art-based biz in Eugene. For: exterior signage; historic renovations; storefront improvement.	$50 application fee. Prescreen; then full application. 30-day determination; fund at closing
Website	**Contact**	**Email**	**Phone**
eugene-or.gov	Aaron Doreen, Business Loan Analyst	aaron.x.doreen@ ci.eugene.or.us	541–682–5448

CREATE YOUR TARGET FUNDING MAP

The final leg in the marathon to develop a target funding map involves reviewing and considering your current business and financial situation, your business objectives and funding goals, and all the information you've gathered about the funding opportunities you've identified, and then mapping out a strategic plan to target the best funding opportunities for your funding goals and overall business objectives. Here is the three-step process for creating your target funding map:

1. **Determine which funding opportunities you want to target.** The criteria for making this determination is unique to each business and each funding situation. Only you and your team know all the factors you need to consider to make this decision. But here are some things to consider:
    -   Which funding opportunities are the best fit for your funding goals? Consider the allowable minimum and maximum amounts, financing terms, application and qualification requirements, cost of funding, funding cycle, funding availability, and so on of each funding source.
    -   Which funding opportunities can be used to meet two or more of your funding goals?
    -   Have you previously used and had a positive funding experience with any of the funding sources?
    -   Have you received high recommendations, or any negative input, about any of the funding sources or funding opportunities?
    -   Do any of your preferred funding sources offer the potential for additional funding down the road?

2. **Determine the sequence in which you plan to pursue the targeted funding opportunities.** This decision is based on your target funding timeline, the funding cycle of individual funding opportunities, and any preparations or milestones that need to be achieved before you target a funding opportunity.

    The funding cycle for certain funding options, like raising equity capital and applying for federal R&D-based

commercialization grants, typically takes several months. So, even if you won't need those funds for another 9 or 12 months, you may need to get the ball rolling sooner than you'd initially thought. Some target funding maps focus on one or two straightforward funding goals—such as a laundromat business with the funding goal of replacing 20 clothes washers and the flooring in one of its units. An edtech startup in its preseed round and gearing up for its seed round will likely have numerous target funding goals and a multiphase target funding strategy.

The key is to routinely evaluate where you are and where you need to be, establish funding goals that help facilitate your business objectives, and target the funding that you need to achieve your funding goals and, ultimately, your business objectives. It can be quite the balancing act, but it is a proactive balancing act— which helps to ensure that you keep all those balls in the air.

3. **Create your target funding map.** This involves assembling your target funding action plan in a format you can use to guide and track the launch and successful implementation of your target funding campaign. It's a simple process.

   3.1 Generate a target funding map workbook (spreadsheet), with the following column headers:
   - Solution (funding opportunity + source)
   - Launch date
   - Specs
   - Eligibility
   - Fund cycle
   - Website
   - Contact
   - E-mail
   - Phone

Following are the funding map pages for the top three funding candidates that our fictitious upcycle home furnishings designer has targeted to fund her new showroom. During my target funding search for this fictitious enterprise, I also identified five other strong funding contenders and two backup funding possibilities as well as resources for no-cost and low-cost services and support (such as Green Lane Sustainable Business Network).

Target Funding Map

Funding: ROBS/Rainmaker Plan at Benetrends	**Amount:** $50,000
Specs: At least 59.5 years old and at least $50,000 in 401(k). Benetrends fee to set up: ~$5,000. Management fee: $150–$200/month.	**Launch:** Immediate
Fund Cycle: 1. Form C corporation 2. Create new 401(k) plan. 3. Roll over existing 401(k) to new 401(k). 4. Sell $50,000 company stock to 401(k). 5. Fund: 30 days.	**Purpose:** Lease, leasehold improvements, website, hire clerk, delivery van
Website: benetrends.com	**Contact:**
Email: customerservice@benetrends.com	**Phone:** 866–423–6387
Notes: Contact Benetrends and speak with ROBS specialist. Discuss with Ben [spouse]. If a ROBS is viable, it can be used to fund this phase of startup without incurring debt.	

Funding: Art Loan at City of Eugene	**Amount:** $5,000
Specs: Up to $100,000 term loan. 50 percent matching. Below-market fixed interest. Flex terms. 50 percent matching funds. Secure with business assets or 401(k). For art-based businesses located in Eugene.	**Launch:** 30 days
Fund Cycle: Prescreen (credit check, etc.); may require consultation with City's business loan analyst. If greenlight, apply online. Determination, 30 days. Fund upon loan closing.	**Purpose:** Storefront improvements
Website: eugene-or.gov	**Contact:** Aaron Doreen, Business Loan Analyst
Email: aaron.x.doreen@ci.eugene.or.us	**Phone:** 541–682–5448
Notes:	

Funding: Small business loan at Community Lending Works (CLW), CDFI, division of Neighborhood Economic Development Corporation (NEDC)	Amount: $20,000
Specs: $7,500–$75,000 term. Fixed interest, 9–12 percent. Up to 60 months. Eligibility: Woman-owned. Uses: To start or expand small business in Lane, Marion, Clackamus Counties.	Launch: 30 days
Fund Cycle: Phase 1. One-page online query. Phase 2. Prescreen and green or red light, up to 5 days. Phase 3. Loan app provided by CLW + biz plan + financial statements and projections. Phase 4. Evaluation/determination, up to 30 days. Close/fund within 5 days of approval.	Purpose: Lease, storefront improvement, equipment, website, job creation
Website: communitylendingworks.org	Contact:
Email:	Phone:
Notes:	

After completing the triathlon of creating a Target Funding Map—all those hours of brainstorming and searching and researching—to pinpoint high-potential funding solutions to target for your funding goals—you may be tempted to give target funding a rest. After all, you've identified some strong contenders for your funding team, and they're not going anywhere soon. So why not kick back and take a breather? Well, I think that's just fine. Make yourself a cup of tea, treat yourself to a couple of macaroons, and congratulate yourself on putting together a strategic funding plan. Then, get busy working that plan. Because it's true: Opportunity waits for no one. In order for the magic to happen, you have to take action.

3-2-1 Target Funding Launch!

Since time is money and since time is always of the essence when it comes to money, there comes a time, usually a week or two into the targeted search for potential funders for your business, when it's time to start asking for the money. When you reach that point—typically because you need to nail down funding ASAP to ensure you meet your funding goal timelines—you might still be on the hunt for potential funders for other funding goals.

That's OK. You can pursue funding solutions you've identified and qualified for while you continue to seek and vet potential funders as backups and for future funding goals. Likewise, if you're turned down by or decide against any or all of the funders you've targeted, which happens, you can continue to look for and research other possibilities. Then again, you might also secure the funding you've targeted with relative ease, as many people do.

Whatever the case may be, the following guidelines will help you to launch, adjust, and successfully implement your target funding plan.

GET YOUR FUNDING DUCKS IN A ROW

After creating their customized target funding map, most people still have some homework and/or legwork to do before they're ready to apply for one or more of the funding opportunities they've targeted. Being prepared increases your chances of getting funded, so it pays off to do an inventory of what you need to know and to have in place in order to apply and qualify for the funding opportunities at the top of your priority list.

Here are some things to check:

- Do you know and understand all of the terms, conditions, rules, and restricting of the funding for which you intend to apply? If you don't, contact the funder to find out and to get clarity on whatever you need to know. Remember the upcycled home furnishings business owner in Chapter 20? She targeted a ROBS from Benetrends as her top priority but wanted to ask the funder some questions about the process and to talk with her husband about using $50,000 of their 401(k). If she were my client, I'd encourage her to make that call and have that conversation pronto, so she could move forward with full knowledge and with her spouse's full support. Record anything you learn and any changes in your target funding strategy on your target funding map.

- Do you have everything in place that the funder requires in order to accept and process your application? Make sure you know or find out exactly what is needed before you begin the application process. Then, make sure you have what is needed in place and/or on hand when you apply.

- Double-check the timing of the funding cycle for each of the funding opportunities you've targeted. Make sure that your targeted date to initiate the prescreening process or the application process allows adequate time to receive the funding when you need it. In fact, make sure that there's enough time if you begin the process today.

Resolve any potential hiccups as quickly as possible. Meanwhile, move forward with any funding opportunities you are prepared for and that are not contingent upon any targeted funding solution still in the balance.

I suggest creating a target funding tracking spreadsheet so that you'll have easy access to all of the critical information you'll need to implement your target funding strategy. This electronic data storage and management tool will also enable you to add and update information as your target funding progresses and is modified. I have found the following data categories to be helpful during the target funding process:

- Name of funder and contact person
- Contact information
- Funding type
- Funding amount requested
- Application opening date (if applicable)
- Application closing date (if applicable)
- Prescreening application required/date submitted
- Application submission date
- Date determination expected
- Determination and date
- Funding amount received and date
- Reporting requirements
- Notes

APPLY TO FUNDING OPPORTUNITIES
AS OUTLINED IN YOUR TARGET FUNDING MAP

Although the application processes of individual funders and for different types of funding vary widely, the process for following the application requirements is similar. The following steps will guide you through most funding applications.

1. Review your target funding map.

2. Review any application information and materials provided by the funder.

3. Add the funding opportunity for which you are applying to your target funding tracking sheet.

4. If the funder prescreens applicants, submit the required prescreening application or inquiry or contact the funder in the manner required.
   - If the funder requests additional information or a meeting, comply with that request if possible and as soon as possible. Make note of the request and your response on your target funding tracking sheet.

- Upon receipt of the funder's prescreening determination, either move forward with the application process as
  instructed or thank the funder for considering your funding
  inquiry. If the funder does not indicate why your request for
  funding was denied, you can also ask, but the funder is not
  required to provide that information.

5. Prepare the application form and any supplemental materials as
   required by the funder. Check all components of your application for accuracy and completeness before submitting.

6. Submit your application to the funder.

7. Update the target funding tracking sheet to record the funding
   application.

8. If the funder requests additional information or a meeting,
   comply with that request if possible and as soon as possible.
   Make note of the request and your response on your target
   funding tracking sheet.

9. If the anticipated determination date passes with no word from
   the funder, wait a week before following up with the funder.
   But do follow up. Things sometimes get lost in the shuffle, and
   funding your business is too important to allow a potential
   funding opportunity to fall through the cracks or to be delayed.

10. Upon receipt of the determination, record the outcome on the
    target funding tracking sheet. Again, if your funding applica-
    tion was denied and no explanation was given, try asking for
    constructive feedback on why and what you might do to meet
    the funder's requirements in the future. If you got a thumbs-up,
    send a thank you note. And celebrate!

CONTINUE TO TARGET FUNDING SOURCES AND FUNDING OPPORTUNITIES

Target funding is sometimes an ongoing or recurring process. You may be
focused on two or more funding goals at the same or at overlapping times,
with one funding goal met while others remain outstanding and continue

to need your attention. The funding opportunities you targeted may not pan out, in which case you'll need to be ready with contingency options. That's why I always recommend sourcing as many potential funding opportunities as possible during the initial search and research of a funding strategy, in preparation for creating a target funding map. But that's also a good reason to continually search for other funding possibilities.

I also think it is important for both your current and future target funding efforts to keep your network in the loop and to keep building your network. You never know when you're going to connect with someone who can connect you with a great funding source—or when you can help connect another entrepreneur with a funding source or other resource.

My favorite business resource is people. People will move mountains and open doors the way no tool and no system can. If you give the people in your life half of what you give to your iPad or tennis game or Zumba, you'll build a support network of superheroes ready to come to your rescue or lend a hand and celebrate your successes. I call that spreading around Karma Dollars, and Karma Dollars go a lot further than money. Those Karma Dollars can also come in handy when you're trying to round up capital and resources to fuel your business—which, for many of us, is more than a business. It's a way to connect with and help other people.

Launching and executing a target funding strategy isn't always a 3-2-1 and done process. Sometimes it's a sprint, and sometimes it's a marathon.

Case in point: For the daycare center I established in Oregon, I targeted a forgivable loan program with a strict deadline and a funding condition that, fortunately, I was prepared to meet. The $25,000 working capital loan was forgivable (meaning no interest, no fees, no payments) contingent upon my hiring five full-time daycare employees over a period of six months. Well, thanks to target marketing, that aligned with my funding goal and my business goals, which included hiring staff for my business. That was a sprint!

On the flip side, when I applied for a loan to purchase my commercial condo, which is designed to provide affordable office space to women and minority entrepreneurs, it was definitely a marathon. Eligibility for the loan program, sponsored through Prosper Portland, required being in business a number of years, providing a lot of documentation, and going through a strict due diligence process. But I'd targeted that particular loan because it was a good fit for my funding goals. In 2008, I purchased the office with only a 6 percent down payment, and my interest rate has been fixed at 0.04 percent for over 10 years.

The point is that even I use Target Funding for my own businesses. Because it works. And it's kind of fun. It's empowering to be in control of, rather than at the mercy of, the funding game.

My hope is that the Target Funding process I developed to help my clients and students find the funding they need for their businesses will also help you find the funding you need to make your entrepreneurial dreams come true.

Acknowledgments

First and foremost, I want to thank all the entrepreneurs who struggle daily to fight for their entrepreneurial dreams, as each of you inspired the vision for this book.

Among the many others who helped bring this book to life, I am most grateful to:

Farmingdale State College, for believing that a young girl could impact the world if given the opportunity to do so.

Capital One Credit Card for sending a $200 credit card after I filed bankruptcy and for inspiring my 15-year journey to uncover funds and resources for entrepreneurs.

Gary M. Krebs (GMK Writing and Editing, Inc.), my amazing literary agent, who believed in my work from day one and always had my back in supporting the best avenue for the book.

The outstanding team at McGraw-Hill, with special recognition to Cheryl Ringer, who was so gracious in supporting this first-time author and believed in the ability of *Target Funding* to be a gamechanger in the maze of finding funds for businesses.

Supportive heroes along the way, including Donya Dickerson for first reviewing my book proposal and Colleen Sell for helping to put the book into a written format and bring it to life.

My gracious mentors along the way, including Steve Strauss, Scott Duffy, Warren Tuttle, Steven Greenberg, Rosalyn Boxer, Tammy Marquez-Oldham, and Angela Jackson, who offered sound wisdom along my journey.

My best friends—Sandra Hoy-Johnson and Elizabeth Sullivan—for all the years of being the best cheerleaders one could ask for.

My ONABEN family, LinkedIn family, SBDC family, UIA family, and National Speakers Association family; I'm proud to be part of their tribes.

My husband and three beautiful sons, especially Caelen, who constantly shows me that autism will never define him or prevent him from being the best version of himself.

My mom and two sisters that have been on the sidelines supporting all my endeavors.

My first therapist, Judy E., who took me under her wings when I was young, afraid, and in hiding and guided me to find myself.

All of my remarkable students, including some who transitioned into wonderful friends—Helen Anderson, Dave Strayer, and Brandon Vaughn.

My darkest villain, who broke me down to nothing, which forced me to become my own superhero and empowered me to help others become the superheroes of their lives, too.

Finally, I am grateful to my past self, who strived every single day to hustle, to fight, to break through barriers, and to never stop believing that a little girl who felt alone and of no value in the world could bring value to the world.

Notes

Chapter 1

1. John Horn and Darren Pleasance, McKinsey & Company, "Restarting the US Small Business Growth Engine," November 2012.

2. Kauffman Index of Startup Activity, 2017.

3. Pew.

4. Kauffman Index of Startup Activity, 2017.

5. Dun & Bradstreet and Pepperdine Graziadio Business School Small Business Survey, 2017.

6. Bank of America Small Business Owner Report, 2018.

Chapter 2

1. *2017 Small Business Credit Survey: Report on Employer Firms*, Federal Reserve Banks.

2. *2017 Small Business Credit Survey: Report on Employer Firms*, Federal Reserve Banks.

3. Katherine Hauge, *Funded: The Entrepreneur's Guide to Funding Your First Round*, Chapter 1, "What Makes a Startup Fundable," O'Reilly Media Inc., October 26, 2017.

Chapter 5

1. Kellie Ell, "Job Barriers Fading for Those with Disabilities," *USA TODAY*, US Edition, August 24, 2017.

Chapter 6

1. *Disparities in Capital Access Between Minority and Non-Minority-Owned Businesses: The Troubling Reality of Capital Limitations Faced by MBEs*, US Department of Commerce, Minority Business Development Agency, January 2010.

2. *Creating Inclusive High-Tech Incubators and Accelerators: Strategies to Increase Participation Rates of Women and Minority Entrepreneurs*, JPMorgan Chase & Co. and Initiative for a Competitive Inner City (ICIC), 2016.

Chapter 7

1. *The American Angel: The First In-Depth Report on the Demographics and Investing Activity of Individual American Investors*, Angel Capital Association, November 2017.

2. Wend DuBow and Allison-Scott Pruitt, "The Comprehensive Case for Investing More VC Money in Women-Led Startups," *Harvard Business Review*, September 18, 2017.

INDEX